MARK
MOVER

MARKET MOVER

LESSONS FROM A DECADE OF CHANGE AT NASDAQ

ROBERT GREIFELD

GRAND CENTRAL
PUBLISHING

NEW YORK   BOSTON

Grand Central Publishing
Hachette Book Group
1290 Avenue of the Americas, New York, NY 10104
grandcentralpublishing.com
twitter.com/grandcentralpub

Originally published in hardcover and ebook by Grand Central Publishing in October 2019.

First Trade Edition: January 2021

Grand Central Publishing is a division of Hachette Book Group, Inc. The Grand Central Publishing name and logo is a trademark of Hachette Book Group, Inc.

The publisher is not responsible for websites (or their content) that are not owned by the publisher.

The Hachette Speakers Bureau provides a wide range of authors for speaking events. To find out more, go to www.hachettespeakersbureau.com or call (866) 376-6591.

Library of Congress Cataloging-in-Publication Data
Names: Greifeld, Robert, author.
Title: Market mover : lessons from a decade of change at Nasdaq / Robert Greifeld.
Description: First edition. | New York : Grand Central Publishing, [2019] | Includes index.
Identifiers: LCCN 2019000524 | ISBN 9781538745137 (hardcover) | ISBN 9781538700983 (ebook) | ISBN 9781478995470 (audio download)
Subjects: LCSH: Nasdaq Stock Market. | Stock exchanges—United States.
Classification: LCC HG4574.2 .G74 2019 | DDC 332.64/30973—dc23
LC record available at https://lccn.loc.gov/2019000524

ISBNs: 978-1-5387-4512-0 (trade pbk.), 978-1-5387-0098-3 (ebook)

Printed in the United States of America

LSC-C

Printing 1, 2020

For Julia.
She has made everything possible.

Contents

MARKET
MOVER

Chapter One

Nasdaq Comes Calling

Nasdaq Names Greifeld CEO

Wall Street Journal, April 16, 2003

I'm six months too late.

That's the phrase that kept popping into my head as I started my job as CEO at Nasdaq in May 2003. I'd been hired to engineer a turnaround at this storied financial institution, which was struggling through perhaps the most precarious period of its three-decade history. It was not a position I'd sought out; I'd initially been hesitant to even take the interview. I knew enough about Nasdaq and its problems to question whether it was really where I wanted to be. But I'm not one to turn away from a challenge. When I got inside, however, I began to wonder if the window of opportunity had already closed.

Earlier that year, I had been happily employed at SunGard Data Systems, a large software and services provider for the financial industry. Prior to that, I'd been a software entrepreneur, co-owner of ASC, which had been sold to SunGard—the second largest acquisition they had ever done. I was promoted quickly, becoming an Executive Vice President responsible for a collection of subsidiaries with annual revenue of more than $1 billion and thousands of employees. It was a fast-moving, stimulating field, and I loved my job. Building new technologies is a deeply creative and satisfying activity. In my heart, I have always loved software—it seems like you have the freedom to create anything. So when the recruiter first called me and told me Nasdaq was seeking a new CEO, I was flattered but hesitant. Did I really want to leave all of this behind for a highly regulated organization that I knew had some serious issues, even one as prestigious as Nasdaq?

"Oh, I don't know, that's not really my thing. I'm a technology guy, not an exchange guy," I told him. "Plus, Nasdaq has so many problems."

That was an understatement. In 2003, Nasdaq was reeling. The dot-com bust had dried up the IPO (initial public offering) market. The tech stars that had lit up the financial firmament only a few years before had lost their luster—and their lofty valuations. The organization was bogged down in transitioning from regulated nonprofit entity to for-profit company. Nasdaq was losing money. The ever-increasing trading volume (and the revenue that goes with it) that had made the platform a favorite of traders during the market expansion of the 1990s was a thing of the past.

Nasdaq's predicament was a classic tale of the disruptor becoming the disrupted. The three-decades-old exchange had once been a technological leap forward: the world's first virtual stock market. Traditionally, exchanges used the "trading floor" model. You've seen it in the movies—traders negotiating, yelling, and gesticulating in the financial world's equivalent of the mosh pit. There were other venues for trading stocks of small companies, like the telephone-based over-the-counter (OTC) market, but these were insignificant and lightly regulated. Nasdaq* was founded in 1971 to bring order and fairness to the OTC market. It was a kind of virtual floor, a centralized system for showing prices. Dealers and traders across the country no longer had to read the daily "pink sheets" or pick up the phone to get prices; they could now see stock quotations in one place, in real time. Instead of making constant calls to keep quotes current, Nasdaq dealers, known as "market makers,"† only had to use a telephone when they wanted to actually execute a trade.

In the excitement that accompanied the long boom of the nineties, Nasdaq found its stride. There had been a time when all America's stock markets played second fiddle to the New York Stock Exchange (NYSE). But in the final decade of the twentieth century, Nasdaq had facilitated and nurtured the rise of a new generation of technology companies, firms like Cisco, Microsoft, Dell, Apple, and Intel. Most of these started small, raising money with Nasdaq back when significant venture capital was hard to come by and NYSE wouldn't list such unproven startups. Nasdaq was their only option, and so it became the public-market parent to hundreds of promising children. Not all of them survived, of course, but the ones that did changed the world. And as they grew ever stronger, becoming national and global leaders, their loyalty

---

* The name was originally an acronym for National Association of Securities Dealers Automated Quotation System.

† Nasdaq dealers acted as middlemen, matching buyers and sellers or filling orders from their own inventory. Given the low volumes typical in the over-the-counter Nasdaq stock market, the market makers were essential to provide grease to the wheels, so to speak, "making markets" in securities that otherwise would have been difficult to trade. As compensation, they generally took a small cut for their service out of the "spread" (or difference) between the "bid" (price a buyer is willing to pay) and the "ask" (price a seller is willing to take).

to Nasdaq persisted. Indeed, as the center of American business began to shift west, away from the industrial factories of the East and Midwest to the sunbaked streets of Silicon Valley, Nasdaq was a primary beneficiary. Its brand became a global signifier of success, technology, and globalization.

In the late nineties, when the boom became a bubble, Nasdaq continued to thrive. In those heady gold-rush days of "irrational exuberance," the promise of internet riches inspired thousands of startups to create online business models. All you needed were enough "eyeballs," and it seemed that investors were smitten. A few such companies, like Amazon, were successful beyond all expectations and became pillars of the global economy. Many more are now remembered only for their sky-high valuations and disastrous flameouts—like eToys or Pets.com. Nasdaq was at the center of all of it—opening the door to a new world of global online trading, stock speculation, and wealth creation that would have been unimaginable a decade earlier. In fact, it would not be unreasonable to claim that there could not have been a dot-com boom at all without Nasdaq. In 1999 alone, the Nasdaq Composite—a weighted index of several thousand stocks listed on the exchange—increased almost 86 percent. But even as its brand reached new heights of prominence, Nasdaq was under threat from a new wave of innovators.

I was one of them. As an entrepreneur in what is now known as the "fintech" (financial technology) industry, I created one of the early Electronic Communications Networks (ECNs) for ASC. ECNs were computer-based trading systems that not only posted quotes but electronically matched and executed orders. On Nasdaq's system, you could see the bid and the offer right there on the screen—close enough to kiss, as I like to say—but the trade could not be consummated without a middleman. Customers still had to pick up the telephone to complete the deal. Indeed, a Nasdaq trading desk at opening bell was almost as loud as the NYSE floor—the phones ringing constantly, the traders yelling into headsets. ECNs came along and automated the last step, empowering customers with direct access, cheaper costs, and greater speed. The future was here and it was digital. And while it might not have been evenly distributed yet (to borrow a phrase from author William Gibson), it was coming soon to a stock exchange near you. Little by little, ECNs were gaining influence and market share, in a market that was exploding with activity.

Indeed, the rise of online brokerages, day-trading, and other nontraditional market activity created massive amounts of new order volume that had to go somewhere. Like a flood of water heading downhill, all of this order flow demanded new methods of trading. It overwhelmed traditional venues and cut new pathways in the extended Nasdaq trading landscape. ECNs rose in tandem with this flash flood of new volume, providing real-time execution in fast and flexible trading forums. The new platforms were online, always on, and global. A massive decentralization and democratization of stock trading was underway. Anyone could do it, and ECNs were facilitating the revolution.

ASC had sold for a good price in 1999, but as the boom persisted and I watched valuations continue to skyrocket over the following year, I sometimes lamented that we'd sold so soon, or hadn't decided to do an IPO in that once-in-a-lifetime bull market. By 2003, however, such thoughts were long gone. The party was over, and the hangover was not pretty. It's always better to sell a year early than a year late.

Over at Nasdaq, the market's tumble was initially not a problem. Volatility and high trading volume are good things for stock markets, and in the immediate aftermath of the dot-com bust, there were plenty of both. But as the IPO market dried up and the economy struggled to recover, Nasdaq's deeper issues became starkly visible. As legendary investor Warren Buffett once said, "It's only when the tide goes out that you learn who's been swimming naked."[1] Ironically, Nasdaq's problems centered on its signature area of focus—technology. The new and more nimble ECNs had surpassed Nasdaq's once-innovative systems. More and more of the buying and selling activity was deserting the traditional dealer marketplace. Nasdaq was uncompetitive, and in danger of becoming an irrelevant sideshow in the new century. Like a large and imposing battleship, it was solid, resilient, and designed for stability. It still commanded all the attention, but it had been built for a different war. Every day, it was being outmaneuvered by a smaller, lighter, faster armada of experimental new watercraft. Sooner or later, the battleship was going to sink.

The Marketplace of the Future?

You can learn a lot about a civilization from its marketplaces: who they were, what they were good at, what innovations they fostered and delivered into society. In the ancient world, marketplaces were hubs for traders in goods and services, cultures and ideas. In the modern world, marketplaces evolved and expanded to be public and private, real and virtual. Now, as ever, when we want to find out what's happened and what will happen next, we look to the marketplace. The marketplace is a reflection of how a culture is changing and evolving. Often, historic events and innovations get their start there. The canon of history's most influential marketplaces includes such names as the Rialto in Venice (fourteenth century), the Grand Bazaar in Turkey (seventeenth century), the Amsterdam Bourse in Holland (seventeenth century), and the New York Stock Exchange (twentieth century). As the twenty-first century dawned, Nasdaq had looked ready to join these ranks as the market that would define the information age. But by 2003, all such aspirations were in doubt.

I hadn't just read about Nasdaq's problems in the papers. I had firsthand experience of dealing with them, often on a daily basis. The main product of ASC was a trade order management system designed for integration with Nasdaq trading desks, and my job involved a constant relationship with many individuals who worked there. It was a frustrating process, to say the least. It took forever to get things done. Nasdaq was unresponsive, slow, and monopolistic. Staff seemed unmotivated and disengaged. From my perspective, it had all the hallmarks of a dysfunctional bureaucracy. It reminded me of my dad's tales of working at the post office. Clearly, whoever took the CEO job would need to do a lot more than update Nasdaq's technology and make it competitive. A cultural transformation was also desperately needed.

When the recruiter called, all of this was going through my mind. It was an honor to be considered, but my enthusiasm for the opportunity was tempered by my knowledge of the organizational dynamics at play. I had no illusions about what the job entailed. Was this the right next move for me? Did I really want to trade in an exciting role at the forefront of a growth industry for a grueling turnaround? I certainly didn't intend to be at SunGard for life, but I had imagined moving on to a new entrepreneurial challenge, possibly leading a startup, not diving into a struggling legacy company. Moreover, Nasdaq was actually a smaller operation than the one I was running. Nevertheless, its brand stature and relevance to the global economy far eclipsed its head count. I had a personal connection to it too: I'd actually written my graduate thesis on Nasdaq, exploring how technology was changing the people dynamics in the equity-trading world. Was this a moment of destiny? I was torn.

Whatever its problems, Nasdaq was a global icon. An organization like that doesn't come calling every day. When the recruiter reached out a second time, I agreed to take an interview. It was a unique opportunity, and I was intrigued by the challenge of turning Nasdaq into the defining market of the twenty-first century.

The next morning my name appeared in the *Wall Street Journal*. This was before we all held the internet in the palm of our hand, and I think I heard the news over breakfast when my phone started ringing. Apparently, there was a story about Nasdaq interviewing me as a candidate for their CEO position. It was the first time I'd ever been mentioned in the *Journal*. It was also my first glimpse of the new world I was entering—fast, furious, and very public.

I talked to Cris Conde, my boss at SunGard. I didn't want to leave him hanging, but I asked him to give me a week to consider the opportunity. I had great respect for Cris and felt loyal to him, and also appreciated that he had seen the value of ASC and paid well for it. He generously agreed to my request. Nasdaq called me in for a video interview with the Board. We didn't have that technology in our pockets in 2003, either, so I was invited to an office in Midtown. On the screen in front of me were several of Nasdaq's

Directors, including Arthur Rock, one of Silicon Valley's original venture capitalists; Warren Hellman, whose private equity firm owned 27 percent of Nasdaq at the time; and Frank Baxter, CEO of global investment bank and institutional securities firm Jefferies and Company. In the room with me was H. Furlong "Baldy" Baldwin, a Baltimore banker, former CEO of Mercantile Bank, and highly respected elder in the financial world.

The composition of the Nasdaq Board was notable for its ties to the technology industry. In particular, Hellman and Rock both had deep roots in Silicon Valley. Rock is a legendary investor who helped found the tech pioneer Fairchild Semiconductor, was a founding investor and Chairman at Intel, and was a key player in the early days of Apple. Hellman, a former President of Lehman Brothers, had gone on to become a major player in West Coast venture capital and private equity. (In San Francisco, Hellman is fondly remembered as the banjo-playing patron of the popular music festival Hardly Strictly Bluegrass, which he endowed generously in his will.)

The presence of these two men on the search committee signaled Nasdaq's commitment to embracing tech as its future. While its listed companies included numerous tech brands, Nasdaq itself was not considered to be a technology company as of yet. It used technology, of course, but the information revolution had not yet rewritten the DNA of Wall Street. Quants, high frequency traders, and algorithmic trading systems had yet to appear on the scene in any significant way. In fact, the old guard—the traders, brokers, and bankers who ran the financial institutions—were not natural technologists. Nasdaq, NYSE, and many other exchanges around the world were undergoing—and in some cases resisting—a generational transition from the nonprofit, cloistered "brokerage clubs" of yesteryear to the more transparent, public, fast-moving, technology-driven, global trading platforms they would become.

This changing face of the industry demanded a new kind of leadership. Remarkably, the Nasdaq Board exhibited great foresight in recognizing the moment. It would have been too easy for them to look toward Wall Street's past rather than its future in choosing a new CEO. The top job at Nasdaq, as with NYSE, conveyed a certain ceremonial power, and it was often bestowed on a respected elder in the financial industry as a kind of sinecure. But Hellman, Rock, and their fellow Directors were clearly not attached to tradition when it came to writing Nasdaq's next chapter.

The first interview went very well; it was clear the Board and I saw eye to eye on the technological and cultural challenges facing the organization. Soon, any lingering questions about why they'd tapped me for the role dissipated. I might not have come from an investment bank or a brokerage firm, but my entrepreneurial background and my technological orientation were part of my appeal. Nasdaq needed that kind of energy.

I began to feel like the job might be mine if I wanted it. However, I'd soon learn that I had serious competition. At some point in our discussions, the headhunter let slip that the other person being considered was Bob McCann, then head of global equity trading at Merrill Lynch. I knew that McCann was articulate, charming, and formidable, and would be hard to best in a traditional interview format. If we both simply answered questions, I feared that the job would be his.

It was only when I considered that I might lose the role to

someone else that I realized how much I really wanted it. *Who are you kidding?* I asked myself. *You're not going to walk away from an opportunity like this.* My entrepreneurial mind had already started to mull over the types of transformations that might help Nasdaq execute a turnaround. The more I thought about it, the more determined I became to do whatever I could to show the Board that I was the right person to lead Nasdaq into a new era. I would take a more proactive approach in my second interview. After all, the struggling exchange didn't need conversational skills; it needed decisiveness and action.

When the day came, I sat down in front of the video screen and before anyone from the Nasdaq Board uttered a word I said, "Here are the five things I'm going to do in the first hundred days."

My plan was simple:

1. Get the right people on board.
2. Reduce bureaucracy.
3. Embrace fiscal discipline.
4. Overhaul technology.
5. Stop being satisfied with No. 2.

I spent about fifteen minutes going through this five-step plan, describing how I would implement each step. No posturing. No sugarcoating. No charm. Just a straightforward, hit-the-ground-running blueprint for change. As I finished, I looked around at the faces on the video monitors (and a couple in the room with me). I could tell I had won them over. Two weeks later, it was official.

Day One

I had a firm point of view on what it would take for Nasdaq to be successful. It was going to involve a significant change of culture. Inevitably there would be ruffled feathers and disgruntlement, and I would need to part ways with some of Nasdaq's existing management team. There was no avoiding it, and only so much I could do to prepare. On the final day before assuming my new role, I decided to do the best thing I knew to keep my mind focused and blow off some tension—I ran a marathon.

As a young man, track had been my preferred sport, and in my adult years I had taken to running longer distances. The only race I could find that particular weekend was in Ottawa, Canada. I brought Bobby and Greg, my two teenage sons, along with me. It was a surprisingly chilly day in late May; in fact, it was so unseasonably cold that our flight home was almost cancelled because the deicing equipment was in storage. *Am I going to miss my first day as CEO of Nasdaq?* I thought as we sat on the tarmac. Thankfully, we made it out. As I watched the skyline of Ottawa fall away, I wondered when I would have the time and opportunity to do something like this again. As it turned out, that would be my last marathon.

The next day, I was sitting in the kitchen of my New Jersey home when my wife, Julia, called from the front room. "Bob, there's a great big black Cadillac parked out front. I'm guessing that's for you!"

As the driver opened the door to the plush private limousine, I reflected on how far I had come. I wasn't bred to be a captain of industry. Growing up working-class, I had worked hard to get an education. I'd not attended private schools or Ivy League colleges. I was lucky enough to have genuine opportunities to advance, but I'd had to earn every one of them. As a hungry young executive, I put myself in a good position to succeed. I got my MBA at NYU Stern, taking classes at night. I helped build and sell a successful company, gained important experience in leadership, and created a good life for my family. But this situation was different. I was stepping onto a bigger stage. Nasdaq was more than an organization or a business; it was an American institution and a global symbol of capitalism—a signature brand that spoke to the aspirations of millions. In my own mind, I was still just a kid from Queens, but I knew that somewhere along the way, I had crossed an invisible line. Private cars and *Wall Street Journal* mentions were only the first indications of that change. There would be more to come.

The car pulled up to One Liberty Plaza, Nasdaq's home office. This imposing skyscraper had originally been commissioned in 1973 by U.S. Steel—a once iconic, top ten American company that today doesn't even crack the top five hundred. If I needed a reminder that there are no guarantees in business, the large steel girders of this architectural giant sent a pointed message.

I could never have imagined then that this massive structure would be my workplace for the next fourteen years—a lifetime in terms of global markets. In the days, months, and years ahead, I would oversee the near death and rebirth of Nasdaq and build it into one of the world's premier stock exchanges, a globally dominant company active on six continents and in twenty-five markets around the globe. I would help Congress and the Securities and Exchange Commission (SEC) overhaul and modernize financial regulations, and shepherd Nasdaq's antiquated technology through a massive restructuring and upgrade. During my tenure, I would have a front-row seat for the Lehman Brothers bankruptcy and the ensuing financial panic. I would be center stage during the frightening Flash Crash, in the spotlight for the infamous Facebook IPO, and caught up in the controversy around high frequency traders. Like everyone else, I would be shocked by the fall of Bernie Madoff, and encouraged by the resiliency and recovery of global markets in the wake of the greatest recession of my lifetime.

Through it all, I would participate in hundreds of successful IPOs, as America's next generation of great companies—in biotech, technology, energy, renewables, medicine, and more—found funding and empowerment in the public markets. It would be a period of tremendous upheaval, and even the nature of my own job, as CEO, would be hardly recognizable by the end.

But that was all to come. On that cool spring morning in May 2003, I only knew that Nasdaq was in a fight for its survival, and there was not a minute to waste. Perhaps I was already too late. I walked in the door, headed up to my new office on the fiftieth floor, and parted ways with three of my executive team before 8 a.m.

Chapter Two

People First

Two Executives Leave Nasdaq As Greifeld Assumes
the Reins

Wall Street Journal, May 13, 2003

Get the right people on board.

That was number one on the list of priorities I had presented
to the Nasdaq Board in my interview. The right people leverage
everything else in a business—even more so when you are undergoing a turnaround and cultural shift. Business, like life, is unpredictable. No matter how good your strategies, you can be sure
you will face unexpected challenges, new opportunities will arise,
and shifting market conditions will take you by surprise. You
can't control circumstances, but what you can do is to ensure that
you have the best people in place so that when the world changes
around them, they can adapt, respond, and step up. That's why
my motto has always been *people first*.

In management circles, we talk a lot about engagement. If you
have workers who show up every day merely because they're getting a salary, your company is unlikely to thrive in the long term.

Engaged employees come to work for more than a paycheck. They show up with purpose and even passion. They want to work hard and are connected to the mission of the organization. That's the type of workforce a thriving business needs. In the early days of any culture change, the critical first step is to find the people who want to work in that new culture—and to part ways with the people who don't.

When corporate leaders say, "People come first" or "People are our most important assets," the message may seem warm and fuzzy. But it's not always a line that a CEO can deliver with a hug and a smile. There is another side to the "people first" principle. Just as the right people are extremely important to the success of any given business, the wrong people—individuals who do not fit, for whatever reason—need to be let go. And letting people go is never easy.

The first firings during my tenure happened immediately. I had done my homework, evaluated the executive team, and already knew several changes in senior management that needed to be made. It was still early morning when the first person came in. This was an individual with a long history at the company. I considered him part of the old Nasdaq and knew that he was not a good fit for a company embarking on the changes I had planned. I needed someone who could get out ahead of our issues; he seemed only able to analyze what went wrong after the fact. It was the right step to take; there was no benefit in dragging it out. "We're taking Nasdaq in a different direction," I explained, "and we don't think your skill sets are aligned with where we want to go. We might as well part ways now and give you time to go look for something else."

He was surprised, of course. Perhaps he'd had an inkling that this might happen, but I could see he wasn't expecting it before 8 a.m. on my first day. Nor were the other two people I let go in that first hour. Around the office, as staff arrived, there was a palpable sense of shock at the events of the day and how quickly they were unfolding. As word got out that personnel changes were already underway, not surprisingly, people were reluctant to come into my office.

Personnel changes can be painful—there's no way around it. The people I said good-bye to on that first day, along with the nearly three hundred I let go in my first year, weren't faceless cogs in a machine; they were colleagues and teammates. Change had come to them uninvited. In these situations, I was glad Nasdaq had the resources to be generous with severance packages. After all, many of these employees weren't leaving because of under-performance in relation to the original expectations of their job. Rather, the expectations had suddenly and dramatically shifted.

I knew that these changes would temporarily impact morale. But I kept in mind a great piece of advice I'd received from a friend and business associate, Vinnie Viola: "Good morale in a bad organization isn't worth much." He is absolutely right. What use is a contented workforce if the business is failing? I was willing to temporarily sacrifice morale if that's what it took to achieve the goal—good morale *and* a great organization.

I also saved myself a lot of time and struggle by acting clearly and decisively from the moment I arrived. The message was immediately and effectively communicated: We're in a new world, and there's nothing to be gained by digging in and defending the old one. It saved us all countless hours of meetings and long, drawn-out culture wars. I didn't want to constantly hear the phrase "This is how we've always done it."

Transparency builds trust and minimizes drama. If you tell people what you are about, right from day one, then when they see you follow through on your intentions and act accordingly—even if that involves making difficult decisions—on some level they'll appreciate that you were up front and honest with them. That will create confidence in your leadership and encourage clarity and transparency in return. If you're not transparent, you set the stage for all kinds of negative drama. There will be gossip, innuendo, and distrust, none of which helps anyone get their job done.

The bottom line was, those changes had to happen if Nasdaq was to survive. Yes, this was an emotionally difficult part of the job, but as I told my team at the time, "We can't operate like a charity. If we don't do the right thing—and make the necessary changes to adjust to financial realities—somebody will acquire Nasdaq and do the right thing for us." As a public company, you're always for sale. The sale price is published every day on the ticker. And if you're running a 20 percent margin business when you really should be running a 35 percent margin business, someone is going to take notice and make a change.

Who's on the Bus?

Most business leaders understand the impact of a bad hire. Zappos CEO Tony Hsieh has said that bad hires have cost his company over $100 million since he opened for business.[1] A study by the Society for Human Resources Management suggested that the cost of a bad hire can reach as high as *five times* that person's annual salary.[2] A bad hire disrupts productivity, saps morale, and can negatively impact the performance of others as well. Plus, the opportunity costs of not having the right person in the role are incalculable. Unfortunately, having the wrong person already occupying a position is similar to making a bad hire. That's why I believe that the same concern and attention that is often brought to the hiring process should always be applied to existing personnel at the start of a turnaround. Indeed, it's helpful to imagine that you are hiring for a new company, one that will exist only when the change process is complete. That will lead you to look at your existing staff freshly, with eyes on the future of the organization.

"I felt like I was interviewing for my job," Adena Friedman told me later, describing our first meeting. "Then, at a certain point, I realized that was exactly what I was doing!" You might recognize her name—she would become CEO of Nasdaq after I decided to move on in 2016, and that role still rests in her capable hands as of this writing. In 2017, *Forbes* would rank her as one of the most powerful women in the world. In 2003, she was a smart young executive with tons of potential. She'd been with Nasdaq for a decade, and exuded dedication, passion, and competency. I quickly recognized that she had no cause to fear for her job in the reorganization. Adena soon became a critical member of my inner circle. A highly effective manager and tough financial negotiator, she would go on to lead a number of strategic acquisitions.

In addition to Adena, there was another executive who would become a central figure in Nasdaq's turnaround: Chris Concannon, my new EVP of Strategy. Industry insiders may know him as the current President and COO of MarketAxess, a large electronic bond-trading platform. In 2003, Chris was an outsider like myself, one of the two people I brought with me to Nasdaq. He had previously worked at an ECN called Island, and then as an executive at its parent company, Instinet, so he was deeply familiar with the ways in which technology was changing the trading landscape. As upstart executives and leaders of ECNs, both Chris and I were disruptors when it came to the Nasdaq marketplace.

Chris was smart, creative, and independent. He had an irreverent, wise-guy personality that brought some welcome levity to our executive team. He didn't just follow directions. He liked to second-guess things. His thoughts on Nasdaq's various projects and business strategies were already proving invaluable in the organizational overhaul, and his skills nicely complemented mine. Indeed, I believe that any good team should supplement each other's skills, abilities, and expertise, not replicate them. I think of this as "checkerboarding your skill sets." Chris would go on to become a thought leader in the organization, who deeply understood how markets and exchanges work, and he helped us shepherd the Nasdaq marketplace into its next phase. I take pride in having helped Adena, Chris, and many others develop from talented young executives with great potential into seasoned leaders who are shaping the future of the financial industry even today.

During my initial days and weeks on the job I would continue to evaluate my management team. Some clearly brought a lot of value to the table, like EVP of the Global Index Group John Jacobs, or General Counsel Ed Knight. I was fortunate to have them on board. However, I ended up parting ways with several others. And instead of immediately searching outside the company for their replacements, my preferred strategy was to look more closely at the people already around me. I was rewarded by the discovery of real talent at Nasdaq that had been unrecognized, undeveloped, or underutilized before I arrived.

Sometimes it's necessary to go outside the company to find the right person for a role. But don't make that a default move. Promoting from within builds morale, incentivizes higher performance, and avoids many of the risks associated with outside hires. The hiring process is unscientific, and interviews last hours at best. People can sound good in an interview, but it's hard to know for sure. I've found that eloquence is often overrewarded in corporate contexts. Internal candidates, by contrast, have essentially been interviewing for years. They are also familiar with company culture, which accelerates the onboarding process. Wherever possible, *promote before you recruit.*

If you find that you can't follow this rule, you may need to do some honest self-examination. If you've been doing your job as a leader in an established company, you should be developing the talent you need. When I couldn't find an internal candidate for a key role, I'd ask myself, *What am I doing wrong?* We invested a lot in developing talent over time for this reason. Of course, sometimes new blood is a good thing, and you don't want to become entirely insular, but as a general guidepost, I like to keep the ratio of promotion to outside recruitment at around 80:20.

Over and over again, I sought out hidden gems at Nasdaq and elevated in-house talent. When I let go of the head of our listings business, a prominent position that required a unique mix of relationship-management skills, marketing talents, and public relations expertise, I didn't just call an executive search agency. Soon enough, on a trip to our office in San Francisco, I met Bruce Aust, a young, charismatic executive with that exact skill set, along with an impressive roster of relationships with key figures in Silicon Valley. There was just one problem: Bruce was a Vice President, two rungs down the ladder of the Nasdaq hierarchy. In order to lead the Corporate Client Group, he'd need to leap over the Senior Vice President and into Executive Vice President territory. Such leapfrogging was virtually unheard-of at the company. In the old Nasdaq culture, you ascended to VP, you put in your two to four years, then you might be considered for SVP positions. Put in another several years, and perhaps an EVP role would be in reach for the lucky few. It was more about time and experience, less about merit and performance. There is value in seniority, of course, but I wanted meritocracy to become a fundamental value at Nasdaq as well. And as I surveyed the existing EVPs, I saw no one with the qualities that I found in this young VP.

My intuition about him was confirmed when I made my first trip as CEO to the West Coast. Bruce organized a dinner with nearly every key player in tech and venture capital in attendance— exactly the sort of people with whom Nasdaq needed to connect in order to position itself as the marketplace of the up-and-coming tech world. The listings business is all about connections. Indeed, the reason I'd parted ways with the former EVP was because he spent too much time sitting in his office: He was a conference room pilot, not a relationship builder. In contrast, it was clear that the organizer of that dinner was more connected than most.

The next evening, after a marathon series of meetings, I cajoled Bruce into taking me to a track meet at Stanford to watch my favorite sport. As we sat in the stands, he turned to me with a serious expression and said, "Bob, as you're making this EVP decision, there's something you should know."

My heart sank; I'd been almost ready to break with tradition and offer him the job—was he going to give me a reason to reconsider?

"I'm gay," he said.

I breathed a sigh of relief. "Bruce, the only thing I care about is that you do a great job!"

Given the climate of the time, I guess he felt it was important to be up front about it. He didn't have to, but I appreciated his transparency. This was 2003, and even in the short time that has elapsed since then, things have changed a great deal in the culture of corporate America—for the better.

Bruce's strengths were clearly compatible with the job he wanted, so I invited him to leapfrog the SVP title and take the EVP job. While I generally do believe in the value of "spending time in the seat," extraordinary times call for extraordinary measures. He was the right person to take over that role, despite not having the ideal management experience. Moreover, his appointment reinforced the culture change I wanted to communicate to Nasdaq: *Don't cling to tradition. This is an era of change.* I myself hadn't risen through executive ranks the conventional way, and I wasn't going to let tradition trump talent. Bruce would end up owning that key role for the next decade.

Little by little, I was filling the crucial seats on the organizational bus. If the bus analogy sounds familiar, it may be because it's borrowed from Jim Collins's best seller *Good to Great.* Success in transitioning companies from moderately successful to world-class, Collins argues, begins with getting the right people on the bus. I was particularly fond of that image because, as readers of *Good to Great* may remember, Collins's metaphor was inspired, at least partially, by Tom Wolfe's *The Electric Kool-Aid Acid Test,* the classic book describing the exploits of Ken Kesey and the

Merry Pranksters in the late fifties and sixties. Kesey had loved to employ the phrase "You're either on the bus or off the bus" in his leadership of that countercultural tribe. The driver of Kesey's bus was in fact none other than Neal Cassady, the hero of Jack Kerouac's *On the Road*. There was something irresistible about a metaphor that connected my role as driver of the Nasdaq bus to the great Beat poets I'd loved in school—though I hoped I was a safer driver than Cassady!

Poetic associations aside, Collins's advice was sound. His research suggested that leaders are best advised to "begin with 'who,' rather than 'what.'"[3] A rock-solid team, he discovered, seemed to be the key first step in any good-to-great transition. The marketplace will shift, strategies will change, but a great team can respond to it all. I had a sense of the type of company I wanted to build, but I knew that inevitably there would be unexpected twists and turns (and bumps) in the road ahead, and exciting new destinations to aim for as well. Having the right people on board would allow Nasdaq to adapt to all those challenges and respond to the opportunities effectively.

People first. To drive the point home, I actually had a couple thousand little toy buses made up and handed out to the Nasdaq staff along with copies of *Good to Great*. The not-so-subtle hint: The wheels of change were turning.

New People for a New Culture

Anytime a company culture dramatically changes, the filtering system for talent will inevitably be affected. To use an evolutionary term, the selection pressures in the organization will be reset, and this shift will reverberate throughout the corporate ecosystem. Often, the people who are right for the new culture are not individuals who thrived under the previous regime. Change the culture, and inevitably, people with skill sets more apropos to the next context suddenly stand out.

Good performers can become great performers when the conditions are right. Over and over again I saw B players become A players when the game changed. My experience is that people want to achieve, to contribute, to help the organization thrive. If you clearly define the mission, remove the bureaucracy and organizational inertia, provide clarity about what is needed in each role, and put in place a good reward and incentive structure, you'll be amazed at how people step up. As the environment shifts, the people come into focus. When we began to make organizational changes at Nasdaq, I immediately noticed that there were certain people whose eyes would light up, who would walk down the hall with a new bounce in their step, who would work a little harder and go the extra mile. They felt uplifted by what was occurring.

Nasdaq's culture was shaped by its history. The company had long been a nonprofit, in the cultural mode of its parent organization, NASD, which is a regulator. People worked there for the good salary, regular working hours, stability, predictable workflow, and good benefits. There is nothing inherently wrong with a culture like that—if the culture fits the mission. But my mandate and mission were different. I wanted Nasdaq to fully embrace the competitive, for-profit world, to be a leader and an innovator in the financial industry. I wanted it to grow, expand, and become the premier equities exchange in the world. To do that, we were going to have to slim down and become much leaner and faster, more nimble and more competitive. We needed a change of mind-set and skill set. It would be disruptive, no doubt, and some would embrace that change wholeheartedly and thrive in that new culture, while others would find it unpleasant. It was up to me, in those first days, to send a clear message about the nature of that change.

I made it clear from the start that Nasdaq's new direction wouldn't be right for everyone. My message was straightforward: "This place is changing. It's going from a nonprofit environment to one that has a faster pace, higher stakes, higher pressure, and greater potential rewards. We're building a performance-driven meritocracy. The energy, the expectations, and the culture will all change. If this new culture doesn't appeal to you, I suggest that you self-select and move on now because eventually that mismatch is going to become clear. Please find another place that is a better fit." It was Nasdaq's great sorting.

In the first year, we cut around a quarter of our staff. Some of that was due to the need to slim down and reduce costs. Some of it was a result of closing unprofitable lines of business. But much of it was driven by the specific cultural change I was focused on. There were plenty of people on staff who liked the old culture—nine-to-five, process-centric, few surprises. Nasdaq, as a human ecosystem, had to function at a higher frequency if it was going to thrive in the fast-moving, rapidly changing ecosystem of global financial markets. The right people for the culture I was determined to create were not necessarily just smart people. It wasn't just about IQ—though I obviously wanted to work with intelligent, capable men and women. IQ is just table stakes; it gets you in the game. Motivation, drive, flexibility, and emotional intelligence are also important attributes that contribute to a company's success. "Bandwidth," for lack of a better word, is another. By that I mean the capacity to fruitfully focus one's attention on multiple areas. That's a critical talent for successful organizational leadership, where a lot comes at you thick and fast. Many people struggle with bandwidth issues, and this can also be true for higher IQ types, who sometimes prefer very specialized domains of expertise. Of course, in certain occupations, like programming, a narrowly focused approach is an enormous value-add, but when it comes to management, bandwidth matters.

When You Have Good People, Listen to Them

Knowing who to bring on board, who to promote, and who to let go is critical in any turnaround. But a people-first strategy means much more than hiring and firing. Any CEO can swing the ax; that doesn't take much talent. Building great companies requires interacting with your team members in a highly productive way, one that encourages creativity, autonomy, focus, and discipline.

In corporate America, we pay well for smart managers. But if you're going to pay for talent and high IQ, be sure to use it. Seek input and honest feedback from your team. And get them involved in your decision-making processes.

One of the ways I sought input for critical decisions was by running a series of head-to-head debates among my executive team. Authentic debate isn't always easy to manage, but it's necessary if you're going to hear what you need to hear in the decision-making process. No issue is black-and-white, and each perspective contains relevant truths. Debate helps to illuminate the inevitable trade-offs and help you make smart and well-informed choices. I liked to mix up our debates by assigning counterintuitive roles. If the topic of the day was, for example, "Nasdaq Japan: Should we keep it or close it?" I might even assign the pro-Japan executive to take the anti-Japan position. It made for some spirited contests. People knew better than to make a weak argument for a position they didn't support; it was clear they were being judged on the quality of their reasoning, not just the content. I firmly believe that most positions stem from rational presumptions, at least from the perspective of the person holding them. Rather than simply dismissing a position we don't agree with, it is valuable to make the effort to understand its underlying rationale, even if we eventually choose another path.

Of course, it's important to not let debate descend into a free-for-all. You don't want shouting in the halls. A culture of argument is distracting. Our debates had structure and rules. They took place in our conference room, and each had an audience of about a dozen additional executives. People argued with passion. At the end, if necessary, I'd give a thumbs-up or thumbs-down to the decision at hand, but often, by that stage, the right answer had become clear to everyone. Occasionally, however, I had to make an executive decision that went against the prevailing winds. After all, the point of the debate wasn't to enact a perfectly democratic ideal. It was to achieve better clarity on all of the issues involved so everyone understood the reasons for proposed changes, and my decision-making was both transparent and much better informed.

This approach was especially critical during my first hundred days as CEO. Nasdaq in 2003 was awash in dead-end projects. The firm had exercised little discipline in this area—it had a process for saying yes to new initiatives, but no processes for tracking their effectiveness or pulling the plug if needed. Certainly, no one had been planning for a downturn in the market when many of them were approved. As often happens in such situations, constituencies within the firm had arisen that protected, or at least were advocates for, many of these projects. I was aware of more than one person who had made a career managing his or her little section of the company without regard to whether that project was critical to Nasdaq's overarching mission, or even profitable. Pruning the project list was a high priority. Still, I didn't want to lose good projects just because I was committed to closing underperforming ones. I wanted to safeguard against overzealousness on my part. The transparent, objective debate style was my chosen method.

I could have handled this in a much quieter fashion. For example, both sides could have created presentations or memos and then submitted them to me for a ruling, and it would have all been done simply and soundlessly. But that method bypasses important aspects of human nature and discounts the reality that people want to be heard. Debate creates energy around a topic. And whether a project lived or died, everyone could be satisfied that a case for its continuation had been well made. That helped to get a deeper level of buy-in from the executive team and ensure that in the aftermath of any decision, we were all rowing together in the same direction.

Input from my team was not limited to these staged debates. In fact, I made sure to communicate to everyone that I wanted them to be honest with me, even when the news was bad. It's natural for people to want to give the CEO the good news, but that's not very helpful. In fact, it can be downright toxic, as was demonstrated all too clearly during the downfall of General Electric, which was helped along by an internal "success theater," as some inside the company called it—the practice of always emphasizing the positive elements of the business and the most optimistic narratives. Enabled by executives throughout the organization, the GE culture became dangerously disconnected from the reality of the business, and it served to keep management from addressing its decline.[4] People won't tell you what you need to hear unless you ask for it, and most important, reward it. Leaders have to counteract people's natural inclination to make reality seem rosier than it is.

It's not enough to hope people will be honest with you. Sometimes you have to create explicit avenues for feedback. It was common for me to open a meeting with "Tell me the problems" or "Give me the bad news." And I didn't want the honesty to be limited to top management. We also instituted regular "town halls" and would invite questions from the general staff for a live Q&A. That gave people a chance to ask anything, and it was a chance for me to interact with our staff in a group setting. Even then, the tougher questions tended to arrive through email.

I also had regular employee lunches. Seven people would join me for a meal, each time from a different area of the organization. I would solicit their feedback, asking "What are we doing well?" and "What are we doing poorly?" And they could ask me anything they wanted. Usually, I found it took about a half hour of conversation before they would get comfortable enough to open up, ask honest questions, and give direct feedback. I found those lunches invaluable and tried to do one a week.

There were several key moments when I had reason to be grateful for one of my team knowing more than I did about a given area of the business. The controversy over MarketSite, Nasdaq's iconic piece of real estate right in the center of Times Square, was a case in point.

For many people, MarketSite is Nasdaq's public face. It is a cylindrical office and event space located in the heart of Manhattan. With its wraparound digital display featuring market news and highlights that appears in the background of practically any event filmed in Times Square, it is natural that many see it as Nasdaq's epicenter. CNBC currently films two of its shows— *Squawk Box* and *Fast Money*—in the main room. Companies celebrate IPOs there, transmitting the opening-bell excitement from the main studio space to Bloomberg, Fox Business, and CNBC. Bloomberg conducts interviews using the MarketSite studio. Companies advertise on the cylindrical tower. Over the years, it's become a major media center and a symbol of American economic vitality.

Early in my tenure, I made a visit to MarketSite. No doubt it had to do with my fiscally oriented perspective at that time, but what I saw was not an iconic expression of Nasdaq's global brand. I saw a gaping money pit. The space had its own photography staff on retainer costing a cool quarter million a year. It had fresh flowers costing us $1,000 a week. It had lavish catering for every event and a round-the-clock party atmosphere. I told John Jacobs, who had recently taken over the Chief Marketing Officer role, that it was a waste of money.

"Close it down."

"Are you telling me to close it," he inquired, "or are you asking for options?"

"You can get me options," I conceded, "but my inclination is to close it." I was imagining the significant amount of money we could save, envisioning all the employees and projects we might be able to keep without that extra cash burn. I just didn't see how this side party, as nice as it might be from a branding perspective, was going to survive a clear-eyed fiscal audit. At this point, fiscal discipline was first and foremost in my mind. Still, I reminded myself that I'd given John this role because he knew things I didn't, so I was willing to hear him out.

Some of the questions surrounding MarketSite were related to the role of the listings business within Nasdaq. It's the public-facing business, what most people associate with the brand of the company. It's profitable, but it's not a growth engine. At that time, Nasdaq's core business was transaction-processing—and that business was failing. Without turning that around, nothing else was going to work. I came from that technology and transaction world and was hyperfocused on getting that business into shape. I knew it was easy for the CEO of Nasdaq (or NYSE, for that matter) to get caught up in the ceremonial glow of leading a national stock market, to fly above the trees, enjoy the limelight, and leave the details to others. But that was not what I was hired to do. Indeed, part of my concern about MarketSite stemmed simply from the urgent need to not get distracted by the shimmer and glow of noncore activities.

Those instincts were correct, but the suggestion to close it down, I eventually realized, was not. In my zeal to reenergize Nasdaq's core transaction business, I didn't appreciate how critical

MarketSite was to the listings business, how much it meant to our companies, and how much, by extension, it meant to the Nasdaq brand. This was brought home to me in my first conversations with CEOs of Nasdaq-listed companies. In those calls, I wanted to tell them about how we were revamping the transactions business to be best in breed and upgrading Nasdaq's service and technology. They wanted to talk about ringing the opening bell in Times Square. They would talk about bringing their mother and father to the ceremony and how great it was. Moments like that were symbolically meaningful to our customers. Business is not all boardrooms and budgets, customers and clients, products and services. It's also that feeling of having a moment in the spotlight to celebrate the culmination of years and years of hard work. MarketSite, I realized, was far more important than the bottom line might indicate.

In the end, we didn't shut down MarketSite. Instead, it was revamped and transformed into a leaner operation, without so many high-priced trappings and perks, but with all the drama and emotion that made it so popular with Nasdaq-listed companies. While the decorations were toned down, MarketSite retained its status as a place to gather and celebrate the achievements of our listed companies (and in February 2018 Nasdaq would announce its intention to make the building its headquarters). We also began to rent out this unique space to others for high-profile events— another way to limit its fiscal impact. This new version of Market-Site could still uplift our brand and provide a powerful publicity boost for our public companies with less drag on our bottom line. That was a decision I didn't expect to make, but my team helped me see the wisdom of keeping it. There is no point in having great people around you unless you trust them to come up with good solutions, even ones that surprise you. Sometimes the right people are the ones who tell you what you don't already know.

Don't Double Down on a Bad Hire

Early one morning, a few months after I started as CEO, I burst into Chris Concannon's office.

"I can't take it anymore," I declared.

"What are you talking about?" Chris asked, surprised by my dramatic entrance. He was starting to appreciate that I tended to be straight, even blunt if necessary, and was not inclined to beat around the bush.

"We have to let him go. We can't keep going like this."

Now Chris knew exactly what I was talking about. One of the two outside hires that I had made when I started at Nasdaq had turned out to be a mistake. His résumé looked great, and he came with stellar references, but it had quickly become clear that it was not going to be a successful placement. Despite being likable, even charming, with an impressive background, he was failing to grasp the intricacies of the job. Everyone knew it. Several months into my tenure, I had to acknowledge that I'd been wrong to hire him and figure out what to do.

"Look, I can imagine it's difficult to let him go, given that you just hired him. It looks bad," Chris acknowledged. "If you'd like, I can work with him, help him out, cover for him where necessary."

"Not a chance. That's not going to work. Covering for him

is not a realistic plan." I appreciated Chris's willingness to help, but I was not going to compromise our team so I could save face. "That's not how I work," I explained. "There is no getting around it. We've got to pull the Band-Aid off."

Needless to say, this was not an easy move to make. I've heard Athletic Directors or General Managers of sports teams say that it's much harder to fire a coach they hired than one their predecessor hired. The same principle applies in business. That reticence may be human nature, but it's very important not to let your ego get in the way of doing what needs to be done. Be prepared to admit you were wrong. Face the reality that you will make mistakes, and don't compound them by avoiding them.

I made the move quickly and didn't let the poor choice linger. My advice to leaders in a similar situation is: Don't defend yourself when it comes to incorrect hires or other faulty personnel decisions. Don't pretend that you should be above such errors. If you made a wrong choice, make the switch.

On the positive side, letting him go was a popular decision in the company. It communicated that I didn't just have "my people" to whom I would be loyal regardless of performance. This wasn't going to be a regime of subtle cronyism; it was a genuine meritocracy. Performance matters—and people know who's not pulling their weight. While this was far from a personal highlight in my career, in retrospect it was actually one of the most important things I did in those early days to win support.

At the end of our conversation that morning, Chris asked, "What are we going to do about his job?"

I looked at him and smiled. "You're going to take it."

And he did. Chris became EVP of Transaction Services, a job that he performed with distinction for the next six years.

People are the lifeblood of any successful business, whether it's an established organization like Nasdaq undergoing a turnaround or a fast-growing startup like so many of the companies that choose to list with us. Listen to entrepreneurs talk about building their businesses and you'll often hear them praise the team they worked with, the joy of getting up every day and creating something with a group of smart, passionate people all focused on one mission. Nasdaq wasn't a startup, but in the transition we were going through, we were definitely starting a new phase of its existence. By the time my first year as CEO concluded, our head count was dramatically down, but the bus was brimming with talent, expertise, and enthusiasm. We were ready to put it in gear.

LEADERSHIP LESSONS

- **People First.** You can't predict the future, but what you can do is ensure that you have the best people in place so that when the world changes around them, they can adapt, respond, and step up.

- **Transparency Builds Trust.** If you tell people what you are about, right from day one, it builds trust in your leadership even when you are making tough decisions.

- **Promote Before You Recruit.** If you've been doing your job as a leader, you should be developing most of the talent you need in-house. Look carefully at your existing people before hiring from outside the company.

- **Encourage Healthy Debate.** It's necessary if you're going to hear what you need to hear in the decision-making process and take into account all the important perspectives.

- **Seek Honest Feedback.** Leaders need to counteract people's natural inclination to make reality seem rosy by seeking out and incentivizing honest feedback and creating explicit avenues for its delivery.

Chapter Three

Triage

Nasdaq Faces Eroding Share, End of Boom

Wall Street Journal, December 24, 2003

"Unbeknownst to all but a handful of insiders and industry players, Nasdaq is fighting for its life... Will Nasdaq survive as a thriving market for tech stocks? It's under assault from all sides."[1]

Thus began a splashy *Businessweek* cover story from August 2003, titled "Nasdaq: The Fight of Its Life." The story was hard-hitting but not incorrect. Nasdaq's situation was dire. We needed to act right away. But more important, we needed to act on the right things, and as Nasdaq's new CEO, it was up to me to figure out what those were.

Why do some CEOs succeed and others fail? After all, most people who make it to the corner office are talented, smart, and experienced. That's why they were hired. Generally, they work incredibly hard. But I'm convinced that one key factor that distinguishes those who thrive at the top from those who only struggle and strive is how they *leverage their time*. They work on the right things—those that will give them the greatest advantage. "Give me a long enough lever...and I'll move the world," said the ancient Greek mathematician Archimedes. Great executives feel the same way about their business. They are constantly seeking ways to increase their leverage—to have maximum impact without maximum expenditure of time or resources.

A common trait of those who fail, I believe, is that they end up working on the wrong things. Time is finite but the CEO's to-do list is infinite, and every item may seem highly relevant at any given moment. Prioritizing the endless tasks is part of the great challenge of leadership at any stage in the growth of a business. During a turnaround, it becomes particularly critical. For a master-of-the-universe CEO type who naturally wants to do everything—and do everything perfectly—this can be a difficult reality to accept. People sometimes think the key to success is doing your job well, but for a leader it is equally important to know what you're *not* going to do well and what you're not going to do at all. It's all too easy to spend time working on things that don't provide high enough leverage to really impact the business. Don't get pulled off course by the seemingly endless priorities and time-wasting task lists. Believe me, you can fix all kinds of problems in a big organization, win plenty of battles, and still lose the war.

I knew I couldn't fix every problem at once. It was time for triage. In the midst of a turnaround, an organizational leader must be prepared to function like an emergency medic in a disaster zone—making quick decisions about which projects, business lines, and initiatives deserve further investment of energy and resources, and which do not. To ensure I was using my own time to maximum advantage, I would need to take stock of our numerous problems, understand the various business lines, figure out which most urgently needed care, and look for the most efficient ways to cut costs and increase revenue.

Bob vs. the Blob

Before I took the helm, I had requested that the existing Nasdaq leadership put together a daily accounting of profit and loss. I always want to be able to demonstrate the economic benefit or cost of every major activity. The report was on my desk on day one. I was pleased with the team's responsiveness, and I wondered if the systems in place were better than I had initially thought. Then I found out we had fifty people working on it. This was clearly an example of an unsustainable business model. Over time, we would develop robust financial planning and analysis systems for internal cost accounting and, more important, a company culture that kept a closer eye on such matters.

What the report told me was that Nasdaq was losing $250,000 every single day. What it didn't tell me was why—which specific business lines or projects were draining our resources. In other words, our cost structure wasn't clear—there was a great big blob of corporate spending that was not being clearly allocated to the appropriate areas of the organization.

Every business has a blob. To some extent it's legitimate—corporate overheads and resources that are used by every department. For example, IT resources, HR resources, or lawyers' time—even the CEO's time. What tends to happen is that because the departments don't have robust tracking systems to know what percentage of these general resources they are actually using, these costs don't get allocated. Sometimes they get allocated by formula, divided up by number of employees or by percentage of revenue. That's better than not allocating at all, but it's rough justice and doesn't really help give you an accurate picture of how the organization's resources are being used. It also doesn't promote accountability throughout the organization. Big companies get into trouble this way, because everyone thinks their project has high profit margins, even while the organization as a whole may be bleeding out.

You can never completely eliminate the blob, but if you can minimize it, you will take a big step toward fiscal clarity and fiscal discipline. When you accurately allocate costs to the place they're being consumed, you promote accountability among the leaders of various business lines and projects. For example, let's say an organization is spending $50 million on data centers. You divide that cost up among the business lines that are making use of that resource, and one of them suddenly finds a big chunk of that $50 million flowing through its particular Profit and Loss Statement. The P&L of that business line doesn't look so good anymore, and that leader has a new incentive to think creatively about using resources. He probably never voted for those data centers, but he's getting billed for them. And so he now has a reason to try to reduce that cost. "Hey, why don't we put everything in the cloud?" he suggests. When people are forced to take ownership of the actual costs associated with their projects, it starts critical new conversations. Seemingly fixed costs might be revisited. As Nasdaq's then CFO David Warren used to say, "All fixed costs are variable over time."

In the leader's quest for leverage, tackling the blob is essential.

Until you can clearly see where the money is going, you won't know how to best focus your time and attention. You can't have a functional organization without cost clarity. And the way you get to clarity is by focusing in on those areas where allocating expenses proves to be difficult. When David began presenting the report to the executive team, I requested that he skip straight to the problem areas. "I don't need to start on page one. I don't need the whole story. Start with the friction points. In what areas have you had trouble allocating expenses?"

Although I think of myself as a fairly positive person, as a leader I consider it my job to focus on what's not working. It's always a balancing act. Optimism is essential if you're to take risks and succeed; indeed, it's probably true that the only people who really accomplish things are the optimists. But that optimism must be tempered by a disciplined and critical perspective. Just as Marines are trained to run toward gunfire, overriding the fundamental human instinct for self-preservation, leaders need to run toward problems and not avoid them. Face reality relentlessly. Override the natural propensity to turn away from trouble or procrastinate. Unlike a fine wine, most problems do not improve with age. Shine the light into areas of vagueness, confusion, or conflict, knowing that there is leverage to be found in creating clarity, alignment, and resolution.

When I asked David to show me the problems, he didn't hesitate. He quickly flipped halfway into his binder. As we allocated expenses, turning vagueness into granularity, our fiscal situation began to get clear. Some of his findings were information I'd anticipated; others were surprises. The meeting went quickly, and I made the final decisions where needed. I think the executive team was a bit surprised how fast things got resolved. The message sent was subtle but crystal clear: *We're not going to waste time in turf battles. We're not going to spend precious hours arguing over details that sap our energy and reduce our focus. We have an enormous challenge ahead of us. We need to be decisive and move fast.*

A Leader's Instinct

How does a leader make decisions, especially big and consequential ones, under pressure? There are many factors, but it often comes down to instinct. By *instinct*, I don't just mean a shoot-from-the-hip reaction or a mysterious intuition. Instinct, as I see it, is the accumulated result of a lifetime of learning that empowers your ability to assess and respond to a situation. Your life experiences, your education, your business acumen, your successes and your failures, your breakthroughs and your missteps—all of it comes together as an internal compass that calibrates to the issue at hand. You find out what you really know in those moments.

Instinct is more than just knowledge. I'm a runner, and I have a wealth of knowledge about my favorite sport, track. When my daughter was racing, I thought I could come up with a data-based training plan for her, a formula for success drawn from the experts in the field. But then I took her to a great coach, Frank Gagliano. I watched, each day, as he would talk to Katie before her workout, and then choose exactly the best training session for her on that particular day. While sometimes his suggestion was straight out of the training manual, at other times it was clear he was pivoting and innovating in real time. It was obvious that his ability to tailor her training regimen far exceeded my own. While he and I had access to the same technical knowledge, he had something I didn't have in that field: instinct. In the virtuous overlap between trustworthy instinct and learned knowledge, effective leadership is born.

In business, I trusted my hard-earned instincts, but I also was a great believer in using all the data available. There were rare times when I had to make an on-the-spot call, but wherever possible I liked to allow time to let the decisions crystallize. The data needed time to settle and integrate with my instinctual algorithms so that eventually a clear direction or decision would emerge. Indeed, I was decisive, but not always in the moment. Often I'd try to sleep on an important issue, letting the information I'd gathered soak through the layers of my mental processes, knowing I would wake up with more clarity. Another of my favorite strategies in the early years was to go for a run—as my feet pounded the pavement, my mind cleared, focused on nothing but the miles ahead. But afterward, in the shower or eating a meal, deeper insight would come. The ability to work with your instinct—knowing when to trust it, when to act quickly, when to take more time, when to seek input or data—is one of the hallmarks of successful leadership. There's no perfect formula for developing this other than time and experience.

During my first summer at Nasdaq, there was no shortage of consequential decisions to be made. We spent an enormous amount of time cutting programs, projects, and expenses. I shuttled back and forth between Chris's and David's offices, as we questioned everything. Some projects were failing; others were flailing. Even many initiatives that showed promise just didn't make sense at that moment, given Nasdaq's financial priorities. It was hard work, and I spent significant time each morning combing through financial reports. But in other respects, it was simple. We needed to cut costs and there were plenty of worthy candidates for the ax.

Here are some of the questions one should ask when evaluating business lines, projects, and initiatives in the midst of a turnaround:

- Where can I stop the bleeding? Which business lines are failing so dramatically that they need to be shut down before they waste any more resources?
- Which business lines are in decent health and can survive for now without significant new investment?
- Where might immediate care and attention make the biggest difference in helping the business survive and grow?
- Is any given project or initiative essential to our core business at this moment, or is it peripheral?
- Which proposed projects would be crazy to even start, with low odds of succeeding?

It's easy to shut down projects or initiatives that are failing outright. The tricky ones are those that limp along, with a handful of loyal customers that embrace the product or service. As I often like to say, the only thing worse than no customers is one customer. You'll upset them if you shut it down. Plus, over time, certain people within a company will get invested in those projects and protect them, despite their unprofitability. It's important to be clear-eyed about what constitutes a success and what doesn't.

Some of the most challenging decisions I faced involved projects that were promising but peripheral. A case in point was a project that Adena Friedman was leading: Nasdaq's first exchange for smaller, "micro cap" companies, known as BBX. It had real potential; it was a valid concept that would serve investors. It was also going to take years to come to fruition, consuming resources and time in the process—most notably, the time of one of my most talented executives. But she was committed to it, and she argued passionately against my suggestion that we shut it down. I respected her all the more for this position, but that didn't change my ultimate decision. It was simply the wrong time for that kind of project.

Six weeks after my arrival, Nasdaq wrote off $100 million in underperforming assets. This was a consequence of cutting through the confusion and analyzing the actual performance of the business. Nasdaq's money pits were no longer buried, vague, or unknown. Thanks to Chris, David, Adena, and others' hard work, we'd identified the problem areas and already taken major steps toward their resolution. My plan was beginning to take effect. I'd focused on *people first* because the right people leverage everything else in a business. I'd begun the essential process of *reducing bureaucracy*. Now we were *embracing fiscal discipline*.

How Healthy Is Your Core Business?

In a turnaround, fiscal discipline is critical. You need to weigh, measure, and count everything that can possibly be weighed, measured, and counted. But it's important to understand that you can't save your way to success. Cutting costs and becoming a leaner operation helps slow cash burn, but there is a lot more to getting your fiscal house in order than reducing head count or closing unprofitable lines of business. You can't cut your way to prosperity.

At some point, you have to find a way to increase revenue and start bringing more customers in through the proverbial door. A new leader needs to quickly wrap his or her head around the company's various sources of revenue and ask the question: *How healthy is my core business?*

Nasdaq revenue in 2003 was derived from three main pipelines. First, the data and indexing business. That includes, for example, the data that everyone sees scrolling across the screen on financial networks such as CNBC, Yahoo Finance, and Bloomberg. We also licensed financial products derived from Nasdaq listings, like the Nasdaq 100 index. As Exchange Traded Funds (ETFs) and index funds became more and more popular in the overall markets, this business was robust and growing—a godsend during the turbulent period from 2003 to 2005. It wasn't our core business, but it was important. Without this revenue, Nasdaq wouldn't have made it. I quickly ascertained that this business was healthy and didn't require too much time and attention. I was free to focus on more urgent matters.

Nasdaq's second source of revenue was its listings business. Companies pay to be publicly listed on Nasdaq. In addition to their yearly fees, there is also a onetime fee associated with the initial public offering (IPO) of shares in the company. It was not the largest source of revenue, but those yearly fees were steady and predictable, and investors loved that consistency. It was also our public face, our flagship business. Indeed, from a branding perspective, the listings business *is* Nasdaq. It wasn't just about money; it was critical for our global brand. Stop anyone on the street and ask them what they know about Nasdaq, and they are not going to wax poetic about trading volume or exchange technology. They are going to talk about Google and Facebook and Microsoft. They are going to tell you about tech companies, opening bells, CNBC's *Squawk Box*, or the latest, greatest tech IPO. Nasdaq is an attractive brand. And part of that was winning the best new IPOs every year, and keeping our existing companies happy with Nasdaq's service and image.

Unfortunately, following the dot-com bust, the listings business was seriously impaired. There were very few IPOs in 2003. Moreover, our longtime rival, NYSE, was competing aggressively for our existing listings. I had confidence that given time, this business line would naturally recover its former health, but time was something we didn't have. The listings business demanded immediate attention; in fact, it felt like an infinite consumer of resources, and I chafed against spending my time on it. It was the very opposite of the type of high-leverage activity that is critical during a turnaround. Listings is a good business, but it doesn't have a very high ratio of revenue output to degree of energy input. A listings victory represents a single account. It doesn't scale well, and it's people intensive. It's what I call an "arms and legs business." In time, however, I would gain a deeper appreciation for the importance of listings to our global brand, but for now, I had more pressing priorities.

The third revenue stream, and the one that was truly our core business, was transactions. Nasdaq charges a transaction rate per share of stock traded on its systems. From an income perspective, this is the most important revenue stream, representing 40 percent of our overall revenue at the time. And it was in trouble. Our revenue from transactions dropped by 20 percent in 2003.

This business was on life support, but I knew what medicine was needed. I knew the industry intimately, and a significant part of the reason I'd been hired was to change Nasdaq's fortunes in this mission-critical area. I arrived with a clear mandate: Invest in technology, focus on the future. While I couldn't control trading trends in the overall market, I certainly intended to regain our footing in the battle for market share in electronic trading. We needed to innovate, compete, and serve our customers better. Transactions was the area where I could get the greatest leverage.

Every business is in a relationship with its competitors but also with the market as a whole. When assessing why a business line is struggling, it's important to consider:

- Is the market as a whole depressed?
- Is the business struggling because we're failing to compete?
- Is the market going through a significant transition?

In the case of Nasdaq's transactions business, the answer to these questions was yes, yes, and yes. There was no doubt that the market as a whole was still struggling to recover from the dot-com bust. In 2003, industry-wide trading volume was down, and revenue along with it. Adding insult to injury, we were rapidly losing market share to competing ECNs, so we were also receiving a decreasing portion of that shrinking industry revenue. But by far the most important thing we were up against was a significant market transition: a sea change in equities trading. In the end, our success or failure would depend on how we met that challenge. As John Chambers, former CEO of Cisco and a longtime Nasdaq customer, reflects, ultimately *"you compete against market transitions, not against other companies.* If you don't stay focused on figuring out what's happening in the market, it doesn't matter if you win a few battles here or there... Disruption can quickly lead to self-destruction if you misread the market and end up fighting the current."[2] Of course, as any leader of a public company who has to report quarterly earnings knows, you have to compete effectively in the short term as well. But from a macro perspective Chambers is right: Market trends can make or break a business. And when they involve technological innovation, there's no sense in pretending it's all going to go away and things will go back to how they were.

A Market in Transition

As in many industries, technology was radically disrupting how trading was done on Wall Street. Every exchange was impacted, or would be soon enough. Like many businesses that find themselves under the unexpected assault of a marketplace in technological transition, Nasdaq had been slow to respond to its changing environment. It had initially been cautious in embracing the emerging world of electronic trading, trying to keep one foot in the old dealer-dominated universe while cautiously embracing the digital future. The company had tried to listen to its customers, and that's important, but sometimes, your existing customers want you to stay the same. In a market that is being disrupted, your customer base can be in flux, and it's all too easy to follow your legacy customers off a cliff. Sometimes it's necessary to forge a more independent path. As Henry Ford allegedly said, "If I had asked people what they wanted, they would have said faster horses." With my arrival, the time had come for a different approach.

In order to contextualize the steps I took to get Nasdaq on track, and the lessons I learned in the process, let me briefly explain the market transition that was occurring, and the changing customer demands that were driving it. A few years before my arrival, Nasdaq essentially had 100 percent market share in Nasdaq-listed stocks, which meant that trades in Nasdaq-listed stocks were entirely controlled by Nasdaq-sanctioned dealers and processed through Nasdaq systems. By the time I arrived, Nasdaq's market share for matching buys and sells in our listed stocks had fallen to 13 or 14 percent. That was how profoundly the electronic revolution was impacting our business. ECNs offered customers alternative venues for trading Nasdaq stocks. So although these stocks were still listed on the Nasdaq marketplace, we had less and less influence over the trading that was happening in that marketplace.

Why was Nasdaq falling short? It was failing to provide two of the critical things any stock market needs—speed and liquidity. Liquidity, simply put, is the ability to buy and sell relatively easily, usually due to the high volume of shares being traded. Liquidity is the lifeblood of any stock market. In trading stock, price is important, but so is the certainty that you can get the deal done. It's Human Nature 101. When we make a decision that we want something, we demand instant gratification. Imagine that you, as a consumer, have spent hours agonizing over the decision to buy Microsoft—weighing up the pros and cons; poring over the research, the business model, the track record, the market conditions, the management team. Finally, you make up your mind: *I'm going to do it.* Getting a good price matters, but it's not your only concern. The last thing you want, at that moment, is to wait for that order to get filled. You want it now! So you will tend to process your order with a trading firm that can assure you it has sufficient order flow to get the deal done fast. It's just like buying produce at the grocery store. You are more likely to go to a busy market that consistently has ample supply, offering you the certainty that you can get what you want.

In the trading business, the phrase that describes this dynamic is "liquidity attracts liquidity." If a particular firm has enough buying and selling activity, then there is usually going to be someone on the other side of any given trade in any particular stock. Naturally, that creates a network effect that attracts more people to want to trade stocks with that firm.

Waiting brings uncertainty. A delay in getting orders filled can cost money as the market continues to fluctuate. Customers were looking for speed, which means certainty, so they were increasingly choosing ECNs. We were losing market share and liquidity, and that was, in turn, causing us to lose more of both. If liquidity attracts liquidity, the opposite is true as well. Compared to NYSE, we might have been faster and more electronically oriented, but when it came to what all our customers wanted, we were slow-footed and a generation behind.

Remember, Nasdaq had pioneered the electronic market all the way back in 1971, providing a central, up-to-date quotation system for stocks of small companies. However, it didn't eliminate the human element altogether. You could see the quotes on the computer screen—close enough to kiss—but you still had to pick up the phone and call a Nasdaq-sanctioned dealer in order to consummate the trade. ECNs automated that final step. They could match your bid with an offer in the blink of an eye. The traditional role of the middleman, the market maker, the broker-dealer, was being bypassed.* ECNs harnessed the latest technology to meet customer demands for speed and certainty. Nasdaq tried to compete with ECNs by building its own version of an electronic order-matching system, known as SuperMontage. It was a step forward, but by trying to include features both for dealers and for new electronic players, the final product ended up pleasing neither. It was a horse designed by committee, and the resulting camel didn't help Nasdaq's position in the market. By the time it was released, in 2002, the market had already moved on. As in any established business being disrupted by innovation, Nasdaq struggled to balance the interests of its legacy dealer network and its customers' new demands for the latest technologies.

By the time I arrived in 2003, the dramatic loss of market share had created more than a decline in revenue—it also contained an

---

* The exception here was in lower-volume markets, where there is very little likelihood of getting simultaneous buy and sell interest. High-volume stocks are perfectly suited to electronic trading networks. But low-volume stocks, which tend to be illiquid, require greater hands-on assistance to function efficiently. In these cases, middlemen can play a critical role in facilitating trading.

existential risk. Some on Wall Street were beginning to openly question whether Nasdaq would survive. Without liquidity, the exchange couldn't perform one of its critical functions accurately: *price discovery.** The more buyers and sellers come together in any one trading venue, the more accurate will be the price of the stock that is being bought or sold. Without volume, all kinds of distortions are possible.

If other venues with more activity were providing the function of price discovery in Nasdaq-listed stocks more accurately than Nasdaq, what advantage did we have in the listings business? After all, wouldn't it be more appropriate for those stocks to be listed on the exchange where price discovery was actually happening? If Nasdaq just became a sort of electronic posting service, showing the "last sale" prices of stock primarily being traded in other electronic venues, the fundamental relevance of the business would start to be called into question. I was deeply concerned that the decline in market share, if steep enough, could become a slippery slope that accelerated our troubles in the listings business—at least that was the scenario that occasionally woke me up in the middle of the night. In my mind, I could hear CEOs of would-be public companies asking, *Why would I list with you, if you are not trading my stock?*

Overhauling our transactions business was a major task, and

---

* A well-functioning stock market doesn't just facilitate trading of any given equity; it also helps determine its price. If you want to know the true price of any asset, the best method is an auction-style interaction, where a group of buyers and sellers all come together in one place and enter bids and offers, until eventually a price prevails. However, that type of auction is dependent upon sufficient volume—there has to be enough activity to arrive at a legitimate price. If there are only two or three people in the auction, you'll never get a trustworthy accounting. It's the same with stocks.

I knew I couldn't do it overnight. I also knew that I needed to move immediately to increase our market share and stop the bleeding. We did have some competitive advantages, including our size, our talent, our lack of any real debt, and a reasonable amount of cash on our balance sheet. That cash certainly wasn't doing us any favors by slowly burning up in unprofitable operations. The short-term solution, I decided, was to employ these assets and buy some market share, in the form of an ECN. And so it was that approximately one year after my first day at Nasdaq, we purchased BRUT ECN from SunGard Data Systems, my former employer.

I have no doubt that several eyebrows were raised at a new CEO proposing to acquire the technology he'd built at a previous company. One very significant Board member, however, was more outspoken in his reservations. Pat Healy had replaced Warren Hellman, of the private equity firm Hellman and Friedman, who owned a fairly large percentage of Nasdaq at the time. Over time, Healy would become a highly valued advisor and someone with whom I would often consult on Nasdaq's strategy. But for the moment, we were on opposite sides of this critical decision. I listened to his reasonable strategic concerns, but decided to proceed anyway. Overriding his objections regarding my first major acquisition was an early test of my leadership mettle.

BRUT was the first major acquisition on my watch. It wouldn't be the last. We needed its market share—it was that simple. Our trading platforms needed it. Our listings business needed it. Our IPO business needed it. Our brand needed it. And frankly, our mojo needed it.

With the acquisition, Nasdaq also received an infusion of new technology, though it still wasn't adequate to address the IT challenges we faced. BRUT was a good system, and it allowed us to level up on the technology front, but it wasn't a foundation upon which we could build Nasdaq's future. Like many ECNs, it was a bit rickety. But it was a step. A small step, perhaps, but my strategy was just getting going, and I knew the next one would be bigger.

From Defense to Offense

As I grappled with how to upgrade our technology and get Nasdaq on the right side of an industry in transition, our fortunes were helped somewhat by an improving economy. In 2004, the IPO market began to pick up. We launched a number of new public companies, twenty-five of which were international, including ten from China. Most notably, Google successfully launched their landmark IPO, trading 22 million shares on the first day. Few knew at the time just how massive an impact Google would have on the global economy, but already it was a tech company with a $27 billion valuation and extraordinary potential. Moreover, it was the first big IPO in the post-dot-com era, and the competition for Google's favor had been intense.

Our victory in winning the listing was a group effort. Bruce, Adena, and I were the team that spent time courting Google's young founders, Sergey Brin and Larry Page, and its CEO, Eric Schmidt. I was excited and more than a bit relieved when we got the good news that they'd chosen Nasdaq.

The Google IPO was a milestone, not just for Nasdaq but for the technology sector as a whole. After the dot-com bust, Silicon Valley had suffered through a particularly grueling period of retrenchment. But it felt like winter was finally receding, and the green shoots of spring were all around. As Larry Page led us on a tour of the Googleplex in Mountain View, California, the troubles of just a few years ago seemed to be fading into memory. A new generation of innovators, unencumbered by the failures of the past, was showing the way forward.

But we still had work to do. As the economic headwinds of 2000–2003 slowly shifted to tailwinds, I knew it was more important than ever to prepare Nasdaq to thrive as the economy picked up speed. It was time to make a move that was not about getting slimmer, smarter, leaner, or even meaner, but was about positioning ourselves for future growth. In a narrow, cost-cutting context, it's not easy to innovate and think long-term. When a culture is focused entirely on thrift, the next big thing is usually invented somewhere else. In other words, we couldn't just play defense; we had to get our offense on the field as well.

LEADERSHIP LESSONS

- **Prioritize Your Time to Get the Greatest Leverage.** The CEO's task list is endless, but time is not, so choose those activities that give maximum return on time spent.

- **You Can't Do Everything Well.** People sometimes think the key to success is doing your job well, but for a leader, it is equally important to know what you're *not* going to do well and what you're not going to do at all.

- **Run to Problems.** Face reality relentlessly. Override the natural instinct to turn away from the things that are not working.

- **Develop Your Leadership Instinct.** Find the right balance of experience, knowledge, data, and advice that works best for your decision-making process.

- **Don't Underestimate Market Transitions.** To win in the short term, you need to compete well against other players in your market, but to win in the long term, you have to get out ahead of major shifts in the market itself.

Chapter Four

Buy the Winners

If you can't beat 'em, buy 'em.

"Nasdaq Agrees to Buy Brut ECN," *Wall Street Journal*, May 26, 2004

"Young man, you don't get it. This is not an admission of failure."

The gentleman addressing me in this fatherly tone was Jim Mann, longtime CEO of SunGard. It was 1999, and he had just told me he was planning to acquire another company that had developed some technology we needed. I'd questioned his move—couldn't we just build in-house the technology he was proposing to buy?

"Give me a fraction of what you're planning to pay for that company and I can come up with our own version," I said.

Mann shook his head, smiling indulgently at my entrepreneurial pride. "It's smart," he told me. "We buy the winners." A successful company, he explained, has already beaten out its competition and proven itself in the marketplace while a dozen others failed. Yes, you pay a premium when you buy. But you save yourself all the time and resources it takes to develop your own product, build a customer base, and outperform your competitors.

And you dramatically reduce your risk of failure by betting on a proven business.

I took his words to heart. At forty-five, with many years in business under my belt, I was at an age where I could appreciate being called "young man." And more important, I learned a lesson that day that I would employ for years to come: *Buy the winners.*

Mann's wise words came back to me as I assessed the state of Nasdaq's technology in 2003 and 2004. Could we develop what we needed in-house, or should I be seriously looking for someone to buy?

Turning Nasdaq into a market leader was going to require more than new tires and a paint job—we needed to overhaul the entire engine of our trading technology. I knew this before I was hired—that was why *overhaul technology* was one of the five points on the plan I presented to the Board. Even so, getting a look under the hood was an eye-opener. Nasdaq was operating on an older mainframe system, while the competition was using faster, more flexible, less expensive UNIX systems or, in some cases, Intel and Microsoft platforms. We had our own way of doing business that was native and proprietary, but the industry around us had become more open-source, fostering a degree of iteration foreign to our internal culture. If an ECN had a problem in executing orders, they'd just tweak it and reboot it, and their system would come back up—no harm, no foul. Like modern software, ECNs were constantly updating and upgrading, in some cases as often as once a day. Nasdaq had no such flexibility. If we went down, even momentarily, it would be on the front page of the *Wall Street Journal.* Our engineers upgraded the system closer to *once a year.*

Yes, our platform was reliable—much more so than our new competitors'. The uptime in our trading systems in 2003 was more than 99.99 percent. In a different time and place, that reliability might have given us a significant advantage. But in this circumstance, it began to look like an albatross. It left us without the critical adaptability that allows innovation to thrive. As a result, we weren't evolving fast enough. It was time for Nasdaq's technology to enter a new era.

I knew the technology behind electronic trading, and I had firsthand experience of building an ECN from the ground up. As I made my appraisal of the state of our technology in 2003, I took a good look at SuperMontage, knowing that the organization had invested enormous time and resources in developing this system. Could we turn it into a platform on which to build Nasdaq's future? Try as I might, I just couldn't see it.

By 2004, we had begun to upgrade the existing transaction system to work with new regulations and keep competitive with existing ECN functionality. We were shifting to a more flexible, dynamic architecture and had even increased our average update speed from once a year to once a month or more if needed. Steve Randich, our CIO, was transforming our IT department into an outfit that valued dynamism and responsiveness, not just stability and reliability. BRUT had helped stabilize our market share. But I knew that none of those changes was sufficient to deal with our fundamental issues. With a technological engine designed to fit a different era, we couldn't just put our foot on the accelerator.

Realistically, that left two pathways open to us. Option one involved some promising but unproven new technology we had developed with Nasdaq Europe, built on a Microsoft platform. It could potentially be the architecture for Nasdaq's next-generation system. But I was hesitant. It was not designed at enterprise scale, and I wasn't convinced it would be easy to get it there. Speed to market was critical. The prospect of integrating a system, however promising, that wasn't yet tested at scale and was bound to encounter growing pains along the way made me slightly queasy. We simply didn't have a lot of margin for error. Spending too much time in development limbo or going to market with a less than bulletproof system was a fate to be avoided at all costs. Furthermore, I had done my previous system-building work on UNIX platforms, and knew the reliability of that computing ecosystem. I was willing to pursue the new technology, but our second option was my preferred path.

What was option two? Simple: Buy someone. And not just anyone, but the best. *Buy the winners.* The winner, in my mind, of the ECN wars was very clear. It was INET (formerly Island ECN). Especially from a technological point of view, INET was the one I coveted. It was robust, sophisticated, and proven at scale. Its real genius was in the simplicity of its construction, often the hallmark of the best software architecture. It was elegant, efficient, and, with its off-the-shelf hardware and open-source software, had a light footprint that made it less expensive to operate than many of its competitors. Plus, it had the largest market share.

To understand how INET technology had earned such a good reputation and why I singled it out, it helps to know something about its unlikely origin story—a remarkable tale starring a few highly motivated outsiders who were determined to disrupt the established Wall Street trading landscape with the new tools of the information revolution (and make a lot of money in the process). By chance, I'd made a brief appearance in one chapter of this narrative, more than a decade before I started the job at Nasdaq, in an unlikely setting—a basement office in Staten Island.

An Island of Bandit Traders

It was the early 1990s, long before the days of GPS navigation systems or ubiquitous mobile phones, and I was lost on Staten Island. I wasn't familiar with the borough; like most New Yorkers, I'd only ever driven through. While Staten Island is just a short ferry ride from Wall Street's soaring skyline, culturally it may as well be a thousand miles away. It is home to lots of working-class Irish and Italians, contains the highest number of gun owners in New York, and, in more recent years, boasted a majority of Trump voters. Some readers may remember it as the home of Melanie Griffith's scrappy character in *Working Girl*. I thought about that movie as I anxiously cruised past blocks and blocks of identical row houses looking for the right address. As a blue-collar kid from Queens, I would have expected to feel at home. But the inimitable character of Staten Island resisted such superficial comparisons.

The founder of ASC, Carl LaGrassa, had asked me to go in search of a trading outfit based somewhere out there. ASC had a back-office software business clearing trades. Most of the customers were small, doing a handful of trades every day. But suddenly, one customer's trading volume spiked dramatically. "Find out what's happening in Staten Island," Carl had said.

I was about to give up any hope of finding the place, when I turned a corner and saw a shiny Porsche, a Mercedes, and a BMW, all parked next to each other on the street. It was an incongruous sight, to say the least. At that time, in that neighborhood, it was like seeing a unicorn tethered on the side of the road. I had arrived.

In the basement of that modest Staten Island home was the operation of Shelly Maschler. This was my first encounter with Maschler; it wouldn't be my last. He was a fascinating character—a big, boisterous bear of a man, full of brains and braggadocio in equal parts. Think Rodney Dangerfield, only with a larger personality and more F bombs. Maschler would become something of a Wall Street legend in the years ahead, making millions by pioneering various trading schemes, many of which riled financial authorities, skirted the edges of regulations, and even ignored them altogether. In a few years, Maschler's small Staten Island operation, Datek Securities, would morph into Datek Online, one of the original day-trading operations, which would eventually be sold to TD Ameritrade in 2002 for more than $1 billion.

Maschler's influence on Wall Street was significant, if controversial. Playing the role of the upstart, little-guy outsider fighting the elites, he used aggressive strategies to help usher in a new age of speed and automation in Wall Street trading practices. But perhaps his greatest impact was helping to recognize the talent and launch the career of Josh Levine, whom I met in his office that day.

Levine was an idealistic, brilliant computer programmer who was just a few years out of high school and had landed a consulting gig working with Maschler and his small team of traders. Levine started out as a technical gofer—an enthusiastic kid still learning the finer details of trading and experimenting with technological enhancements that would help give Maschler's team an edge. However, as the whole industry would discover in the years ahead, Levine had bigger goals. He believed in the promise of computers to change the world and, more important, to level the playing field on Wall Street.

At the time we met, Levine was helping Datek capitalize on rule changes in the Small Order Execution System (SOES), an early computer ordering system that automatically processed the orders of small investors. SOES had been devised as a response to the infamous Black Monday crash of 1987, when smaller investors were furious that Nasdaq dealers didn't answer their calls as stocks plummeted. From the dealers' perspective, the unprecedented volume of trading that day meant that their phone lines were overwhelmed, and they simply couldn't get to every call. Telephone, after all, is a nonscalable technology. Whatever the reason, the result spelled disaster for the small investor. So new rules were proposed to help protect them. The SOES system would automatically fill stock orders for small investors at a market maker's current, posted quote (up to a thousand shares).

As with many seemingly innocuous rule changes, the SOES rule spawned a new class of opportunities for savvy traders willing to exploit this automated system to their advantage (and ignore the spirit of the rule). Maschler was the most prominent of these "SOES bandits," as the dealers called them. Given that any dealer or market maker worked in many Nasdaq stocks at once, and entered their posted stock quotes manually in their computer terminals, it was often hard to keep fully updated with small changes in each stock. At any given moment, two market makers might have different posted quotes, especially for stocks that were on the move. These were small differences, to be sure, but that was all a smart trader needed. For example, one dealer might have a posted quote of Microsoft at 25¾; another might have it at 26. Sitting in his basement in Staten Island, Maschler, or one of his traders, could buy from the first dealer and sell to the other in a split second, making money on the difference in price. One might make only tens or perhaps hundreds of dollars at most on any given trade, but repeat that many, many times a day, and pretty soon you are making real money.

By any contemporary standard, it wasn't technologically sophisticated. But when the other guy is unarmed, even the simplest weapon wins the day. And it wasn't long until Levine devised a way to automate the process—a computer trading system that would carefully seek out the best trading opportunities on its own (it was appropriately called "the Watcher"). Other algorithms followed, and Levine's reputation spread, helped along by another young trader in Maschler's orbit, Jeff Citron. They showed me the system that day as I toured their Staten Island office. Watching their algorithm track "risers" and "fallers" among Nasdaq stocks, I suddenly wondered where they were getting this up-to-date information. There was no hard line attached to this house, as you might find on Manhattan trading desks. This was long before the days of mobile phones, high-bandwidth cable, or even dial-up internet. As I contemplated this seeming miracle, Maschler walked me outside and pointed up to the roof, where a satellite dish hung precariously.

"Check out our data feed." It was another anomaly in this sleepy neighborhood.

"The neighbors must think you're communicating with aliens," I remarked, only half joking.

With this innovative setup, Levine, Citron, and Maschler brought attention to the advantages that the smart use of new technologies could give the savvy (and sometimes unscrupulous) trader, increasing their trading speed and access to information. Soon, copycat strategies would be ubiquitous on Wall Street, even as they became increasingly sophisticated.

Not surprisingly, the establishment was not happy about these developments. The SOES system was designed to help brokers act on behalf of small, retail investors—mom-and-pop investors around the country calling in their orders—not to enrich a fleet of high-energy, super-motivated day traders pushing the boundaries of speed and arbitrage. (The extent to which the SOES bandits were legitimately representing investors was often a point of contention.) Market makers did everything they could to have them censored. A technological and regulatory arms race proceeded between the SOES traders seeking new advantages and market makers looking to defend their turf. Datek Securities was repeatedly fined. Maschler and his young crew saw themselves as scrappy Davids taking on the old boy network of fat and happy Goliaths who didn't want the world to change. They didn't seem to care too much if they needed to bend or even break a few rules in the process. Needless to say, Nasdaq market makers saw it differently.

Regulations eventually did evolve in response to these trading strategies, but the technology genie was out of the bottle on Wall Street. Trading was becoming faster, more automated, more democratized, and more accessible, and information more transparent. Perhaps it was inevitable. After all, *information wants to be free*—to borrow a phrase from the emerging world of computer hacker culture that Levine represented (a saying that, incidentally, goes back to one of the fathers of the personal computing movement, Stewart Brand, who had been on that bus with Ken Kesey).

Maschler would eventually cash out of Datek Securities and walk away with millions, but he would also incur one of the largest fines in history and be personally banned from the securities industry for life by the SEC. Jeff Citron would go on to work with Levine on his new ventures before leaving Wall Street altogether (he was banned along with Maschler) to help found the telecommunications company Vonage. But the part of this story that was destined to intersect again with mine and with Nasdaq's was Levine's.

In the years following our first meeting, this young savant would parlay his initial efforts at automated trading into a new ambition—building a virtual marketplace where buyers and sellers could come together without the need for a middleman. He envisioned an electronic exchange that would match Nasdaq trades efficiently, immediately, and transparently. It was the culmination of his dream to build a platform where every trader in the market was on equal footing, whether they were in Milwaukee or Manhattan—a sort of protected, virtual "Island." He built Island ECN using Linux OS, the open-source UNIX operating system, running on Dell boxes, in another basement, this time at his company headquarters on Broad Street in Manhattan. The servers were set atop wooden pallets to protect them from flooding (another reason for Island's name).

Many of the world's great technical breakthroughs seem simple and even inevitable—*in retrospect*. That's part of the illusion created by innovation. Our backward-looking narratives so easily fill in the blanks. *All the pieces were already present*, we might think to ourselves. *It was a natural evolution of the market.* Yes, that may be true, but only with the benefit of hindsight. It takes genius to put all the pieces together in a new way. Take Steve Jobs and the iPod. Or Tim Berners-Lee and the World Wide Web. Maybe someone was going to create such breakthroughs, sooner or later. But no one had, until them.

In his book *Where Good Ideas Come From,* author Steven Johnson posits that creative genius is less about dramatic, singular leaps of invention and more a creative fusion of many smaller ideas put together in novel ways. Levine's Island ECN was like that. Trading automation, distributed computing power, near-universal online access, a decade-long bull market, cheaper Intel-based hardware that could compete with mainframes, a version of UNIX (Linux) that was open-source—all of it came together in the right creative fusion. Levine devised an ECN that was built around the Linux kernel, so it was reliable. It could also run on distributed Intel servers, so it was cheap and scalable. Its coding was lean, so it ran fast. Levine understood the market structure down to its fundamentals, so his programming was elegant. And he understood trading, so Island's feature set was built for the new wave of traders entering the market. Was it an inevitable evolution of trading technology? Maybe. But no one else did it quite so brilliantly.

Island ECN grew quickly. It became the preferred platform of the wave of electronic traders entering the market in the mid-nineties. By the end of the decade, Island had established itself as a major player, and Levine's reputation had grown along with it. Digital luminaries of the era, like Jerry Yang of Yahoo! fame, made the pilgrimage to his New York office to check out the system, and a highly talented technology team formed around Levine and his creation, including my future partner Chris Concannon. In

1999, a glowing article about him in *Wired* began: "Forget Nasdaq. Island ECN is tearing down Wall Street."[1]

A few years later, in a strange and simple twist of fate, it was Levine's carefully crafted and brilliantly simple ECN—now known as INET—that would help rescue Nasdaq from its doldrums. I could never have predicted such a turn of events at that original meeting, where Maschler, with his brawny intensity, was chewing on his cigar and barking orders at his youthful acolyte. Who knew then what market-changing genius was germinating in that basement office?

Perhaps, however, it's not so surprising. Business leaders should always cultivate an attentive disposition toward outsiders, especially in industries impacted by technology. Always be on the lookout for new ideas, products, and technologies happening on the edges of your business ecosystem, where outsiders are developing a different picture of your future in apocryphal (and sometimes actual) garages and basements. Of course, you have to distinguish the mad from the madly creative, but it's always wise to give some attention to what today's outsiders are planning for tomorrow's establishment—one day they might be right.

Today, Levine's fingerprints can be found all over Wall Street's trading systems. In 2017, when I took over as Chairman of Virtu Financial, a company whose computers are deeply embedded in Wall Street's operations, I quizzed them about their IT systems. In a frank moment, one of the engineers told me, "Well, you know, it basically runs a lot like Nasdaq's INET." Moreover, Nasdaq still sells trading technology based on INET IP to more than one hundred exchanges all over the world. In other words, Levine's handiwork is now ubiquitous in the world's electronic markets—a quarter century after I first met him.

A Necessary Risk

In April 2005, Nasdaq bought Instinet, the company that owned INET. Of the forty-five acquisitions we made during my time as CEO, all were by choice, except this one—it was by necessity. This was the one we *had* to do. I felt we were at institutional risk otherwise. After all, if Nasdaq couldn't call itself a worldwide leader in trading equities, what exactly was it? If we couldn't command a premium share of the market for transactions in our own listed stocks, what were we doing in the listings business? If we weren't leading the market in technology, how long would we continue to be the stock market of choice for the tech industry?

The acquisition wasn't cheap. We had to take on $955 million in new debt, leaving Nasdaq highly leveraged. Our debt was actually junk-rated at the time. It was a calculated risk, but a risk nonetheless. If we'd hit the great recession in the months after the INET deal we could have been dead in the water. Luckily, we had time to get the company back on a sound financial footing.

The private equity firm Hellman and Friedman provided much of the funding for the deal, along with Silver Lake Partners. The deal wasn't simple—Instinet included several subsidiaries, including an institutional brokerage business that we didn't want and agreed to sell to Silver Lake, meaning that in effect we had to work through multiple deals at the same time. The marathon series of negotiations was led by Adena Friedman on the Nasdaq side. Adena worked incredibly hard on the deal and established her reputation as a persistent and smart negotiator, a role she would reprise again and again in future Nasdaq acquisitions.

Mike Bingle, the representative from Silver Lake, proved a tough counterpart. As he and Adena sparred over the various issues at stake in the deal, progress slowed to a crawl. Perhaps it was just that they were both smart, intense negotiators, but I began to worry that we weren't moving fast enough. During negotiations like this, long hours and sleep deprivation don't do any favors to clear thinking. People become less rational, more irritable. As I watched the time tick by and the energy of our team wane, I grew concerned that it was all going to fall apart.

Sometimes in dealmaking you need to stage a reboot. In a bid to get progress restarted, I called Glenn Hutchins, cofounder of Silver Lake Partners, and told him, "Glenn, you have to come in here or this isn't getting done." Hutchins showed up, well rested and ready to get things moving. He and I negotiated directly. Facing a second all-night session, I was exhausted but determined to get the deal across the finish line. As we went back and forth, trying to wrangle this complicated multistakeholder deal into submission, Hutchins and I got to know each other well. In fact, out of the chemistry we developed in the heat of the negotiating battle, a real friendship was formed. Hutchins would later serve on the Board of Nasdaq and we would eventually go into business together. In the last act of the drama, we sketched out the final series of agreements on a conference room napkin. After two days and two nights of nonstop dealmaking, everyone was happy (and exhausted), and Nasdaq had its prize.

A Balancing Act

Over the next year, we consolidated the SuperMontage matching engine, the BRUT matching engine, and the INET matching engine into an integrated system: one platform to rule them all. It was a herculean undertaking and involved significant new functionality. For example, we had to write new code to handle opening and closing auctions for the markets—technologically tricky processes to get right. This was not something that BRUT or Island had had to worry about in their pre-Nasdaq incarnations.

The team, who had come over from INET, had a distinct culture—rebellious and idealistic. After all, they had built Island ECN as a revolt against the Wall Street empire—to democratize access and let Main Street trade on equal footing. Now they had become part of that empire, but they had retained all of those anti-authority, antihierarchical, nonconformist leanings in their group culture. It was all jeans and sandals, not coats and ties. It was half corporate culture, half hacker culture. The team had real talent, without question, and the attitude to match it. They had the exuberance of youth, focused on what they could create, not on what could go wrong. They didn't want to submit to any traditional, buttoned-up corporate oversight. Under normal circumstances, I believe in creating cultural consistency throughout the organization. But I decided the time wasn't right to overly enforce this, so I made a calculated compromise. Sometimes you have to break your own rules.

It wasn't long before that decision cost me my CIO. He clashed with the incoming group, and he probably knew that this culture was not right for him. I respected his decision, and he found a great opportunity elsewhere. I was reminded that the right person for one moment is not always the right person for another moment. So I promoted Anna Ewing to CIO and put one of our newly acquired engineers, Jonathan Ross, in charge of the development of the new exchange platform.

Jonathan was talented, had a remarkable understanding of the inner workings of the equities market, and, like many highly capable engineers, loved building things and writing great code. He had a bit of a cowboy attitude, but without question, he was the right person for the job. Anna used her considerable skills to negotiate all of the culture and personality clashes and became a trusted colleague who served Nasdaq as CIO for the next decade.

In the end, the culture clash wasn't too problematic. After all, the INET people were doing great work. If they wanted to wear casual clothes to the office and resist certain operational structures, what the heck did I care? Were they producing? The answer was a resounding yes.

The team ran almost like a startup, meaning that we gave the engineers unusually free rein to remake our trading systems. They controlled most aspects of the process—functioning as their own quality assurance department, and deciding when code went into production. We ran without a lot of the checks and balances you would have in a more conventional production environment. My remaking of Nasdaq IT from an old-style, mainframe-oriented, slow-adapting, reliable, nonprofit work culture into a fast-iterating, technology-first, trust-the-engineers, startup-like work culture was never as fully realized as it was during this period. In any IT organization, there is a trade-off between radical efficiency and careful oversight, between engineering and operations, between speed to market and quality control. In this production process, we erred to one side of those dichotomies. We calculated that the existential challenge Nasdaq was facing necessitated that kind of approach. We were trying to survive and play catch-up in the new universe of automated trading functionality. Every release cycle seemed like it could make or break us, and speed to market was critical.

Today, we hear a lot about the "fail fast" ethos of startup culture. *Move fast and break things* was Facebook's unofficial motto in its early days. The idea is to not get bogged down in analysis paralysis, to get to market fast so you can get feedback, and then to iterate and change things on the fly as needed. For a startup, it makes sense. In that kind of environment, engineers rule. Operational oversight is minimal. Speed is everything. But for an established company with highly regulated legacy systems like Nasdaq, whose computers are central to the entire equities market, it's not so simple. We had other responsibilities. We had to be reliable. Uptime had to be close to perfect. So while I was trying to remake our culture to be more nimble, innovate more quickly, and get to market faster, I also had to ensure we kept one foot in each world. We couldn't abandon our conservative roots. It was like riding two horses at the same time without a harness to keep them going in the same direction. As time passed, we would rein our startup side back in, and reestablish a more conservative operational oversight. But for the moment, it was an unbalanced situation.

Looking back on it today, I'm still amazed by what the team accomplished. Their productivity was through the roof. In any normal production environment, integrating two independent matching engines would have taken at least two years. We did three in one year. The advancement they made on the IT front was unprecedented and might have rescued the company. By 2007, not only had we saved a great deal of money on synergies from the Instinet acquisition; we had built a trading platform that was industry leading. Frankly, it still is today. My conviction that INET had been the right technology to acquire was vindicated and then some. The buy-the-winners strategy had worked. Even the high cost of the acquisition and the leverage Nasdaq took on ended up being a small price to pay for the long-term boost to the business. After years of technological missteps, Nasdaq had finally got it right. We had a transactions platform that was best of breed and a technical team to match it.

The price of riding those two horses would be paid much later. In business, as in life, every decision comes with inevitable trade-offs. Context and timing is everything when it comes to strategy. We were in a desperate situation, and my hands-off approach to my touchy but talented engineering team was necessary for their success. And I don't just mean the dress code. I let them keep the black box of their technological universe partially opaque and resistant to traditional forms of operational management. No doubt, that's partly why they were superproductive. It also meant, however, that we didn't have sufficient visibility on all the ramifications of the technology. We didn't have fail-safe procedures to vet all of it in real-world situations. Their extraordinary work would deliver us great returns and power Nasdaq's transactions platform for years to come. In 2007 it was all upside. The downside would come later. Unfortunately, it would reveal itself during one of the most publicized IPOs in history, that of another company famous for its unorthodox "hacker" culture—Facebook.

From the Basement to the Boardroom

Disruptive innovation often comes dressed in countercultural garb. The electronic trading revolution, like many rebellions, had started on the fringes—cultivated by outsiders, built by computer engineers, and indirectly financed by hordes of investors across the country who wanted a more direct pathway to sharing in the riches of the economic boom. The upstarts were ignored, resisted, feared, banished, and eventually embraced as allies. ECNs traveled from Wall Street's basements to its most illustrious boardrooms in just a few years. Along the way, they dealt a mortal blow to the cloistered, insider clubs of Wall Street, where cigar-smoking men gathered in wood-paneled rooms filled with leather chairs to count their money over cognac and discuss the winners and losers of the day (at least in Hollywood legend). It was the end of an era.

I reflected on this unlikely journey when I sat down to lunch with Josh Levine at Nasdaq's headquarters, shortly after our purchase of his creation. INET had come a long way in its short life. The once antiestablishment ECN was now integral to our establishment exchange, and we were beginning to assimilate our trading platform into its technology. Chris Concannon had invited Levine to connect and celebrate the acquisition. As young entrepreneurs and executives at Island, they had dreamed of the day when their ECN might actually vanquish Nasdaq, wresting control from the old-style market makers and remaking Wall Street trading in the image of their creation. In a sense, that day had arrived, though perhaps not in precisely the way they had envisioned.

Levine himself, dressed down in his usual T-shirt and jeans, was a pleasant dining companion. A private, unassuming person who always shunned the limelight, he had moved on to new horizons in alternative energy and lost interest in the markets. Perhaps he felt his contribution to the Wall Street technological revolution was complete.

A new elite was rising—the quants, coders, and engineers who were more likely to be found in chat rooms and data centers than in high-ceilinged men's clubs. Wall Street was slowly being remade in the image of ones and zeros. As someone who watched the revolution unfold from its earliest days and helped coax the old guard into the new world, I was convinced the changes were mostly for the better, but like any innovation, they came with plenty of disruption and involved significant new dangers and regulatory challenges—as the years ahead would make clear.

LEADERSHIP LESSONS

- **Buy the Winners.** There's no shame in using smart acquisitions to gain much-needed market share or technology, even if you pay a premium in the short term.

- **Sometimes You Have to Break Your Own Rules.** A good leader can be flexible as circumstances demand—even knowing there will be trade-offs involved, and what's right today won't be right tomorrow.

- **Today's Outsiders Are Tomorrow's Establishment.** Don't ignore those on the fringes of your business ecosystem—they just might be creating your future.

Chapter Five

From Apple to Zillow

Six Big Board Stocks Join Nasdaq

CNN Money, January 12, 2004

In my entrepreneurial days at ASC, I did my time in sales (along with HR, accounting, product management, cooking, and bottle washing, as is the way in any small company). Back in the early nineties, as the public face of the company, I often found myself calling on potential customers, doing demonstrations, and making pitches. One particularly memorable sales call involved the hedge fund D. E. Shaw, then relatively new and focused on using cutting-edge computational technology. When I heard they were getting into the market-making business, I called up one of their executives and told him that I'd like to come over and demo our system. Despite being state-of-the-art at the time (twenty-inch cathode-ray technology), it still required a few decent-sized boxes, which I loaded into the elevator in a Midtown Manhattan building and wheeled up to the room where I was to give my presentation. I'd begun assembling my demo station, bumping into walls, tripping on cords, and struggling to set things up in this tiny, Spartan office, when my contact, some guy named Jeff, told me to stop.

"Just explain to me how it works. That's all I need," he said. I thought that would be a professional mistake. Customers generally needed to actually see our software in action. But he insisted, so I reluctantly agreed to do the demo verbally. I started giving my best visual description of how the screen would appear and operate. Lost in my own efforts, it took me a few minutes to realize that my would-be customer had leaned back in his chair and closed his eyes. *I hope he's not falling asleep!* I thought. For a brief moment, this sales call seemed to be breaking bad.

I soon realized, however, that he wasn't sleeping. He was listening. He was completely focused—immersed in his own visualization. He was building, in some imaginal realm, the working demo I was describing verbally, envisioning our system in his own mental universe. As I went through the whole setup, he followed every word. By the time I was done, it was as if he had built it himself. He grasped the interface and intricacies better than most customers. In the end, I didn't make the sale. But I learned an important lesson, nonetheless. Sometimes you don't really know who you're talking to—or rather, who they might become. That day, I made the acquaintance of Jeff Bezos. I can testify that he is a visionary—in the most literal sense of the word.

I would encounter Bezos on a few other occasions pre-Amazon. Amazon went public in 1997 on Nasdaq, raising $54 million for an overall market valuation of around $440 million. For new disruptors in the digital landscape like Amazon, Nasdaq was the venue of choice for raising money in the nineties. Indeed, in those days, NYSE didn't take startups. They considered themselves to be the stock market for established companies, and they expected all significant national businesses to switch over to NYSE once they reached a certain size. Dick Grasso, NYSE's CEO when I joined Nasdaq, used to boast that he'd reserved the prestigious one-letter ticker symbols M and I for the anticipated defection of Microsoft and Intel. But it didn't happen that way. As Nasdaq nurtured a generation of young technology companies, it earned their loyalty. After all, Nasdaq was providing them with critical funding in the public markets at a time when there simply was no other significant source of capital available. This was long before the days of a venture capital marketplace awash in money. I give my predecessors at Nasdaq credit for walking a delicate line—embracing promising startups while keeping their listings standards high enough to earn credibility in the eyes of investors.

The result, over time, was the creation of a national duopoly. Most countries have one primary stock exchange that provides listings services for national companies. There is one in Paris, one in London, one in Madrid, one in Tokyo, and one in Sydney. America has two: Nasdaq and NYSE. Inevitably, this leads to an intense competitive dynamic. Think Coke and Pepsi, Airbus and Boeing, Android and iOS.

I knew that in the long run, our greatest competitive advantage was to be found in transforming our transactions business through technology. But I couldn't ignore the other business in which we went head-to-head with NYSE: listings. My client relations team wouldn't let me. "Grasso is in our accounts," they kept telling me, in my first weeks and months on the job, meaning that NYSE's CEO was whispering in the ears of our companies, offering them enticements to switch their business to his exchange.

A hardscrabble guy who had worked his way up from floor clerk, Grasso was an intelligent, tough competitor with a fearsome reputation on Wall Street. I respected Grasso's work ethic and knew he was not to be underestimated. He certainly wasn't going to back off just because we were going through a painful reorganization. He was always working the phones—a seemingly omnipresent behind-the-scenes rival, trying hard to convince Nasdaq companies to bolt for NYSE, and in the process forcing me to spend much more time on the listings business than I had planned in those first years on the job. (Interestingly, when he left months later, my life got much easier.) Hence, in my role as CEO, I found myself doing sales once again—working hard to entice the next generation of technology startups to choose Nasdaq as their home and to keep our existing clients happy lest they take their listings elsewhere.

The Human Side of Business

When it comes to a business that is built on relationships, you can never take anything for granted. Before I'd even started the job, I had a conversation with John Jacobs, the longtime Executive Vice President of Nasdaq's Global Index Group. I asked him, "What do I need to know about Nasdaq that I don't yet understand? What don't I get about this job?" His response was prescient. "I know you have a deep understanding of the transactions business. You have extensive technology experience. You have a good sales and operations background. But the listings business is a different animal. It has an emotional component that will surprise you. Companies don't choose to list with Nasdaq or NYSE for purely rational or financial reasons. You're often dealing with CEOs and founders and their pride, ego, life aspirations, and concerns about their legacy. Nasdaq may be less expensive than NYSE and offer a better package of services. But that alone seldom wins the day."

Over and over again, I discovered that Jacobs was right. There were all kinds of reasons why companies chose Nasdaq over NYSE, or vice versa. It wasn't simply about the bottom line. What made the listings business challenging—and interesting—was that our customers were the founders and leaders of some of the world's biggest companies. In leading the listings business, I had to work directly with these iconic figures and try to figure out what made them tick. More often than not, it surprised me.

Yes, some CEOs were eminently rational: "What can you offer me that NYSE can't? What's the benefit?" they wanted to know. Others were transactional: "What could my company sell to Nasdaq if I list with you?" Some were social or tribal: "What are other companies in my industry doing?" Many were emotional, their choices based on personal aspirations or childhood ambition: "I always dreamed of ringing the bell at NYSE," or "I want to see my company's name listed among the world's best technology companies on Nasdaq." In these latter cases, I eventually realized, trying to sell the benefits of Nasdaq's superior trading statistics was beside the point. How many CEOs did I put to sleep by regaling them with the underappreciated benefits of Nasdaq's micromarket structure before I learned that such matters were probably not driving their decision-making?

Certain CEOs put more value on the personal relationship than on a cost-benefit analysis. They would list with whichever stock market had developed the best connection with the CEO (or executive team). Some thrived on engagement and joint partnerships. Some made a decision, and you barely heard from them again for years—like Jeff Bezos and Amazon. Some needed reminders every so often that Nasdaq was still the best partner for their business. Some were loyal, no matter what, to the exchange that had been the venue for their IPO. Others were always wondering if the grass might be greener down the street.

A key factor, I discovered, was often brand affiliation. Why did technology companies want to list with Nasdaq? An important reason was simply that other technology companies did the same. Our affiliation with innovation and technology was unmatched by our rivals. Indeed, the brand identity of the two exchanges was quite clear in most CEOs' minds. It all came down to "Who are you as a CEO?" and "Who are you as a company?" *I've arrived, I'm established*—that was NYSE. *I'm growing, I'm innovative, I'm entrepreneurial*—that was Nasdaq. We worked hard to make "Nasdaq-listed" a badge of pride for the world's best companies. And it was a virtuous circle—our companies liked to associate with Nasdaq, but we also built our brand through association with them. But this sometimes made it hard to convince companies outside the tech world to list with us as well. In every sale, it seemed we were either leveraging that affiliation to our advantage or fighting tooth and nail to escape that brand box.

I quickly realized that being a likable social presence and an effective CEO-to-CEO networker was an integral part of my role, and key to representing Nasdaq on the national and world stage. Of course, there were perks as well. I had the opportunity to meet probably more CEOs than just about anyone in business. I sat in hundreds of conference rooms, from Apple to Zillow, and heard their leaders' visions as I pitched Nasdaq's wares. Inevitably,

I spent a lot of time in Silicon Valley, talking to executives all over the peninsula, attending industry events at Stanford, visiting venture capitalists on Sand Hill Road, and schmoozing with social media savants in San Francisco.

John Chambers, longtime CEO of Cisco, was kind enough to throw a party for me on my first trip to the Bay Area, introducing me to the leaders in the Valley. It was a bit nerve-racking, as this type of public profile was new to me. I was fascinated by the unique ecosystem of Silicon Valley and, in particular, the symbiotic relationship between the university, the business community, and the venture capital firms. The executives at the event, many of whom had attended Stanford, mingled with professors, technologists, startup founders, and venture capitalists (VCs). Money, ideas, business savvy, and intellectual firepower were all richly interwoven through the community in a fertile network of talent. Many Stanford professors had spent time in Silicon Valley businesses or VC firms, or started their own, and some business leaders now taught at Stanford.

I remember staying at the gathering late into the California evening, something that seemed perfectly natural in the warm, Mediterranean climate of Palo Alto. That would have been rare in New York business, where everyone is eager to make it out of the city as soon as the workday is done. California's casual dress code and laid-back attitude were novelties to me, but I soon learned not to make the mistake of thinking my new West Coast friends were any less driven than their New York counterparts. I came to look forward to my visits to the West Coast as one of the more enjoyable aspects of my job. And there would be plenty of them, as the competition for the tech company listings ramped up.

Changing the Competitive Landscape

In 2003, when I started as CEO, no company had ever switched its listing from the New York Stock Exchange to Nasdaq. If they moved at all, they went the other way. As Nasdaq had become a more established brand, the flow of companies wanting to switch their listings to NYSE had slowed dramatically. But it was still unheard-of for large, established American companies to switch from NYSE to Nasdaq.

I was determined to change that.

Bruce Aust and I put our heads together and came up with a strategy and a list of companies to approach. One of the first was Charles Schwab, the innovative financial management company based in San Francisco that was still run by its famous founder, Chuck Schwab. I flew out to the Bay Area, and Bruce and I met with Chuck and discussed the opportunities available with a Nasdaq listing. Usually, our sales pitch was based on tailored packages of offerings and talking points. These included a series of marketing "gives," things like cobranded advertising and promotions that we tweaked and tailored for each customer. Finally, we would leverage our brand as "the Silicon Valley stock market." That was a real selling point for companies like Schwab that were trying to position themselves as part of the new information economy.

Schwab was receptive. But he wasn't ready to abandon NYSE yet. "What about dual listing?" he asked us. Dual listing? Bruce and I looked at each other with a mixture of confusion and curiosity. It wasn't something companies had done before. At first,

I thought Schwab was saying this just as a way to get out of the meeting—throw something out that isn't going to work, and then move on. But I quickly realized that he was serious. My mind started turning even as the discussion continued. After all, a listing switch is as much a marketing victory as an economic win. A dual listing would largely accomplish that without requiring the same level of immediate commitment. "We'll look into it and get back to you soon," we told him.

Sometimes your customers give you great ideas. They have a unique view on your business. Always pay attention to their feedback. Maybe a suggestion will be embedded in a complaint, disguised in a rejection, or hidden in a throwaway remark, but listen closely and the nugget of wisdom is there. That being said, you never want to limit your vision to your customers' demands. They are usually focused on incremental changes to existing products or services. Genuine leaps of innovation happen when you envision the thing your customer doesn't yet know they need.

Dual listing wasn't a leap, but it was a real step, and no one had tried it before. If Charles Schwab was willing to put one foot into the Nasdaq ecosystem, surely others would follow. Given that we were having difficulty convincing companies to switch outright, this was a much easier proposition, allowing us to build long-term relationships with new companies, even as they evaluated Nasdaq's offerings. Over time, our hope was that we could outwork NYSE and win the listings outright. So Nasdaq set out to find a group of companies willing to dual-list. We wanted at least five or six to announce all at once.

Soon, we got a boost from one of Silicon's Valley's most celebrated companies, Hewlett-Packard. Bruce and I met with Carly

Fiorina in her office at HP's headquarters and pitched the benefits of dual listing. Fiorina was open to the idea and, with her characteristic assertiveness, had a meeting on the spot with her CFO and decided right then and there to go ahead. Her willingness to rationally think through the benefits and her capacity to act quickly and make an immediate decision were very impressive. We were thrilled, even knowing that part of her motivation was likely to be in a better position to sell HP technology to Nasdaq's back-end trading systems.

By January 2004, we had six companies ready to go. We put out a press release announcing the program, and the companies that had joined up—Hewlett-Packard, Walgreens, Cadence, Charles Schwab, Countrywide Financial, and Apache. All of them were significant market cap companies. There would be many more over the years. But this was a great first step—a shot across the bow to NYSE.

Walgreens, in particular, was a coup. This wasn't a technology company. (These days, every company is a technology company to some degree, but this was before that became the reality of the business landscape.) It was a heartland mainstay, headquartered in Illinois, an icon of Middle America. And yet, more than most, they were willing to see the benefits and take the risk. I loved our reputation as a technology stock market, but I didn't want to be limited by that. We needed to be able to represent all kinds of companies. Walgreens was exactly the kind of business that affirmed that strategy, as was Starbucks, another early and loyal nontech Nasdaq company. Starbucks was one of the first nontechnology companies that stuck with Nasdaq as it blossomed into a global retail brand, and affirmed that we were much more than a market for high-flying Silicon Valley companies.

One More Cup of Coffee

Winning a customer feels great, but it's really just the beginning. Like a marriage that has to be renewed every year, Nasdaq's relationships with its listed companies can never be taken for granted.

As a case in point, some years later, Bruce came into my office with a worrisome message: "We have a problem with Starbucks."

"Starbucks! Are you kidding? What's going on?" The iconic coffee chain had been with Nasdaq for almost two decades. Led by celebrated CEO Howard Schultz, Starbucks was always a much-loved customer at Nasdaq's headquarters—and not just because they had a store in the lobby of One Liberty Plaza that was frequented by my executive team. Over the years, the company had grown into one of America's truly great brands, and we had been along for that remarkable ride the entire way. We had done plenty of joint promotional activities, including a market open at MarketSite with Howard Schultz and Jamie Dimon, launching a Starbucks Rewards Visa card. They had even been featured in a Nasdaq advertising campaign, and one of their executives was on our Board. What could possibly be wrong now? Bruce didn't know the details, but he had heard rumblings of discontent from his contacts at the company. It was clear we needed to get out to Seattle and make sure the relationship was on a good footing.

I called John Jacobs, who had a close relationship with

Starbucks's CMO. Jacobs worked in Nasdaq's DC office. "Have you heard anything?"

"I haven't been able to find out any details," Jacobs replied. "In fact, their CMO doesn't know anything either. Maybe NYSE has been whispering sweet nothings into Howard's ear."

"Yes, maybe. But we can't lose Starbucks. Pack your bags. We're headed to Seattle. I'll set up a meeting with Schultz."

When we arrived in the Pacific Northwest, I huddled together with Jacobs and the customer account person for Starbucks and prepared for the meeting. I'm not a coffee drinker (I consider myself self-caffeinated), but that day I made sure I had a Starbucks mug in hand as we were shuttled into an office with Schultz and his CMO. Sure enough, we soon learned the seats in which we were sitting had recently been occupied by our competitors. "NYSE was just out here and they are willing to knock down brick walls for me and Starbucks," Schultz told us as the meeting began.

Schultz and I had developed a positive relationship over the years. He had grown up working-class in Brooklyn before his ascendance to fortune and fame, and I always felt a kinship with such an inspirational, bootstrapping biography. He was the type of CEO who was always tending his company's brand. Perhaps Nasdaq had been remiss in providing Starbucks the full capacity of our promotional power. Perhaps he wanted reassurance that Nasdaq was still in Starbucks's corner. Sure enough, the conversation soon turned to Schultz's forthcoming book, which told the story of the creation of Starbucks. Clearly, he was hoping the book would give the brand a boost, and he was looking for our support. In fact, it seemed to have become a kind of test of our partnership.

John must have realized the same thing, because before I

could respond, he jumped in: "Just so you know, Howard, Nasdaq has a lot of plans for your book. I think it's a remarkable, inspirational story, a must read for C-suite executives at Nasdaq companies. We're planning to buy several thousand copies, and we're going to send them to all of our listed businesses."

As Jacobs outlined plans for the book launch, the tone in the room changed. Schultz looked encouraged, and his interest was piqued. John continued, laying out plans for Starbucks's fortieth anniversary the following year, with an opening bell in Seattle. "It would be the first time it has ever been done out here. It could be a great cobranded event with Starbucks and Nasdaq."

I smiled to myself. I knew John was improvising to some degree, but that was okay. He was doing what was needed in order to keep an important customer satisfied. This is why you have talented executives, so they can stay one step ahead of a client's needs. And when they fall behind, for whatever reason, they find a way to scramble back into the lead.

John's quick thinking saved the day. We did do the opening bell in March 2011 at Starbucks's first store in Seattle's iconic Pike Place Market. I took the stage with Schultz at 6 a.m. on a rainy morning. We opened the trading day together, launched Starbucks's new logo, and celebrated a wonderful twenty-year relationship, with lots of highly caffeinated onlookers. Schultz, a remarkable entrepreneur who built his company up from essentially nothing to more than seventeen thousand stores in fifty-five countries, gave a powerful speech about preserving and extending the values and culture of Starbucks. For my part, I resolved to preserve and extend Nasdaq's relationship with Starbucks as the years went by.

Opening-bell events always were a hit with our companies,

even more so when they were on location. The first time we did one remotely was with Cisco in 2005 in San Jose. Nasdaq employs a great deal of Cisco equipment in its technology back end, and the idea of doing a virtual opening, using Cisco equipment, was too good to pass up—especially given that Nasdaq was the world's first virtual stock market.

When a company celebrates an IPO or an anniversary, as it was with Starbucks or Cisco, it's a chance for a business to reflect for a moment on itself. It's like a significant birthday for a whole organization, and especially for a public company. I was always struck by how much interest there was in these celebratory milestones, whether it was popping champagne corks before the opening bell at Nasdaq MarketSite in Times Square, or all-night "hackathons" with the employees of Facebook before their morning IPO, or Starbucks fans sipping early-morning lattes in Seattle, or remote openings in various cities in Asia. I have such fond memories of all those occasions. Like few people in business, I was able to vicariously participate in hundreds of landmark moments in the lives of the organizations in the Nasdaq ecosystem.

Just like individuals, organizations also need to celebrate milestones, to reflect on where they came from, their accomplishments, their role in creating economic opportunity, and the investors around the world who believed in the vision. Nasdaq is a go-between for these companies to interface with millions of shareholders and stakeholders around the world. Its function is more than the facilitation of trading; it's providing a connecting point between the great companies of the world and the capital— both economic *and* social—that makes them viable.

A President in Waiting

"He's waiting. Get here as soon as you can."

Bruce sounded agitated, and I understood. "I'm leaving now: I'll be there as soon as possible." Unfortunately, in New York, "as soon as possible" could mean anything, and I was already behind schedule. I had just left Nasdaq's headquarters and was headed uptown to meet Donald Trump at Trump Tower in Midtown Manhattan.

As I hung up the phone, I looked out the window at the bumper-to-bumper traffic on Sixth Avenue. Not a good sign. Among Nasdaq EVPs, my reputation for punctuality was...well, less than stellar. But sometimes there just were not enough hours in the day. This was 2005, and the future President was just a larger-than-life businessman. He had reorganized his casino business and was looking to list again on public markets. His name was quite the popular franchise, and I certainly wanted to win the listing. A half hour later I pulled up to the front of the gold-accented tower with Trump's name emblazoned above the doors, and headed up to meet the man himself.

Many years later, this building's lobby would become the scene of frenzied media activity as a breathless horde of reporters blanketed the entrance after Trump's 2016 election victory, while his government-in-waiting strategized on the floors above. But for now, it was just another bustling office building in New York, and I hurried up the escalator with some urgency.

Trump didn't seem at all fazed by my tardiness. He was charming and gracious, inviting us to have a seat. As we began the conversation, and Trump launched into his plans for Trump Entertainment Resorts, I felt something was slightly off, but it took a moment to realize that it was our relative height—we were sitting lower than Trump, who sat noticeably higher, behind a huge desk, smiling down on us, his broad face perched over his red power tie.

Whatever your politics today, it's impossible not to notice that Trump has authentic star power. I had first encountered the Trump phenomenon some years before, when I met him at a MarketSite opening bell for Nextel, the wireless communications company. They had formed a partnership with NASCAR, and Trump was being paid to help promote the brand. I'm impressed that even then Nextel recognized Trump's appeal to the working-class demographic that is NASCAR's primary audience. I rang the opening bell, standing next to Trump, Melania, and Kurt Busch, that year's NASCAR Cup champion. After the event, we walked out into Times Square together, and Trump was simply mobbed with fans. I'm not sure I could explain his magnetism, but it was remarkable to see up close.

In that meeting at his eponymous tower, Bruce and I offered Trump the TRMP ticker symbol and talked about what Nasdaq could offer the company in terms of trading, investor relations, and publicity. After some high-profile bankruptcies and a damaged reputation, his business star was rising again, and his celebrity power along with it. The IPO market was still depressed in those days, and any new listing helped. Winning a celebrity IPO wouldn't hurt, either. As we discovered in the meeting, we had the inside track due to Trump's bad experience with NYSE.

"Just so you two know, I hate the New York Stock Exchange,"

he told us. This was long before Trump met Twitter, but already, I suspected he was not one to mince words.

"Well, it probably goes without saying that we are not huge fans of the New York Stock Exchange either," I replied. "What happened with you?"

"I had some of my casinos listed on the exchange, and they ran into trouble. The business went bankrupt, and we had to delist. The people at NYSE were very nasty about it."

Bruce looked at me, and then at Trump, before responding very deliberately: "Just so we are clear, Mr. Trump, if you go bankrupt while on Nasdaq, we will also delist you." And then he paused, continuing with a slight smile, "But I promise that we'll be super nice about it." And that was exactly what happened. A few years later the business did go bankrupt, and we—very nicely—delisted it.

The Once and Future Capitalists

In 2006, Nasdaq managed to attract two-thirds of the available IPOs in the market. Indeed, in the perpetual contest with our competitor down the street, we felt an increasing edge. We were making headway on my fifth priority: *Stop being satisfied with No. 2.*

The search for competitive advantage, however, was not circumscribed by our nation's borders. At home, we were competing with NYSE; on the world stage there were two other competitors with global reach: London (LSE) and Hong Kong (HKEX). A particularly rich market for new global listings was China.

I spent a fair amount of time there, courting the executives of upstart firms. Listings was an unpredictable business on American soil; it was doubly so in this unfamiliar culture.

It was on my first trip to China that I began to realize just how much the Nasdaq brand meant worldwide. I simply wasn't prepared for the kind of media coverage we received. My team had arranged a press conference, and a veritable horde of journalists showed up, writing down every word, snapping my photo like paparazzi chasing a movie star. For a brief period, it seemed like I was at the center of the media universe, and I will confess to having a moment of self-inflation. But it was fleeting. I quickly realized that my newfound fame had nothing to do with me personally. Those paparazzi weren't chasing me; they were hoping to get close to the Nasdaq brand, and to American entrepreneurialism. It was quite an experience to feel, so directly and powerfully, the Chinese interest in our economic model. Granted, my exposure was to a certain slice of the population, but my impression was that the Chinese are natural capitalists. What still amazes me, after many visits to their great nation, is not that they have embraced entrepreneurial capitalism, but that they ever turned away from it in the first place.

I did witness an evolution in my visits to China. In my early trips, during 2003 and 2004, it seemed that anything American had a certain golden aura. Companies wanted to be like American companies—a Chinese version of Google (Baidu), for example. But that changed over the years. By the end of the decade, business leaders expressed less interest in copycat formulas; rather, they aspired to their own innovations. Their confidence in their independent economic vision was growing.

Occasionally, on those trips, I encountered some surprising cultural mismatches. Before one appointment in Beijing, I read in my briefing notes that the CEO I would be meeting liked to hunt. I've shot some birds in my day, and thought this line of conversation might be a way to bond with a prospective customer.

"What do you hunt?" I asked.

"Chickens," he replied.

Chickens? "How do you hunt a chicken?" I inquired, trying to hide my surprise. Was something getting lost in translation?

"They're in a pen. We shoot them," he explained enthusiastically.

As I regained my poker face, I made a mental note to excuse myself from any proposed hunting trips.

There were other memorable moments of cultural dissonance— some funny and incongruous, others surprising and strange. We would often end our evenings with a bountiful dinner party with plenty of food and endless toasts. It must be said that the Chinese palate embraces a wide variety of foods that are not found on the Western plate. In one dinner table conversation, a new Chinese business associate explained the Chinese relationship to food through a joke.

"Imagine that an ET came to Earth," he began, leaning over with a slight conspiratorial air as we sat around a large dinner table. "The Americans would do everything they could to study and scientifically understand ET. The Russians, on the other hand, would try to figure out how to turn ET into a weapon. But the Chinese"—he paused for dramatic effect, and I waited for the politically incorrect punch line I was sure would follow— "the Chinese would spend all of their time figuring out which part of ET was best to eat!" He had burst out laughing before the joke was finished.

In most respects, the cultural differences were easy to overcome. It's a cliché but it's true that people are people all over the world. Beyond the superficial particulars of culture and geography, there were so many ways in which the Chinese executives were just like their American counterparts. I made lots of new friends and developed many good business relationships during my trips. What's happening in China right now has little precedent. It's the biggest migration into the middle class in history. They have tremendous challenges ahead, but the business community is learning fast and evolving at a remarkable speed. Nasdaq-listed companies like Baidu, Weibo, and JD.com are now globally recognized and respected brands. It was an honor to help facilitate, with Nasdaq's investor credibility, the evolution of their access to global capital and public markets.

Indeed, this was the deeper meaning I found in leading the listings business, both at home and abroad. Amid all the hoopla of pomp and celebrity, and the thrill of the competitive spirit, it reaffirmed for me that Nasdaq is not just a business—it is also a global platform for supercharging innovation and entrepreneurial capitalism in our society. I know that sounds like a line out of an annual report, but I came to see truth in it. There is very little historical precedent for the global reach, scale, and public transparency that Nasdaq (and other similar exchanges) brings to the world of investment. Money may make the world go round, but it's only money well allocated that actually transforms economic capital into social and technological progress. That enables visionaries to do what they do best—rewrite tomorrow with a script that reads better for us all.

LEADERSHIP LESSONS

- **Build Your Brand Through Affiliation.** Your customers are often your best brand ambassadors.

- **Not Every Sale Is a Cost-Benefit Analysis.** Human choices are driven by multiple factors, some personal, some tribal, some transactional. Take the time to understand what really makes your customers tick.

- **You Don't Win a Customer Just Once.** Great customer relationships need to be tended to and constantly renewed.

Chapter Six

A Political Education

SEC Alters Rules on Stock Trading in a Narrow Vote

Wall Street Journal, April 7, 2005

If you had the chance to chat one-on-one with the great innovator of our time, what would you talk about? When I found myself alone with Steve Jobs for ten minutes, strangely enough, the conversation turned to regulation.

It was sometime in the mid-2000s, and Nasdaq was hosting a meet-and-greet with political leaders and CEOs over breakfast in Silicon Valley. Recently appointed Treasury Secretary Hank Paulson was the speaker that day. I arrived early, and when I entered the room only one of our guests had arrived. Jobs was sitting quietly off to the side. After years of working and negotiating with the world's top business leaders, I'm not starstruck easily, but Jobs had a certain aura about him that was unmistakable—a quality of unusual intensity and focus. After exchanging pleasantries, we struck up a conversation.

"We're going to hear about politics and regulation today,

right?" he asked. "Thank God I don't have to deal too much with that world."

"Unfortunately, I can't avoid it," I replied. "For the most part, Nasdaq can't make a serious business move without oversight and approval. It's just something we live with."

Jobs looked sympathetic. "I can't imagine trying to function in a business that is so highly regulated. It's not something I've ever had to do. I've been lucky. All my business initiatives have been in largely unregulated areas."

"I'm used to it now," I reflected, "but I admit, there are moments when I feel like the beaten stepchild of the SEC."

His expression took on a new appreciation. "How can you be creative, get things done, with that kind of oversight?"

Before I could answer, Paulson and the other guests showed up, and that magic moment of private conversation was over. It wasn't profound; it wasn't life-changing, but it was memorable nonetheless. And Jobs was certainly right about the challenge of innovation under the regulatory apparatus. At Nasdaq, we weren't living the unregulated life. Like it or not, regulation was in the very air we breathed. In fact, without decades of regulatory action in the financial markets, Nasdaq would likely not even exist. We couldn't shed our SEC skin. We had to embrace it, roll with it, work with it. As entrepreneurs and disruptors, we chafed against it. But over time, we found the right rhythm to our innovation that included the slow machinery of the SEC approval process. And to my surprise, I began to realize that regulation could even be an ally in increasing our competitive advantage and fulfilling the final step in my five-point plan: *Stop being satisfied with No. 2.*

A Political Education

Mike Oxley wants to talk to you.

When I first heard that phrase, I was surprised. I'd only recently taken on the Nasdaq job, and my education in the ways and means of politics was about to begin. Oxley was the powerful Congressman from Ohio who served as Chairman of the Committee on Financial Services in the United States House of Representatives. His name was on the Sarbanes-Oxley legislation that had defined a new era of financial regulation. Oxley ran the committee that oversees the SEC, which oversees Nasdaq, making him one of the most powerful people in our industry and, by extension, in the country as a whole. And he wanted to talk to me?

Initially, I admit, the thought bolstered my ego. That was, until Chris brought me back down to earth. "You know he wants to raise money from you, right?" Oh, right. This was politics. The rules of Washington, DC, were different, and there were times in those early days when I felt like a freshman student in a world of long-tenured political experts and professors. Negotiating our financial regulatory structure and engaging our nation's political class was simply not a skill set I had brought along with me to Nasdaq.

Yet, it certainly mattered. Our every operation had to be authorized by the SEC, and any changes made to our trading systems had to be approved. Regulations could make or break us; they could encourage good behavior or spawn bad (or both). They could make markets work better—helping securities trading become more equitable and efficient in its allocation of precious capital—or they could do the opposite. They could reward innovation and encourage technological transformations like those we had embraced at Nasdaq, or they could stymie and delay those changes, and shore up our entrenched competitors. They could level the playing field or they could stack the deck. I understood the incentives and motives of businesspeople; politicians, not so much. I needed to know what made them tick, what constituted a win for them. I had to get up to speed in the ways of Washington—and quickly.

As it turned out, I would soon become accustomed to hearing that Oxley wanted to talk to me. He and I would work together on many projects over the years and become good friends. A fellow sports fan, he helped me to understand that sports and politics have much in common, each involving intricate strategy and gamesmanship. I have fond memories of him recounting great moments from games gone by—unforgettable football plays, epic golf shots, and other sporting highlights. He would segue from describing the strategic sequence of plays in a fourth-quarter comeback from a long-past Ohio State–Michigan football game to describing the legislative pathway and political positions adopted around a particular bill, with the same curiosity and insight, revealing the similarities. His remarkable, near-photographic memory also served him well in Congress, where he easily recalled names, faces, events, details of a bill, who said what in a committee meeting, and so on.

I wish there were more people in government like Oxley. His eponymous Sarbanes-Oxley Act of 2002—passed in the wake of the Enron and WorldCom scandals and designed to improve accounting standards and transparency in American business—was not popular in corporate America, to put it mildly. The financial industry chafed under its increased oversight and complex reporting requirements. However, Oxley's affable, engaging personality managed to transcend his legislation's reputation. After his retirement in 2007, we ended up bringing him on at Nasdaq as a nonexecutive Vice Chairman. Executives from our listed companies enjoyed the opportunity to meet with this pragmatic, middle-of-the-road former Congressman, and they were fascinated to hear his behind-the-scenes stories and get his advice on dealing with the intricacies of Washington. Before his untimely death in 2016 from cancer, his service to Nasdaq was greatly valued.

In my political education, I also benefited a great deal from the guidance of Ed Knight, Nasdaq's general counsel, formerly at the U.S. Treasury Department, where he had served under Bob Rubin and Lloyd Bentsen. His thoughtful advice and deep well of wisdom regarding both law and politics were invaluable. I relied on his expertise, his knowledge of financial regulations, and his personal relationships with key players both in Washington and on Wall Street throughout my time at Nasdaq. For businesspeople, Washington can feel like a world apart. Like anyone thrown into a foreign culture, you need friends who understand the language and know how things get done.

I made many friends in Washington, but had my share of policy disagreements as well. My relationship with Bill Donaldson, head of the SEC from 2003 to 2005, was a case in point. Donaldson's impressive résumé was a testament to success, power, and privilege in both the public and private sector. He was steeped in the old world of equity trading, and a veteran of the floor exchange model. In fact, he'd once been CEO of NYSE, which troubled me, to say the least.

My initial meeting with him, soon after I started at Nasdaq, was a sign of things to come. Ed Knight walked me over to the SEC offices one summer day. We invited Baldy Baldwin, Chairman of the Nasdaq Board, to join us, hoping he and Donaldson would connect given their shared history as U.S. Marines.

"I was just talking to my colleagues about how great the New York Stock Exchange is," Donaldson declared, as we began the meeting.

NYSE? Even if he thought that privately, why say it at that moment? Surely he knew we were advocates of a completely different model. We were ready to talk to him about the ways NYSE's trading practices and outdated regulations were holding back progress and competition in the equities market. Was he being deliberately provocative? Was he absentmindedly reliving his own past glories as CEO of NYSE? Or did he simply mistake whom he was talking to? To this day, I don't know. But it was a worrisome sign, and indicative of his loyalty to old-style trading.

Some of the initial challenges in my relationship with the SEC had to do with understanding its role. Formed after the 1929 market crash, the SEC had the explicit purpose to help bring more order to stock trading and to protect investors. To that end, it was primarily concerned with rules and regulations and how the various players on Wall Street were following them. It goes without saying that this is an important function. But the narrow focus of the SEC was brought home to me when *Businessweek* published its 2003 cover article questioning whether or not Nasdaq could survive—a concern that many on Wall Street shared at the time. It accurately mentioned that we were losing money every single day. Yet no one from the SEC called or even seemed to notice.

They cared about the minutiae of a rule filing but didn't seem too concerned that we might be going out of business.

Later, I challenged Donaldson about this. Wasn't that important information? Nasdaq, after all, is a fairly critical piece of the Wall Street machinery. If a big bank were going through the same issues, you can be sure the Federal Reserve would care about its viability! Of course, the stability of our nation's banking system is part of the explicit mission of the Federal Reserve. That's why we hear phrases like "too big to fail," "stress tests," "systemically important institutions," and so on. Officially, the SEC has a three-part mission—to protect investors; maintain fair, orderly, and efficient markets; and facilitate capital formation. Notice that health and viability are not on that list, though obviously they should be related concerns. The mandate of the SEC revolves around policing markets. As Ed Knight explained it to me at the time, "The SEC is more like the Justice Department and less like the Treasury Department. The SEC has rooms full of lawyers, not economists."

This may seem like an obscure point, but it had huge implications in the financial crisis of 2008. Much of the trouble started with unseen risk-taking on the balance sheets of the investment banks, which were regulated by the SEC, not the Federal Reserve.* But like punitive parents who care only about their child's behavior, not their health, the regulators missed the cancer on the balance sheets at Bear Stearns and Lehman Brothers.

In contrast, stability was job number one over at the Federal

---

* Technically, the SEC and FINRA—the financial regulatory authority that grew out of the combined regulatory arms of both NYSE and Nasdaq—were overseeing these institutions, but the SEC played the primary role.

Reserve, and it's telling that the commercial banks weren't the primary source of the troubles. Obviously, there were many causes of the financial crisis. But in retrospect, my 2003 conversation with Donaldson about Nasdaq's precarious financial position and his lack of concern for our financial well-being was an ominous foreshadowing of the troubles that would start with the investment banks and eventually threaten the world economy.

Lobbying Is Education

It's worth stating that I've never had a strong political ideology about regulations in financial markets. I'm a firm believer in capitalism, but not without clear boundaries. All markets benefit from smart, transparent, and consistent rules, and these need to be updated as markets evolve. To borrow Oxley's favorite analogy, think about sports, where competent officials enforcing clear rulebooks are essential to enacting healthy competition on an even playing field. Likewise, good regulation allows capitalism and markets to thrive. Bad rules easily degrade the game, causing the public to lose faith in the fairness of our markets.

Where possible, I prefer market forces to work their magic without regulatory intrusion. But good regulation is an essential feature of modern markets, and certainly of the equities markets. I also believe that genuine competition is good for consumers—no less so in financial markets than in other parts of the economy.

In Washington, I embraced my role as an advocate for Nasdaq's particular perspective when it came to regulatory oversight.

This usually meant I was promoting the ongoing transformation of equities markets into customer-focused, technology-driven, for-profit businesses, functioning in a competitive ecosystem. The insider networks of traders, dealers, and manual market makers—however appropriate for another time and place—were becoming less relevant in the modern world. We were for "lit" markets, and by that I mean exchanges in which everyone can see the buyers and sellers operating in the market. As Louis Brandeis once said, "Sunlight is said to be the best of disinfectants." I believed that these characteristics were the way of the future and would eventually prevail. Progress was coming, fueled by new technologies, and I didn't want to be on the wrong side of history. I had no interest in protecting what I considered to be old and outdated ways of trading securities. We were working hard to compete, innovate, survive, change with the times, serve our customers, and make decent profits. I thought others should have to do so as well.

Representing Nasdaq also meant representing more than our particular organization and its needs. In the public mind, we were associated with innovation, entrepreneurship, and economic vitality, and people in Washington wanted to meet with me to take the pulse of the market. "What are CEOs telling you?" "Where is innovation really happening?" they would ask me. "How is the VC world doing?" "What is your sense of the economy right now?" "How are financial markets operating?" Questions like these were constant. As Ed explained it to me, "When we come to Washington we represent not just Nasdaq itself, but also the state of the tech economy and the several thousand companies listed on Nasdaq. We embody their aspirations, challenges, and also their collective impact on American business."

Of course, those several thousand companies had their own questions. When I visited CEOs, they would ask me, "What's happening in Washington?" "What are the politicians thinking?" "What regulations are coming?"

All of this meant many trips to Washington, lobbying Congressmen and Congresswomen, and testifying before the Financial Committees in the House and Senate. As in most fields, personal relationships matter in politics, and so I spent time with the politicians and government officials, got to know them as individuals, and put in the effort to develop trust and rapport.

In many respects, it was a fascinating journey. I was introduced to a new world and met people who were quite foreign to my background and life experience—individuals like Richard Shelby, the powerful head of the Senate Banking Committee, a larger-than-life southern power broker right out of central casting. During my tenure, I developed relationships with many public servants on both sides of the aisle—people like Massachusetts Senator Barney Frank, Connecticut Senator Christopher Dodd, Treasury Secretary Hank Paulson, New York Senator Chuck Schumer, the aforementioned Mike Oxley, and many others. In general, my experience was that the politicians I engaged with were hardworking and dedicated public servants. Nevertheless, there were many elected officials who surprised me with their inability, or unwillingness, to grasp the basic dynamics of the equities market. For all those whom I came to deeply admire, there were others—on both sides of the aisle—whose inattention, ineffectiveness, and outright incompetence disturbed me.

Indeed, my colleagues and I spent a great deal of time lobbying political leaders and teaching them about the nature of financial markets—how they function, how they serve investors, how they have evolved over the years, and how they could change for the better. Lobbyists have a bad name right now, and perhaps deservedly so. I don't hesitate to acknowledge that the quest for political influence leads people down some questionable paths. But effective lobbying, in my experience, has an important educational role to play. Not many Congressmen or Congresswomen have experience in the markets before taking office. In fact, if I were in Congress, I would bring people in to talk to me all day long, even if I didn't need to fund-raise a dime, just so I could learn from the people on the ground.

Yes, we had a particular point of view, and our competitors had different ones, no doubt, and that is as it should be. But these conversations were not just a partisan effort at winning the argument. In fact, when I sat down with an elected official, I tried to represent both sides of the argument, and to frame them in the context of the larger issues at play. At its best, lobbying is what gets all these important perspectives on the table, so legislators and regulators can actually make informed decisions.

It's easy to get frustrated or even cynical about what goes down on Capitol Hill. But for a business leader, such an attitude is neither smart nor strategic. Don't feel like you're above politics—none of us are. Learn to work with it and do your part to create a fairer world in which to do business. Even if your industry has not yet been subject to regulatory oversight, you never know exactly when that will change.

Leveling the Playing Field

Much of what we aimed to do with our initial regulatory push at Nasdaq was to change the rules of the market so that we could actually compete with NYSE on a level playing field.

In those days, we were fighting a battle on two fronts. The armada of new ECNs was only one side of the challenge facing Nasdaq; the other was our ongoing competition with the older exchange down the street. We competed with them for listings, and we also were intent on gaining market share in trading NYSE stocks. In 2003, NYSE controlled around 80 percent of trading in stocks listed on their exchange. However, this wasn't a sign that they were competing well in the new world of electronic trading. Quite the opposite—they were avoiding competing altogether, with the help of sympathetic regulations.

The regulatory structure at the time favored NYSE's manual style of trading, in which specialists controlled most of the order flow of any given stock and negotiated prices by trading with others at the exchange. If you wanted to trade NYSE stock electronically, outside the context of the exchange floor, it was hard to give the customer a truly up-to-date price. The floor brokers and specialists controlled most of the liquidity, and it took them about thirty seconds to execute a trade. Whereas if you wanted to trade a Nasdaq stock like Apple, all you would need to do is pull up your terminal and look across at various ECNs for the best offers. Then you could execute that trade in a millisecond.

However, while NYSE might have been more effective at holding back the electronic trading future for the time being, inevitably it was going to catch up with them. After all, much of what the digital revolution was doing was cutting out the middle-man. In 2003, NYSE trading specialists were still shouting on the floor like it was 1969, but sooner or later progress would do to floor trading what it did to rotary phones. However, there would need to be a regulatory change to allow it to happen. Progress, in this case, needed a nudge.

In 2004, an opportunity presented itself, in the form of a regulatory package designed to "modernize and strengthen" our securities markets. Known as Reg NMS (Regulation of the National Market System), it was a chance to improve the efficiency of stock markets, encourage their technological evolution, and change the rules of the game to our advantage—all at the same time. My role in the process was to help legislators and Commissioners understand some key aspects of how equities trading worked, and how the proposed rule changes could help it work better. Lobbying is education, and sometimes these important but technical matters took some explaining.

My three kids were playing soccer in those days, which inspired a helpful analogy. Let's say I'm at one of their soccer games on a hot day, and after leaving the field, I look around for some refreshment. Just down the street, there is a store with a sign in the window—*Soft Drinks, $1.79*. Then I turn my head and see another sign, far in the distance, across a suburban six-lane highway, over a median, around a turn. I can just make out the advertisement—*Soft Drinks, $1.69*. All things being equal, I might choose the cheaper price. But it might take me twenty minutes to get to that other store. It's late in the day; it's getting dark. By the time I get there, the store might be closed. I'm thirsty now and so are the kids. The choice is simple.

In 2004, however, as I explained to lawmakers, when it came

to financial markets, that choice was anything but simple. In fact, the regulatory structure at the time *required* that you take the "best price" on any given trade, wherever you might find it. The "trade through rule," as it was known, stated that you could not trade through a posted quote, meaning ignore it for another, slightly more expensive quote listed somewhere else. This created a problem. *If NYSE had the best price, you had to take it.* That may sound like a good idea, but the NYSE trading floor was like a black hole where time slowed down. Trading speed was measured in tens of seconds, compared to milliseconds on Nasdaq's marketplace (today, it's microseconds). On the NYSE floor, they literally had runners who would carry paper quotes between trading desks. The image of middle-aged men shuffling across the floor captures the anachronistic reality of that trading system.

The Nasdaq ecosystem, meanwhile, was not constrained by human athleticism. If I saw Exxon quoted at 100 on Nasdaq, I could execute an order in a moment and be done with it instantly. At the same moment, I might see Exxon quoted at 99.98 on NYSE. That price difference might save me hundreds of dollars on a large order, but since that trade is happening through human specialists on the floor, I have to wait for the order to be processed. Nothing good happens in that time gap. By the time that order is finally ready to be executed, the shares may not even be available at the same price. It's like dragging my kids across the highway only to find that the drinks have gotten more expensive or even sold out. Any quote is temporary. The market is always moving, and as the clock is ticking, I can quickly find myself losing money.

Customers wanted the option to choose certainty, even over price. Just like the thirsty parent coming out of the ball game, investors want to get the trade that is available immediately, not the cheaper one that comes with so many uncertainties. Simply put, the regulatory structure at the time didn't provide a pathway to get from the floor-based past to the electronic future. We needed new regulations for a new world.

Finally, there was the questionable information advantage that NYSE specialists had over everyone else. The specialists had the ability to trade in a proprietary way. They weren't simply objective auctioneers, dispassionately interested in matching bids and offers. They could place bids themselves. I've never been a trader, but give me unique knowledge of the whole order book in a certain stock and a thirty-second information advantage, and I could do pretty well!

In 2004, I testified before the Senate Banking Committee with a clear and unequivocal message. "The trade through rule is the primary obstacle to competition amongst our nation's equity markets," I explained, "and competition is the driving force in making the U.S. markets the strongest in the world, the best for investors large and small, and accountable to the public." I also stressed that the markets had uncovered a fundamental truth: "Electronic trading is best for investors."

The proposed regulation change was important to Nasdaq, but we weren't waiting for it to save the day. After our purchase of INET and BRUT, Nasdaq had successfully begun to trade NYSE securities on our own system. Little by little we were having success, building up liquidity in our electronically traded order book. If a customer ordered a NYSE stock from us, sometimes we could fill that order from our own book immediately. If we weren't able to do so, we would then send it down to the NYSE floor and get it filled that way. This was helped along by our purchase of BRUT, as the ECN was a broker-dealer and became a member of NYSE, licensed to trade on the floor.

Around that time, our BRUT executive was invited to a party over at NYSE and ended up chatting with the Chairman of the NYSE Board.

"Who are you with?" he asked our trader.

"BRUT," he replied.

"That's interesting. Perhaps we could have a party here at NYSE, sponsored by your company and featuring your champagne."

At this point, a NYSE employee, overhearing the conversation, quickly pulled the Chairman aside and explained that BRUT was an ECN that was part of Nasdaq, and not associated with the bubbly wine we all enjoy!

Mistaken identities aside, Nasdaq was determined to compete in trading NYSE stocks. As our market share grew, our execution time improved, and our liquidity did as well. After all, customers wanted the option of trading electronically. Our hope was that Reg NMS would provide a massive push in that direction.

In retrospect, the proposed changes in Reg NMS seem obvious, essential, and even inevitable. But at the time, getting it passed by the Commissioners at the SEC was a nerve-racking process. NYSE had significant influence in Washington and a powerful brand. For many, the floor of NYSE represented the center of American capitalism. It's an international tourist attraction; it looks great on TV. I remember the first time I visited—the crowded floor, the commotion, the colorful jackets of the traders, the incredible energy of the place, the sense that you had entered the living heart of financial markets. We were proposing changes that would potentially undo or alter it significantly. That gave people pause, and, understandably, it sometimes overshadowed the merits of our arguments. NYSE was able to translate its rich history into significant mind share as well as market share. Its name commanded immediate attention in Washington. We certainly developed a healthy respect for our rival's political clout, if not its business acumen.

Over time, I came to better understand the incentives that dominate the mind-sets of policy makers. With help from my team, we put in the time and effort to persuade them of our point of view, and in the process we developed good relationships with key political leaders. And yes, we hosted our share of campaign fund-raisers. It's an unavoidable truth that political contributions are part of what gets you access in Washington. But it's naïve to think the biggest check was some kind of skeleton key to unlock political favor. The merits of the argument still dominate the decision—at least that was my experience in the decade and a half I spent wrangling with the various Commissioners, Congress members, Cabinet members, and other curious creatures that constitute our nation's political class. There is a certain rough pragmatism that operates in Washington, and that's a good thing.

Imperfect Progress

In the end, Reg NMS struck down the trade through rule in non-electronic markets. It basically said that *if a posted quote for a security was not electronically accessible, you could trade through it.* That changed everything. The father no longer had to cross the busy highway to buy his daughter a slightly less expensive but relatively inaccessible drink. NYSE was betting that even with the change of regulations, their exchange had so much liquidity that people would still trade on the floor. That proved to be wrong.

In 2005, after Reg NMS was passed (but not yet implemented), I testified again before the Senate Banking Committee and commended them for the rule changes. I told them that I believed that Reg NMS would remove a substantial obstacle to competition among our nation's equity markets and establish incentives for floor-based markets to move toward electronic trading. What I also believed but did not say was that those incentives were about to hit the NYSE floor like a ton of bricks. Following the adoption of the rule, their market share of trading volume in their own listed stocks fell precipitously—from 80 percent to 20 percent. Quickly, they were forced to get up to speed on electronic trading. They'd already made moves in that direction, buying an ECN in 2005, but their ambivalence was costly. In a post–Reg NMS world, they have never recovered their former dominance.

Nasdaq was a beneficiary of this regulatory shift. In 2007, we became the largest exchange by trading volume in the country. Our competitive advantage had increased significantly. *Stop being satisfied with No. 2.* We had finally succeeded in tilting the rules back toward parity. We could now compete with NYSE and other exchanges on a more even playing field—and we were good competitors. For the first time since the rise of ECNs, manual markets were no longer the weak link in the national market system, slowing down trading, while specialists on the floor, with their distinct time-and-place advantage, attempted to execute and match orders that computers could handle more efficiently.

As Reg NMS was implemented, the once-bustling NYSE

floor, where generations of traders had plied their skills for over a century, grew quiet. A new generation of trading—defined by speed, computation, and automation—had finally infiltrated the core of Wall Street's empire. The machines had come for the specialists. For some, this was a cause for consternation. For me, it was natural evolution of a market in transition. My intention, in the process, was to make that transition something that benefited investors, increased the healthy functioning of markets, and reduced costs for all involved. I would argue that for all the bumps and bruises along the way, electronic trading has delivered on all of that and more.

I think it may be some natural law that every major new regulation spawns unforeseen avenues of market evolution. Every new set of rules has unintended consequences, both good and bad: possibilities for legitimate gain, but also for exploitation and even abuse. Closing one loophole may open another. The SOES bandits in the late eighties and early nineties took advantage of the Black Monday rule changes. The ECN explosion in the early 2000s was empowered by a 1997 regulatory overhaul known as Reg ATS. Progress is never a straight line, but the trend line does matter. Has the world of stock market exchanges and trading— even with its problems, breakdowns, and scandals—become more equitable, more transparent, less expensive, more accessible, over the last decades? I think the answer to that question is an unequivocal yes.

Reg NMS was no exception to this principle of imperfect progress. In fact, I had predicted some of the troubling issues with the new framework before it was passed, centered on the fact that the trade through rule still applied to the entire electronic marketplace.* I would have preferred to see it removed altogether—for reasons that would be borne out in the following years.

In practice, Reg NMS allowed for a proliferation of exchanges and a fragmentation of the market, creating a much more complex landscape. While the intensive discussion, testimony, and research that led to the SEC rule changes involved economists, traders, brokers, institutions, bankers, academics, exchange experts, and many others, there was one significant group missing from the deliberations—engineers and the people responsible for day-to-day operations. Reg NMS was the first set of regulations that was developed and implemented in a largely computerized trading ecosystem, so this was a regrettable omission. Hence, the actual consequences of Reg NMS implementation on the structure of the day-to-day trading market were insufficiently considered. Not enough thought was given to the downsides of this new structure, how it could go wrong, how resilient it would be under adverse conditions, and how it would evolve. We developed a great engine and a finely tuned transmission, but didn't think carefully enough about the need for emergency brakes.

This would come back to haunt all of us in a rather dramatic fashion during the Flash Crash of 2010, when more than $1 trillion of market value was lost and regained in a very short period of time. The exact causes of the Flash Crash are still debated, but it was clear that the new, more fragmented structure of the equity

---

* I attempted to lay out my concerns in a *Wall Street Journal* op-ed published December 8, 2004. Titled "Millions of Momentary Monopolies," the piece explained to the public why mandating "best price" might sound good in theory but in reality could create problems—as it did, in the long run.

market was deeply implicated. The increased connectivity and proliferation of exchanges may have had many benefits, but they also resulted in new fragilities. Negative feedback loops, driven by computerized trading, presented poorly understood dangers, like those that spun out of control on that day. In the aftermath of that brief but frightening crash, the equity-trading world, in coordination with the SEC, woke up and got very serious about instituting safeguards that were needed in this new trading environment. We developed circuit breakers and new security features. We established limit-up and limit-down mechanisms for individual stocks, instituting a pause in trading in the case of sharp rises or declines. We introduced safeguards in the connections between exchanges, inoculating the overall market against the temporary failure of any particular institution or trading pool. Today, equity markets are much improved as a result of these changes, but the original lesson is still relevant—always consider the downsides and include those who can best anticipate adverse scenarios.

In the end, no market structure is without weaknesses and trade-offs, and no regulation is a cure-all. Reg NMS was a step along the way—a positive step. Nasdaq was pleased with the outcome. In fact, I think just about every exchange not named NYSE was happy with the new rules. When a business doesn't adapt to changing times, it will get left behind. But when regulations don't adapt, whole industries can languish. Reg NMS allowed equities trading to change for the better—and no doubt there is more change to come. Today, a new generation of regulators is examining the markets, and efforts to reform Reg NMS have been ongoing for the last few years. As I often say, the right answer today is not the right answer tomorrow. The last vestiges of the old Nasdaq were falling away. In the hallways and conference rooms of

One Liberty Plaza, we were already thinking more about Nasdaq's future than its past. And we'd created a regulatory pathway to pull the industry into that future with us.

LEADERSHIP LESSONS

- **Don't Feel Like You're Above Politics—None of Us Are.** Learn to work with it and use it to increase your competitive advantage.

- **Lobbying Is Education.** It's an opportunity to get important perspectives on the table so legislators and regulators can actually make informed decisions.

- **Politics Has Its Own Schedule.** Don't pin all your hopes for success on swift changes in law or regulation.

- **Know Your Stakeholders.** Sometimes a business has unconventional stakeholders that are critical to achieve success—politicos, regulators, VCs, community leaders, investors, etc. Build those relationships early and often.

Chapter Seven

The Global Imperative

Nasdaq Lands OMX for $3.7 Billion

Wall Street Journal, May 26, 2007

One morning in early 2004, I walked into Chris Concannon's office. "I have a crazy idea I want to run by you."

My EVP of Transaction Services looked at me with a mixture of wariness and curiosity. "What did you have in mind?"

"I want to buy the New York Stock Exchange."

Chris and I had been working together for almost a year and I imagine he was already starting to realize that when it came to the business of Nasdaq, I was determined that we would play second fiddle to no one. Nasdaq was fast becoming a different type of organization, and I was thinking about how we might begin to grow the business through acquisitions.

NYSE, on the other hand, was reeling. This was well before Reg NMS had passed, but a CEO compensation scandal had just rocked our competitor and their reputation was at a low ebb. John Thain had recently been hired from Goldman Sachs as the new

CEO, with a mandate to clean up NYSE's reputational damage and restore some sense of positive momentum to the old-world exchange. I thought NYSE's days were numbered, at least in its current form. Sooner or later, I knew that the ruthless efficiencies of capitalism were going to transform the place—whatever its remarkable history. Also, as the financial world became more global, I imagined that there was likely to be consolidation among the various exchanges in developed economies. I intended for Nasdaq to be at the crest of that wave, not get caught behind it. In other words, it seemed a good moment to pounce.

Even at the time, we knew it was going to be a long shot. First of all, NYSE would have had to agree, and that was unlikely. There is a certain hubris that is almost infused into the grand architecture of the Corinthian-column-lined building on Broad Street and that seeps into many of the individuals who work there. Of course, in some respects it's a vestigial pride—at that time, NYSE had been the biggest stock exchange in the country for about two centuries, the Goliath of global markets, overseeing capital formation in the most successful economy in world history. By this time, however, we were actually making more money than they were. Nevertheless, they tended to see us as an upstart irritant, always trying to punch above its weight—an attitude that didn't exactly invite talk of mergers. Moreover, our federal antitrust regulators might have had a thing or two to say about the national listings duopoly of Nasdaq and NYSE becoming one. Still, fortune favors the bold. And I didn't get paid for being passive.

Chris called Silver Lake Partners, the private equity group that owned part of Nasdaq, and asked them about financing. They loved the idea—if we could pull it off—and agreed to help provide the money. We were ready, but this was going to have to be a friendly takeover, a merger of equals. We were barely a public company, and NYSE was still a nonprofit, so it wasn't possible to launch an uninvited bid. I called up John Thain and asked him to get together. We chose a hotel in Soho where we could avoid being seen together by the press. No doubt he was expecting a friendly welcome-to-the-stock-exchange sort of meeting. My actual intention took him by surprise, to say the least, and was not welcomed. It was a short conversation, and that was the end of my first attempt to buy our rival down the street; it wouldn't be the last.

In hindsight, perhaps it was for the best. Soon, Nasdaq would buy Instinet, and integrating our new acquisition would keep us occupied over the next year. However, the entire episode awakened in me a new sensibility. I realized that we had to seriously consider how we might eventually expand our national and even global footprints. It seemed to be part of our destiny, for lack of a better word. In trying to buy NYSE, I might have been "ogling the unobtainable" (to paraphrase one my favorite poets, Lawrence Ferlinghetti), but I was nothing if not persistent. In 2005, a different opportunity would present itself.

The Dawn Raid

There is a wonderful scene in *The Godfather* where Al Pacino's character, Mike Corleone, goes to Las Vegas to buy out a hotel that the family had bankrolled. The hotel's proprietor, Moe Greene, is offended by the overture. "You don't buy me out. I buy *you* out!" he declares. I was reminded of this classic moment of drama during a series of events that unfolded in 2005 and 2006 between Nasdaq and the London Stock Exchange (LSE).

In 2005, Clara Furse, then CEO of the London Stock Exchange, contacted me with a request. Could we get together in New York? She and her team had something they wanted to talk to us about.

"What do you think she wants?" I asked Chris and Adena one afternoon as we discussed strategy in my office.

"She wants to buy us," Chris responded without hesitation. "She's seen our depressed stock price and looked at our balance sheet. She thinks we are ripe for acquisition."

I thought Chris was correct. I also suspected that there was another issue in play. There had been speculation that Euronext was trying to buy LSE. In London's view of the financial world, they're situated at the center, and a bid by rivals in Europe was almost certainly unwelcome. Furse was likely struggling to fend off their overtures and remain independent. That meant she was also looking for a white knight to help protect the company. A merger with Nasdaq could accomplish that. Independent of the strategic consequences, it would increase LSE's size such that it would be impossible for Euronext to buy.

When the team from London arrived, we sat down together, and Furse laid out her proposal exactly as we had anticipated. Her manner was gracious and her logic was convincing. She framed a Nasdaq-LSE marriage as a beneficial "merger of equals," and in many respects it would have been. As she listed the synergies between the two businesses and presented her vision of the combined future global company, I could see the appeal. In fact, I was a little chagrined that I hadn't come up with the idea myself. I like to always be a step ahead of our competitors, and in this case, I was a step behind. The meeting opened my eyes to Nasdaq's position in the global ecosystem of exchanges.

As I reflected on a possible merger with LSE, I became more convinced it could work. But clearly, Furse had assumed that LSE would play the lead role in the aftermath of the deal. In most of these deals, there is a so-called contribution analysis of each company's share in the future income statement. Based on those numbers, one side generally ends up with more equity in the future company. In her mind, LSE was likely contributing more future profit to the deal and would naturally be the dominant partner. It may have genuinely been envisioned as a merger of equals, but to paraphrase George Orwell, some companies are more equal than others.

However, there was an interesting twist to the plot. In buying Instinet earlier that same year, not only had we purchased a good deal of extra revenue and market share in the deal, but we were also on track to save an incredible amount of money in costs from the combination of companies. All of which meant that our anticipated revenues and profits were actually much higher than our recent earnings statements would have indicated. Our stock price didn't yet reflect the new and improved Nasdaq. But it soon would. I wasn't going to do a deal based upon a market valuation that had yet to price in the synergies of the Instinet acquisition.

At a certain point during that meeting, I got out the latest Nasdaq forecasts. Those numbers, and subsequent analysis by both teams, revealed that Nasdaq's P&L would be greater than LSE's by the time any merger was consummated, and therefore we would be contributing more to the future income of an LSE-Nasdaq business. Essentially, that meant that LSE wouldn't be buying us; we would be buying LSE.

Furse's enthusiasm for a merger of equals mysteriously waned after she learned LSE would *not* be the bigger partner. In fact, we couldn't even get her to take our calls. The logic of the deal was still appealing to me, however, and I was glad Furse had brought the idea to my attention. A merged company would be in a position to take an extraordinary leadership role in the trading of pan-European equities and become the dominant global listings franchise.

Like NYSE, LSE had a long and storied tradition—it was one of the original and truly great centers of capitalism, dating all the way back to Elizabeth I. Indeed, it was the epitome of an elite, old-school exchange—the type that probably had a spectacular boardroom, an incredible wine cellar, an expense structure to match, and a bureaucratic infrastructure appropriate for another era. Those were always happy hunting grounds for Nasdaq and the transformations in efficiency and technology that we were championing. Show me an exchange with those characteristics, and I would show you a business that we could revamp and rebuild, unlocking incredible value. A potential Nasdaq-LSE merger had all those enticing elements. We couldn't just let it go.

In March 2006, we made an unsolicited bid to purchase LSE for £2.4 billion or £9.50 per share of their stock, a substantial premium over its market price. The offer made great business sense for Nasdaq, but actually taking this step was quite a Rubicon moment for me, personally. After all, it had only been three years since I walked in the door. Given the situation then, it was almost unfathomable that we would so soon be in a position to pursue an acquisition like this. NYSE was a known quantity—it's down the street, literally. This was another country, another culture, another history.

I traveled to the UK with Nasdaq's Chairman of the Board, Baldy Baldwin, to meet with his counterpart at LSE, Chris Gibson-Smith. At first, this overture backfired as well. Baldy called Gibson-Smith in the late evening, an apparent faux pas in London's still more traditional business culture. The 24/7 world had not yet arrived across the pond. The world of international dealmaking is always littered with cultural landmines, and it's wise to tread carefully at all times.

Eventually, we met with Gibson-Smith and Furse in the LSE offices and presented our offer. Furse's pained expression made clear that she was against it from the start. Our connection with Gibson-Smith was more cordial, but at the end of the day, he too seemed less than enthusiastic about the deal. The LSE Board immediately rejected it. We thought our bid was generous, but they announced that it "substantially undervalued" the exchange.

My own opinion was that the LSE Board was doing a disservice to shareholders in dismissing our bid out of hand. I understand the reluctance to be bought—I felt the same way about Nasdaq, and I considered it my job to act as entrenched management every day by executing on our business plan and doing our best to succeed and stay independent. But if a serious bid came in, I knew that was the time to start acting as a fiduciary of the shareholders and give it due consideration. As management, you don't own the company; the shareholders do, and you work for the shareholders. I didn't feel the folks in London were fulfilling that duty.

So we went directly to the shareholders. After our first offer was rebuffed, we made an uninvited bid, bypassing the Board and management. We were in the middle of an off-site planning session with the Nasdaq executive team in November 2006 when news of our intention was leaked to the press. One minute we were having a relatively uneventful weekend, working on strategy and spending time together socially; the next we were all over the news. The tone of the retreat abruptly changed as we got down to planning next steps with our bankers. On Monday morning, November 20, we initiated what is known in the mergers and acquisitions world as a "dawn raid." We started buying LSE stock in the open market with Nasdaq cash, and sent them a public letter announcing our intention.

Over the months that followed, we went through a number of phases in our attempted takeover, many of them dictated by the clear and specific rules outlined by the UK Panel on Takeovers and Mergers. We accumulated a large stake in LSE, reaching up to 30 percent of their shares (we needed at least 50 percent to gain a controlling interest). We managed to get a couple of LSE's largest institutional shareholders to sell us their entire stakes. By this time, we were paying a premium, around £12.50 a share. As often happens when a large potential acquisition in is the air like this, a number of big hedge funds had also taken their own significant stakes in LSE. They had no long-term interest in the company, but they hoped to drive the price up and turn a fast profit.

John Paulson, then a relatively unknown investor who would later become famous for successfully shorting the U.S. housing market, was one of these new shareholders, as was Sam Heyman, another New York hedge fund manager. I was happy to learn I could pursue my ambitions across the pond simply by walking down the street—such is the global nature of finance. I engaged them both in a series of meetings, hoping to purchase their shares, which would have pushed us over 50 percent. (It was somewhat interesting to me that they each had the exact same price. As someone once told me, hedge funds hunt in packs.) Ironically, both hedge fund managers—short-term specialists by nature— tried to convince me to "think of the long term" and not worry about paying a premium for their shares.

The banks supporting our bid assured us that they would lend us the money necessary to meet Paulson and Heyman's price. Initially, it was intoxicating to think that control of LSE was within our reach. All we had to do was give the go-ahead. It actually surprised me how easy the money was to obtain. It was a period when credit was readily available. (Looking back, that seems a bit ominous.) But the more we considered the possibility, the less appealing it became, until finally we decided the asking price was simply too high. We dropped the bid, right at the one-yard line. We'd set ourselves a maximum price we were willing to pay, and we'd already exceeded it. I knew it was time to let it go. Our balance sheet was already so highly leveraged from the Instinet acquisition that we would have had no cushion. I didn't want to put too much debt on our books. In hindsight, I'm glad I made that call. This was only a little more than a year before the 2008 financial crisis, and taking on that much debt at the top of that business cycle might have proved disastrous. While I had no special insight into what was to come, I understood that excessive leverage brings real risks, seen and unseen.

It's Not Personal

It's never easy to walk away from a deal that you've pursued for weeks, months, or even years. In a moment like that, it can be easy to keep reaching for the finish line just because you've already come so far. Economists call this the "sunk costs fallacy"—the reasoning that further investment is warranted simply because time and resources have already been invested and cannot be recouped. It's not logical, but it's easy to fall for. You think of all the sleepless nights, stress, and time that can't be reclaimed. Maybe you pay a little more than you planned, give up a few items on your nonnegotiable list, compromise more than you intended. But sometimes that's not the right choice.

We were in love with the LSE deal, no doubt. It fit our strategic direction; it seemed the best option on the table. But we didn't *have* to do it. We weren't that smitten; we knew we had other strategic options. Indeed, the only acquisition I ever felt we *had* to do was Instinet. LSE was a choice, not a necessity. And it's important in moments like that to know the difference.

What also helped me keep a clear head was the knowledge that it wasn't personal. Sure, I was invested in every deal I pursued, but in the end, it was business. The success or failure of the deal didn't reflect on me or my leadership capacity. I tried to adopt an attitude that I'd learned from the venture capital world. VCs expect nine out of ten investments to fail, so they learn to take setbacks in stride. By contrast, some of my counterparts in negotiations over the years seemed to treat these deals like life-or-death struggles. An unsolicited offer was a personal affront. A buyout was a sign of personal failure. And a deal initiated but not completed was something to be ashamed of. In high-profile, public acquisitions, the press can fan these flames.

The financial press covered the LSE saga in great detail, especially in London, with some hand-wringing about the "barbarians at the gate" who were seeking to take over critical UK assets.

For Nasdaq, it was a setback. But it did have some positive outcomes. It was a real learning experience—I learned a lot about European takeover rules and the culture of business in the region, lessons I would apply effectively in the next acquisition attempt. Second, we would eventually sell our LSE stake for a significant profit—almost $431 million! I joked with my executive team that we were probably the most successful hedge fund in the country in 2007.

Joking aside, I was disappointed not to have a chance to remake LSE in Nasdaq's image. But there was no time to waste worrying about what might have been. The need to expand globally was still an urgent concern, and our attention quickly shifted to other areas of the map. The sweet spot for our acquisition interest would be an exchange that was aligned with Nasdaq's strengths, provided robust synergies and savings, expanded our business into adjacent areas, but was operationally a step behind the technological and business efficiencies we had embraced—in other words, one where we could simultaneously reduce costs and add real value to both businesses. Soon, our attention alighted on a target.

Colder Climates, Warmer Negotiations

I first got to know about OMX, a collection of Nordic exchanges, over a glass of champagne (or three) with its CEO, Magnus Böcker. He had organized a tasting event for potential customers in New York City, and we quickly connected. Never one to do things by halves, Böcker had hired one of the foremost champagne experts in the world to be our guide for the evening. Böcker was a warm, charismatic people person with a magnetic charm. We began what would be a lasting friendship that night, and his company, OMX, caught my attention as well. The more I looked, the more I was intrigued.

Here was a collection of recently demutualized Scandinavian exchanges under one roof, a business that we knew intimately. Here was the dominant global brand in the exchange technology business, which played to our technology strengths. Here was a business that synergistically extended Nasdaq's product lines, with its derivatives exchanges and clearinghouses. Here was a profitable business, but not so well run that we couldn't find great efficiencies in a merger. Here was a company with deep connections not only in Europe, but also in exchanges around the world that were OMX technology customers. A Nasdaq-OMX merger began to look like a fantastic opportunity.

From the beginning, the negotiations were friendly and professional, with shareholder value at the top of the agenda—a marked contrast to our previous merger attempts with LSE. We agreed upon a price of $3.7 billion, 19 percent above the stock price at the time we announced the merger. Böcker agreed to come to New York to serve as President of the combined company. All the major stakeholders gave the deal a green light. We also lined up positive endorsements from OMX's major investors, including the most significant Swedish shareholder, Investor AB, which is the investment arm of the Wallenberg family. At Nasdaq, we were thrilled with the deal. Despite regulatory hurdles in both countries that were still to be overcome, we were confident that it would go through.

There were a number of reasons why it was a win for Nasdaq. In the world of stock exchanges, there was a consolidation occurring—local exchanges were becoming regional, and regional ones were becoming global. OMX, which had recently acquired most of their own regional exchanges—including ones in Finland, Iceland, and Denmark—was a perfect example of that trend. We wanted to be in a position of strength as that process played out.

On the branding side, we wanted to protect our listings business. At that time, there were essentially four stock exchanges that had a robust, global listings business—Nasdaq, NYSE, London Stock Exchange, and the Stock Exchange of Hong Kong. NYSE had just done a deal with the Paris-based Euronext, which had itself been formed out of a series of mergers and acquisitions between exchanges in Paris, Brussels, and Amsterdam. For us, that created a competitive concern. If a global footprint became a significant wish list item for companies looking to IPO, Nasdaq needed to be able to check that box.

Even more critical was preserving our competitive position with our existing premier companies like Microsoft and Google. If our big technology companies began to value having a listings exchange with global connections, we didn't want to be caught on the back foot. (As it would later turn out, this fear was unfounded. Global reach is still critical, but for the most part, companies list on national exchanges and investors can reach them from all over the globe. There are some minor exceptions, in particular Chinese companies, who often seek North American investment capital, and Israeli companies, who regularly list on American exchanges.)

OMX was also the unquestioned leader in the exchange technology business—selling technology to exchanges around the world. That could allow us to dominate the next wave of technology upgrades as emerging markets around the world developed their own exchanges. This high-margin software and services play had great promise. I was surprised when some of our investors and some employees didn't understand its potential. "Are you going to sell it off as part of the deal?" they would ask me. Why would I sell a business that was in our strategic sweet spot, had huge growth potential, leveraged our technology, and had fantastic margins?

In our meetings, I was also encouraged by OMX's culture. At first blush, it was too bureaucratic—lots of committees, extra people, endless analysis, and a consensus-driven decision-making process that could be frustrating and time-consuming. But we found some elements that were scrappier and more entrepreneurial than I had expected. They had started as upstart outsiders before acquiring the various regional exchanges, and still retained some of that energy in their cultural DNA. Throughout the organization, we found pockets of great talent and innovative spirit. Their original founder, Olof Stenhammar, had cut his teeth in American business and imported some of its values when he returned to Scandinavia to start the original OM options exchange. Their entrepreneurial DNA was buried, but the basic blueprint was there.

All in all, the merger was an exciting prospect, a positive move forward for Nasdaq's global ambitions, and our first significant step to becoming a truly international company. We announced the deal in May 2007 with much celebration on all sides. It was a match made in stock market heaven—or perhaps I should say

Valhalla. That is, until we got a call from Dubai, and the whole deal started to fall apart.

Adventures in International Dealmaking

Borse Dubai was a government-controlled exchange operator in the United Arab Emirates. In August 2007, about two months after our initial announcement, they launched their own takeover bid for OMX that valued the company at 14 percent above our offer.

After I got over my initial surprise and irritation, I worked to understand the nature of their interest in OMX. On closer inspection, it was part business, part family rivalry. OMX's founder, Stenhammar, had two protégés, two sons, so to speak—Magnus Böcker and Per Larsson. Larsson served as CEO for seven years after Stenhammar became Chairman in 1996. He and Böcker were friends and also competitors. Böcker took over Larsson's position in 2003. Larsson went on to become CEO of a Borse Dubai subsidiary, the very company that was trying to outbid Nasdaq for OMX. We were caught in the crossfire of a global power struggle, but also a local dynastic rivalry.

Beyond the family dynamics, why were they interested in making a bid? What was the business case? How serious were they? Was there a possibility of a three-way deal? As a matter of due diligence, I immediately flew to Stockholm to convince the powers that be of the superior value of a Nasdaq-OMX merger, and I launched a backchannel communication to Dubai to meet for negotiations.

We agreed to meet in London. I invited Pat Healy, a Nasdaq Board member who lived in London, to join us, adding some international experience to the team. As a newbie to dealing with Middle Eastern business, I was concerned about potential cultural landmines, but as it turned out, my worries were unfounded. The executives from Dubai, Essa Kazim and Soud Ba'alawy, were highly educated, smart, ambitious businessmen, and our negotiations had a tone of mutual respect from the get-go. We met with them on a number of occasions, culminating in a seventy-two-hour marathon session in a hotel near Heathrow Airport in September 2007. The deal on the table was one in which the Dubai group would become major shareholders in a newly merged Nasdaq-OMX company and also receive the rights to the exchange technology business in certain countries, as well as a chunk of Nasdaq's plentiful LSE shares. Nasdaq would take a stake in the fledgling Dubai International Financial Exchange. All in all, it was a complicated negotiation. I sometimes felt like we were playing a game of Risk, shuttling between conference rooms and carving up the world. Adena was in her element, demonstrating extraordinary endurance and masterfully juggling the complex three-way deal.

Negotiations like this can go wrong in a myriad of ways, and I developed a set of personal rules that served me well.

1. **Don't Make Big Decisions When Jet-Lagged.** Always sleep on important decisions. Many times the answers reveal themselves in the clear light of morning.

2. **Put Yourself in the Shoes of the Other Party.** Part of good negotiating is knowing and appreciating what the other

person is trying to get out of the deal and working toward a win-win.

3. **Remember, It's Never Black-and-White.** In dealmaking, there are always shades of gray, and it's part of your job to wrestle with the complexity. If it was simple, you wouldn't be making a premium salary.

4. **Identify the Facts That Matter.** There may be fifty facts on the table, but you need to figure out which are the most important ones. Smart people can always come up with more and more relevant facts, but good negotiators can identify which facts are dominant.

By the middle of that week, we finally had the basic components of a deal in place. We knew we couldn't keep the information under wraps for long, so we decided to fly to Stockholm and announce it right away. Our communications team called a press conference, and every press outlet in the region immediately agreed to come. In Sweden, this was a big deal, and it was covered as a nationally important story.

As we looked out at the assembled reporters, once again it seemed like we had reached the finish line in this multimonth process. But when I took the microphone to give my own remarks and take questions from the audience, a curveball question took me completely off guard. One of the assembled reporters asked, "What do you think about the Qatar bid?"

What? What Qatar bid? What the heck is this person talking about? I thought to myself. *Are they mixing up Qatar and Dubai?* Obviously, Qatar and Dubai are different places, but in my sleep-deprived state I confess to a split second of doubt.

It turned out that neither the reporter nor I was geographically challenged. The *Wall Street Journal* had just broken a story reporting that the Qatar Investment Authority was now making a bid for OMX. In fact, they were already buying up shares and had urged the OMX Board not to finalize anything yet. Suddenly, it felt like Nasdaq and OMX were caught in the middle of a struggle between rival Middle Eastern powers.

Exhausted and exasperated, I wondered if all of this was destined to come to naught. We'd been up for three days negotiating with the Dubai team, and at the very moment of victory, our thunder had been stolen by this new development from Qatar. I knew I couldn't adequately respond to this new information in my current state. *Don't make consequential decisions on no sleep.* I just wanted to get home to New York, recharge, and figure out next steps.

At the end of that crazy, exhausting whirlwind of deals and counterdeals, knife-edge negotiations, bland hotel rooms, and bleary-eyed globetrotting, Adena and I headed to the Stockholm airport together. She had done an incredible amount of work in the previous few days and had been a reliable, smart negotiator, not to mention a trusted advisor. I can only imagine how we must have looked. As we said our good-byes, the emotions of the moment caught up with us both. She started to tear up, and as I went to give her a consoling hug, I realized I was tearing up as well. In the end, even though dealmaking isn't personal, we're all human.

I was often reminded, in times like this, of the importance of what I like to call executive fitness. Business is a marathon, not a sprint, and to be a leader in the marathon takes an unusual degree of fitness—mental, emotional, and physical. Late nights, long days, international travel, intensive negotiations, stressful situations—all of these are part of the job and inevitably take their toll. Wherever possible, minimizing distraction and stress in the rest of one's life helps. A stable family life makes a big difference, as does maintaining good health, staying active, spending quality time with loved ones, and getting enough rest and relaxation. Being a leader takes more than talent; it takes significant energy and endurance. My executive team had all of these attributes, and I was proud to run the long miles beside them.

One of the great joys in life and business is working hard with a close-knit team to accomplish shared goals. There is nothing quite like that sense of commitment and camaraderie that happens when people employ all their talents and capabilities to achieve something together. This is especially true in moments of extreme difficulty, challenge, hard work, or mutual sacrifice. Negotiating the OMX deal was certainly one such memorable moment, when deep bonds were formed and lasting relationships sealed. I'm proud of what we accomplished, but I'm even more appreciative of the people I shared the journey with. I like to think it was those experiences of courage under fire in the trenches of global dealmaking that helped make Adena the tremendous leader and formidable CEO that she would become for Nasdaq more than a decade later.

The Finish Line

In this case, I decided it still made sense to complete what we had started. I went straight to Investor AB. As a public, shareholder-owned company, OMX had to respect the bid from Qatar. But I was also confident that they preferred the Nasdaq-Dubai acquisition offer. It took some tough negotiating, and a sweetened bid, but I eventually struck a deal with Börje Ekholm (representing Investor AB) that presented a formidable challenge to the Qatar group. We negotiated a structured agreement in which Investor AB agreed to vote for the Nasdaq bid, assuming the price difference between the two offers was within a certain range. That locked up their shares (unless Qatar made a super-premium bid), ensuring their support of our offer. As a result, the Qatar group eventually dropped their bid for OMX and sold their stake.

We passed the national security tests, and Dubai's stake in Nasdaq was approved. Nasdaq would have the benefit of a global partner. Our new name would be Nasdaq-OMX. Our head count more than doubled overnight, and our global presence increased exponentially, as OMX had customer relationships with more than sixty exchanges around the world. Nasdaq now had a presence on six continents. Our wish for a global footprint had been fulfilled, in spades. I described the combined company as the largest global network of exchanges and exchange customers linked by technology.

On the downside, we had paid a handsome price for OMX and lost some of our value in the bidding war. We paid for it in both cash and stock. Buying OMX is one of those decisions that looked positive at the time, but over the course of the next few years, as global markets swooned, I was forced to cast a more critical eye on the merits of the merger. In business, however, the long term trumps all, and over time, the Nasdaq-OMX merger would prove fundamental to our success.

Nasdaq was becoming a significant software and services

business serving international exchanges—a true growth market around the world. We also benefited tremendously from the infusion of capable talent from OMX into Nasdaq's global workforce. None of it would have been possible without OMX. Now all we had to do was make the marriage work.

On a more personal note, the OMX merger was an initiation for me. It was my first deep foray into international dealmaking, and what a trial by fire it was. At the end of the entire saga, which went on for well over a year, I felt like I was a different person than when I started. Somewhere along the way, amid the international intrigue, European politics, Middle East power struggles, hedge fund brinksmanship, and hostile takeover bids, I had left the upstart kid from Queens far behind. And at no moment was this clearer to me than the day I found myself driving down an avenue lined with peacocks on my way to meet with His Highness Sheikh Mohammed at his palace, accompanied by our new Dubai partners. Nasdaq was becoming a global player, and in some respects, I guess I was, too.

LEADERSHIP LESSONS

- **Dealmaking Is Never Personal.** It's easy to get caught up in the high drama of negotiation and let it cloud your good judgment.

- **You Don't Get Paid for Passivity.** You won't succeed at every deal you aim for, but in business you have to be audacious at least some of the time.

- **It's Never Black-and-White.** The best dealmakers try to see all sides of a deal and understand what constitutes a win for the counterparties. They embrace the complexity and the inevitable compromises and find their way through to a workable outcome.

Chapter Eight

Grappling with Growth

Nasdaq to Acquire Phil-Ex for $652 Million

Wall Street Journal, November 7, 2007

When my boys were young, they liked to bowl. Julia would take them to the local lanes, rolling balls and knocking down pins. I've never been much of a bowling enthusiast, but there is one simple lesson I did learn: Aim for the center pin or, even better, just to the right or left of center. Years later, I would find myself repeating the same instructions to my executive team—only this time, the bowling alley had become the much higher-stakes game of mergers and acquisitions.

When evaluating a potential acquisition, I told my team, let's make sure that we don't jump too far from our existing strengths—which included transactions processing, running efficient exchanges, and trading technology. I was fine about expanding through acquisition. But I didn't want Nasdaq to become a disparate collection of barely related companies. I wanted us to grow, but not indiscriminately. I valued integration and alignment, two things that become harder at scale. One bowling pin to the right or left of that center was fine. Over time, our sweet spot would expand. But we should be very careful about trying to knock over pins outside that frame. We could very quickly end up in the gutter.

This was not always a popular approach. In the financial markets at the time, the equities business—our central bowling pin—was not the sexiest. Derivatives were all the rage, as those were higher-margin businesses. For those not familiar with derivatives markets, I'm referring to exchanges that trade contracts whose value is based on a "derivative" of an underlying asset. Trading futures in soybeans is one example. Options are also types of derivatives based on the value of the underlying stock. CME (Chicago Mercantile Exchange) and ICE (Intercontinental Exchange) were (and are) the most prominent derivatives exchanges in the country. At the time, their success put pressure on us to expand our business to compete in those markets. I had nothing against derivatives, but I didn't want to chase margins in businesses that were too far from our core strengths. I was very disciplined with my team about our strategy.

In *Good to Great*, Jim Collins writes wisely about the use of acquisitions in building a great company. His key piece of advice is to be wary of using an acquisition as a distraction or a crutch, or a way to "diversify away [from] troubles."[1] Companies truly making the good-to-great transition, he observes, are able to use acquisitions to supercharge an already established, successful, and disciplined strategy. At Nasdaq, this was the approach we took. We knew our core business and our foundational strengths. Acquisitions became a method of building momentum in those areas, not diving into completely unknown businesses outside of our sphere of expertise.

A perfect example of that strategy was our purchase of the Philadelphia Stock Exchange (known as Phil-Ex) in 2007. It was actually the oldest exchange in the United States, founded in 1790, and the third-largest equity options exchange in the country. It was in our sweet spot, one bowling pin away from center. When Phil-Ex shareholders decided it was time to go public or sell the exchange, a bidding war ensued between Nasdaq, NYSE, and a couple of other exchange consortiums. We came out ahead. We paid well over $600 million for the exchange and outbid our competitors, but I was confident in the value we were getting.

Why? We did our homework. First, we had already experimented with equity options internally, allowing us to learn the business from the inside out. Second, we used sophisticated analytics—"big data," in today's parlance—to give us insight into the Phil-Ex market. When it comes to bidding wars, knowledge is power. Phil-Ex revealed itself in our models to be a stronger and deeper market than our competitors perhaps realized, hence our higher bid.

During my tenure at Nasdaq, we did more than forty acquisitions. Some were for technology (like the transformational purchase of Instinet), some were to expand globally (like the merger with OMX), some were to move into related markets (like the purchase of Phil-Ex), and some were for market share (like BRUT). I insisted that the acquisitions we did must be accretive to our Earnings Per Share (EPS) by the end of the first year. They helped Nasdaq grow into a dominant national exchange and a significant global one. We prided ourselves on doing them well, and I learned a lot in the process. In truth, however, this was the continuation of an education that had begun long before I accepted the CEO job at the exchange. My former employer, SunGard, built itself largely through acquisitions, which opened my eyes to the possibilities. By the time I left, I had learned a great deal. I brought that knowledge with me to Nasdaq, where I was able to hone it and put it to the test on a much bigger scale. Over time, my team and I became real experts on the subject, especially when targeting other exchanges. In the early days, we were particularly adept at transforming fat, manual, labor-heavy exchanges into fast, lean, efficient, scalable, technology-centric trading enterprises. Later on, we became primarily focused on technology-based acquisitions.

I called this strategy "leveraging the mothership." We had developed the top technology platform in the cash equities universe. Now we could leverage it by acquiring other exchanges and integrating them into the Nasdaq transactions business, using our considerable technological know-how and deep understanding of the business of exchanges. Indeed, in one busy period of about a year from 2007 to 2008, we acquired three exchanges in addition to OMX—the Boston Stock Exchange, Phil-Ex, and Nord Pool (a Nordic energy exchange).

Acquisitions were a critical part of Nasdaq's growth strategy. Part of our effectiveness was our technical proficiency. Part of it was our discipline. But I also believe some of our success could be credited to our capacity to understand the opportunities and mitigate the risks associated with any acquisition. Acquisitions can add tremendous value to a company and supercharge growth. But they come with inevitable risks and potential minefields.

Evaluating Acquisitions: The Four Elements of Risk

I believe that there are at least four elements that must be taken into account when considering the risk-reward profile of any given acquisition and the potential challenges of effectively integrating the newly acquired company.

1. **Core Business Risk.** *The further a proposed acquisition is from one's own core business, the greater the risk.* That shouldn't be surprising, but it's something to take very seriously. As Nasdaq, equities exchanges were obviously in our sweet spot. That was our business and we knew it well. Moving away from that business—into, say, exotic financial instruments or other types of nonequity derivatives—would add risk to the acquisition. We didn't have the internal intelligence to evaluate those businesses with the same degree of accuracy. Again, it *can* work, but the further you venture away from your core business in the acquisition target, the more risk you are taking on board.

2. **Geographic Risk.** *The further a proposed acquisition is from one's geographic center, the greater the risk.* Today's business world is global, and communications technology has brought us closer together, but geography remains a factor to carefully consider. Buying a business on a different continent with customers thousands of miles away is inevitably more complicated and risky than buying a business just across town. That's not to say that mergers between geographically diverse organizations cannot work well. Our merger with the Nordic-based OMX proved to be a resounding success. But I was fully aware of the increased risk and the challenges we would face because of distance.

3. **Cultural Risk.** *The greater the cultural difference with any proposed acquisition target, the greater the risk.* There are at least two aspects of culture that must be considered: the internal *business* culture of any given company and the *local* culture surrounding any given company. Often in acquisitions, a company ends up taking on board a very different business culture. That creates potential problems. Trying too hard to combine and balance two distinct business cultures is a recipe for trouble. Obviously, transforming business culture is not as easy as flipping a switch, but as a general rule I think companies need to have one overarching business culture. More than likely, the acquiring company will need to impose that—to establish clear principles and expectations. That should be done early and often after an acquisition. There should be no confusion about what business culture is going to predominate. But there is one caveat to that advice when it comes to local culture—the national or regional traditions in which the company is embedded. Don't overreach and start stamping out the distinctive flavors of local culture. Those are natural and important, and there's no reason not to make space for them. I was happy for the OMX team to find ways to express their local culture, which was largely independent of the business culture we were working to establish.

4. **Size and Head-Count Risk.** *The greater the size and head count of a proposed acquisition (relative to one's own company), the greater the risk.* Size equals complexity. Much of that is simply head count—with great numbers of people come greater numbers of issues to be navigated. But in most cases, size also means activities spread across more businesses, more regions, more markets, and so on. When an acquired company is bigger than your own, you also need to consider the cost and complication of the

managerial infrastructure needed to deal with the larger head count. This also means that cultural mismatches will inevitably be harder to accommodate. Indeed, when you more than double your head count overnight, don't underestimate the demands of integrating the company. In a very real sense, the size and head-count risk compounds other risks. It makes everything more difficult and uncertain. That's not to say it's not worthwhile, but as the risk profile of acquiring a company ratchets up in any given scenario, it's important to make sure the corresponding potential of the reward does as well.

All of these were risks I carefully weighed before each of Nasdaq's major acquisitions. They helped me to assess the wisdom of buying any particular company, and they also helped me to look ahead, down the road, and prepare for the challenges that I would face once the deal was done. When a long and difficult negotiation like the OMX deal finally comes to an end, it's tempting to breathe a sigh of relief and pat oneself on the back. But the real work has hardly begun. Too many companies do a merger but then don't really do a successful integration. Without that extra element, you don't get the full benefit of the merger. I always found that in order to get employees to buy into the vision of a new, combined company—and benefit from a higher level of engagement—you have to start to "feel" like one company. Otherwise, you'll never get that higher level of "buy-in" from the various teams. That requires real work at integration. It demands clear leadership and smart management skills. The OMX integration was a real test of everything I'd learned in the various chapters of my business career.

In Search of Vikings

"Magnus, we need to find the Vikings on your team."

Magnus Böcker, former CEO of OMX, laughed in his easy way. "There's one right there."

He was pointing at Hans-Ole Jochumsen, who was just teeing up on the sixth hole. The light was spectacular on the golf course, especially considering that it was midnight. We were meeting for a few days in Iceland, the top executives from both Nasdaq and OMX, and working on the postmerger plans for the two companies. The Nasdaq-OMX company actually owned the Iceland Stock Exchange, and it seemed a good in-between place to convene an executive retreat. With its location near the Arctic Circle, Iceland also offered a unique sporting opportunity during the summer months. It was easy to work long days, and with ample light lingering late into the evening in this "land of the midnight sun," nighttime golf is a popular activity.

"Okay, great. That's one. It's a start." I laughed. Magnus, more than others, always seemed to bring out my lighter side.

What I meant by "Vikings" was simply those OMX employees who were intense, competitive, and ready for change, who wanted to embrace the Nasdaq approach and move forward with us into the future. Overnight, we'd become a larger, more diverse, global company, and I knew it was critical to integrate at a cultural level.

Just as I had done in my first weeks at Nasdaq, I met with the team in the Nordics and delivered a clear and unequivocal message: We are remaking this culture. It is going to be hardworking, performance focused, lean, efficient, profitable, and growth oriented. I told them that we would respect their local culture, but Nasdaq would define the business culture. I understood that for some of them, this would not be the business culture they desired or the one they had signed up for. That was perfectly fine. I encouraged people to self-select and move on. There was no shame in this. It wasn't their fault that the company culture was shifting.

I enjoyed my time in the Nordics and grew to love both the cold climate and the warm local culture. I also learned that the business cultures are far from homogeneous among the Scandinavian countries. For example, the Swedish business culture has a long history of producing big industrial companies—Ericsson, IKEA, Volvo, and so on. Danish business culture, on the other hand, is less industrial and known for producing traders and negotiators—perhaps due to the country's geography, situated between several different economic centers and closer to continental Europe and Germany. While such cultural generalizations must always be taken with a grain of salt, it was also true that the person I came to rely on to run the Global Trading and Market Services business at OMX was Hans-Ole Jochumsen, the highly capable Danish "Viking" Magnus had pointed out on the golf course. Hans-Ole became a critical part of Nasdaq's executive team and ran European transactions at OMX for Nasdaq after the merger. Eventually, he ran global transactions and later became President.

Some stereotypes about Nordic culture are true—at least partially so. Our Nordic friends tend to be more consensus driven and communally focused. Those qualities are neither good nor bad. Like all cultural tendencies, they have upsides and downsides— the key is to maximize one and limit the other. Nordic cultures also have safety nets that would surprise Americans. They do take long vacations in the summer, like many of their European neighbors (six weeks is the average annual vacation time).

Despite these differences, the Nordic team was far from incompatible with American business culture. Over time, in many ways, they imbibed the Nasdaq culture as well as the Americans. Our postmerger experience certainly gave the lie to any idea that Nordic cultures lack entrepreneurial drive. In the end, we did find our Vikings. They have drive and business intelligence, along with an international sensibility. And they have truly been a great blessing to Nasdaq's business fortunes.

Learned Knowledge vs. Lived Knowledge

One of the great advantages of growing through acquisition is the opportunity to eliminate overlapping cost structures while increasing revenue. By integrating and streamlining the businesses, you can cut costs quite significantly even as you grow. My team was very good at doing this, but before they could go in with the scalpel, I always cautioned them to go slowly and ensure that they truly understood the company we were about to remake. Before you start cutting costs, you'd better understand exactly what makes the business tick. Before you try to make it highly efficient, you'd better know what makes it effective. Otherwise, your well-meaning efforts at improving efficiency can be remarkably counterproductive.

Effectiveness before efficiency. That was one of my mantras. It's easy to get carried away in spreadsheet simulations, plotting the synergies and savings that are possible. But that's only learned knowledge, not lived knowledge. *Lived* knowledge comes from actual experience running a certain type of business. Lived knowledge allows you to see around the corner and know what obstacles might present themselves. *Learned* knowledge allows you to logically connect A to B, but it doesn't allow you to extrapolate the nonlinear trend line, to anticipate the bumps and curves. Both kinds of knowledge are valuable, but when you confuse the two, it can get you in trouble. If you try to make big changes to a business based solely on learned knowledge, it's easy to make equally big mistakes.

When you've just acquired a company, it's important to balance the fresh perspective you bring as an outsider with the seasoned experience of the insiders. I applied this advice to myself when considering one of OMX's large technology development projects soon after the merger. It had a big budget: more than $100 million. And it seemed to be going nowhere while still burning cash. I was itching to shut it down, but first I asked around. I wanted to make an informed decision and not rush to judgment. Maybe I didn't fully grasp its importance. Interestingly, it was almost impossible to find any defenders of this initiative. Yet it was still weighing like a stone (as a capitalized development cost) on the balance sheet. In the end, after due consideration, that particular project couldn't be justified, so I felt confident in pulling the plug.

Managing a Global Enterprise

Of course, there are limits to how far one can delve into the details of a fast-growing global business and still be an effective CEO. But that's a hard lesson to learn. It's a common sin of CEOs—getting lost in the details at the expense of the larger picture, wanting to be the best in the room at everything, and not letting good people do what they do best. Master-of-the-universe types find it hard to believe that they don't know better. However, the opposite attitude can be equally problematic: flying too high above the ground (sometimes literally, as in cases where a CEO spends too much time jetting around on the company plane) and losing sight of the important operational realities of the business. As a company gets larger, it becomes easier to fall into this trap. That is why I tried to stay as closely connected as possible to the performance of all of Nasdaq's business lines. "Bob never forgets a number" was a common refrain among my team. I hope it was true. If someone told me that they would hit a certain P&L target, my intention was to hold them to it.

I have found that the best executives become "player-coaches"— able to call plays from the sidelines, but never forgetting how to block and tackle. They learn how to delegate wisely but retain a level of direct knowledge about the businesses they oversee. For a good CEO, that means finding points of leverage that allow you to keep tabs on the business units, have a real impact, without losing touch or getting bogged down in the details.

For me, the acquisition of OMX represented a sea change in Nasdaq's identity and challenged me to level up my management game. Once an American-centric company (and largely New York based), we were now a legitimate global enterprise running multiple businesses on two continents and serving exchanges in several others. In some ways I was thrown back to management lessons I had learned earlier in my career.

In my entrepreneurial days, as a partner of ASC, I had been a micromanager. My natural instinct back then was to get involved in all the details, and in that situation I knew it was for the best. I felt as if the company was my baby, and I had a hand in everything that was critical to our success. In that situation, micromanaging made sense. Research on close-knit human social groups suggests that "tribes" can naturally function well with around 150 members. Beyond that, you start to need new kinds of organizational structures and leadership approaches. At ASC, we were essentially a business tribe, and I was the leader. I had less than two hundred employees, and we mostly worked in one big office on a common project. It was an enjoyable context, all of us focused on the same goal, creating an exciting new product together without any extra management or bureaucratic layers to the organization.

When ASC sold to SunGard, I harbored some concern about how long I'd last in a larger organization with all the inevitable complexity and bureaucracy that came with size. But SunGard valued autonomy more than I'd expected. It was a distributed system, with lots of discrete, franchise-like business tribes, or "Burger Kings," as I called them. These separate businesses within the larger organization ran essentially as autonomous units, supported by a few common functions shared across the enterprise. Part of SunGard's pitch when they bought ASC was "We'll leave you alone." Management would not unduly interfere with what was already a successful, growing business.

Soon, I'd been promoted a couple of times and found myself overseeing many of these independent units. At this new level of scale, I could see the downsides of too much autonomy—the potential synergies wasted, the duplication of functions, and the disconnection of employees from a larger mission. My management challenge became: How do you get numerous teams to row together without compromising the relative autonomy that drives innovation, ownership, and execution? I had gone from leading my own little "Burger King" with minimal interference to being the manager seeking to interfere! "I have met the enemy and it is me," I told myself wryly as I started knocking on doors and proposed knocking down various organizational walls, working to knit together a disparate collection of sixty separately functioning business units into a more cohesive system. Suddenly I was moving at right angles to my previous focus—seeking better integration across the enterprise while also ensuring that various businesses stayed disciplined and focused. Now I was building a large, functional organization, not just singular products—but I was determined to do so without succumbing to the bureaucratic inertia that is the death of any innovative technology company. It was an invaluable learning opportunity.

Managing a global enterprise demands that a leader find the right balance between hands-on management and smart delegation—a transition that often eludes entrepreneurs as their business grows. With thousands under your leadership umbrella, it's simply not possible to be involved in everything. In a startup, you can walk the halls, talk to people, ask the right questions, and get an almost tactile sense of how the business is operating. In a large, global enterprise, there are far too many halls, and some of them are thousands of miles away.

In the year after the OMX merger, not only was I attempting to integrate numerous autonomous businesses, but I was attempting to do so on two continents. I needed to find people I could rely on to run a business that was far from Nasdaq's home base. Magnus ended up coming to New York for a period. Several of the other OMX executives moved on from the newly combined company in the year after the merger, through either natural attrition or simply a cultural mismatch. In the end, Hans-Ole was the only senior executive from OMX who stayed and thrived in Nasdaq's culture—his efforts were essential to our successful integration. Most important, much of OMX's younger talent would end up being leaders at Nasdaq over the medium and long term.

Every morning in the year after the merger, I would get up early in my New Jersey home and head for Manhattan. I would usually get to the city by about 6 a.m., in time for a workout before the business day started. Several days per week, on the way to the office, I would take advantage of the time difference and call Hans-Ole to check in about the transaction business at OMX in Copenhagen. I received the numbers every day, but nevertheless I wanted to get the touch and feel of the business directly, especially since I couldn't walk down the hall and take its pulse. Those calls reassured me that he understood what it took to make that transactions business work in our postmerger business environment. I kept up those conversations with him several times a week for the first year in order to develop the confidence that my faith in him was justified. Over time, it became clear that it was.

Where Silos End

Encouraging autonomy while fostering integration is always a balancing act. I wanted people to feel complete responsibility for their business lines. I always felt that if someone had to interact too much with an entirely different business line during their normal day-to-day work, the organizational chart was probably flawed. But I didn't want to go so far that we had an exclusively "eat what you kill" mentality. In a healthy company, there needs to be some degree of cross-fertilization so that people feel connected to the success of the whole company.

In my first few years at Nasdaq, a consistent complaint I heard in the hallways was "We are too siloed." To some extent, that was intentional on my part. The organizational chart was designed that way. But I took the feedback seriously and looked for ways to encourage cross-department and inter-silo engagement and cooperation. The most important of these strategies was a Monday morning executive team meeting that I called the "where silos end meeting." It was required attendance for all SVPs and EVPs and soon expanded to include the OMX team via videoconference.

The meeting had a twofold purpose. Besides breaking down the silos for everyone present, it also gave me an opportunity to ground myself in the details of each business, ask direct questions of a wide range of executives, evaluate my leadership team, and take a closer look under the hood of every part of Nasdaq. Each week, I got to know exactly what were the primary concerns of my managers—what was at the top of their minds. Most important, it kept me from getting lost in the CEO bubble. Indeed, the higher up you go in an organization, the more people want to put you in a bubble. No matter what was going on during the week, every Monday morning I would get a 360-degree view of the entire business. It helped me to let go of the reins without letting go of the horse.

Another strategy I employed was to structure compensation in such a way as to encourage accountability and independence but also goodwill and collaboration across the company. I wanted to find that sweet spot between healthy competition and dynamic collaboration. Much of this comes down to the proper incentives. In my experience it is often true that people don't do what you tell them to do; they do what they are paid to do.

Our compensation was made up of three components: a base salary, a cash bonus, and an equity award. I wanted everyone to have some equity in the company; that was the glue that put us all in the same boat, tying our financial fate together in the larger success or failure of the company. The cash bonus was where I was able to build in some creative incentives, both individual and collective. So 20 percent of the bonus was tied to specific corporate goals and targets, and 80 percent was tied to the success of the individual business unit. Finally, 10 percent of that 80 percent was based on an employee survey, at least for anyone in a leadership role. We wanted to know: How happy and engaged are the people on that leader's team? How connected are they to the mission? In my book, you have to lead by acclaim. You have to fundamentally garner the support of those you are leading. That doesn't mean everyone will be happy with the decisions you make, but good leaders should have the essential support of their employees.

I also wanted to discourage misuse of power. When you give people significant power in a corporate context—or any context, for that matter—there are always some individuals who have a tendency to turn into little dictators. Over the years, I spent a great deal of energy and effort thinking carefully about the kinds of questions we would ask in those surveys. Obviously, we were measuring a specific kind of satisfaction. We didn't want these surveys to simply become a repository for fruitless frustrations. What I wanted to measure, as closely as possible, were the leadership qualities that were helping foster engaged employees. I believe that over the years, the various components of our compensation package helped encourage Nasdaq leaders to compete, innovate, collaborate, and demonstrate financial accountability—all while incentivizing our collective "better angels."

Not everything comes down to financial incentives, of course. But with part of the compensation tied to individual performance, part to company performance, part to corporate goals, part to equity ownership, and part to employee satisfaction, I felt like we had a robust way of encouraging our team at Nasdaq to deliver on their business priorities while supporting the trajectory of the entire enterprise.

Clouds on the Horizon

With Nasdaq's purchase of OMX, our series of smaller acquisitions, the expansion into new business lines, and our enlarged global footprint, it felt like we had reached a culmination point in our growth-by-acquisition strategy. For the moment, I was hesitant to expand further; more stood to be gained in internal transformations. We focused on taking advantage of the synergies and opportunities provided by the merger. It was a period of nation building within Nasdaq, so to speak. Our success prompted *Forbes* magazine to declare us "Company of the Year" in 2008, and that same year we entered the Standard & Poor's 500. We added 177 new listings to Nasdaq, and we even convinced nine more companies to switch over from NYSE, worth $79 billion in market capitalization.

But in 2008, only one story really mattered. Indeed, the glow of Nasdaq's success, and of several years of consistent market growth and expansion, was overshadowed by the storm clouds that amassed on the horizon. In March of that year, Bear Stearns unexpectedly collapsed, requiring a last-minute shotgun merger with JPMorgan Chase to survive. Global markets reacted nervously, and the economic tailwinds that had driven markets forward for years seemed to have exhausted themselves. By the end of that summer, as Wall Street's finest returned from their brief, American-style summer vacations, optimism seemed in short supply. But even at that late date, few understood the true dimensions of the gathering storm.

LEADERSHIP LESSONS

- **Leverage the Mothership.** When growing through acquisitions, stay close to your core strengths and be aware that the risks increase as you move further away—in size, culture, geography, or primary area of focus.

- **Effectiveness Before Efficiency.** Make sure you have a good business and know how it really works before you try to streamline it into a highly efficient one.

- **Always Be a Player-Coach.** Stay connected to the business on the ground even as you keep your eye on the big picture.

- **Incentives Matter.** Understand the importance of employee incentives and build compensation to match. Employees who have skin in the game tend to be more engaged with the success of the whole enterprise.

Chapter Nine

Blood on the Tracks

Wall Street's Fears on Lehman Bros. Batter Markets

New York Times, September 9, 2008

Where were you when Lehman failed?

On Wall Street, that question will likely be asked for many decades to come. After all, the collapse of Lehman Brothers, one of the leading investment banks, was the biggest bankruptcy in U.S. history and the critical inflection point of the financial crisis that swept across global markets in September 2008.

I was at a party. My host, Maggie Wilderotter, was the dynamic CEO of Frontier Communications, a significant telecommunications company that I was soliciting to switch its public listing to Nasdaq. (I would eventually succeed, though it took several years.) We had become acquaintances, and I was subsequently invited to a gathering at her Westchester, New York, home on Sunday, September 14, 2008. Her husband was a winemaker, and together they owned a vineyard in the Sierra Foothills region of Northern California. On this particular day, he was sharing his wines, and she was a gracious hostess, entertaining guests in the grounds of their beautiful house, when the pleasant hum of conversation was abruptly punctuated by multiple phones buzzing. The breaking news rippled through the party: Lehman Brothers, one of the oldest institutions on Wall Street, was rumored to be going bankrupt. Looking around at the Gatsbyesque scene—the manicured lawn, the well-dressed guests, the dappled sunlight reflecting off the wineglass in my hand—I had the sudden sense that it was all precarious, the calm before a gathering storm. Was this how people felt at the end of the Roaring Twenties, just as the Great Depression was about to hit?

Before I could reflect any further, I found myself the center of attention. Everyone seemed to want my opinion about what this meant. It was largely a New York crowd, but not necessarily from the finance industry, so I became the de facto expert. I didn't have much to offer by way of reassurance. The markets already seemed to be hanging by a thread, and this was not the good news we were hoping for.

I generally consider myself to be a reliable person in a crisis— the one who stays calm as others start to panic. But in this situation, my mind was racing. What were the ramifications? What would it mean to the financial markets? How would it affect the equity exchanges? Lehman Brothers was a huge player in investment banking, with tentacles in every corner of the industry. Compared to Bear Stearns, Lehman was a much bigger institution—and an important player in derivatives, which would be challenging to unwind in an orderly fashion. I knew Lehman's size would likely mean that its impact and contagion risk would be many orders of magnitude greater than Bear Stearns's. How would that affect the psychology of Wall Street? What would it mean to Nasdaq? Amid all of the unanswerable questions, there was one thing I was quite clear about—all hell was going to break loose the following morning. There was going to be blood in the streets.

Eventually, my racing mind settled on a simple truth. The one thing I could do was to take care of Nasdaq's particular corner of the financial markets and ensure that it functioned superbly. That wasn't a simple matter, because I knew we were about to see a flood of orders hitting our servers. For equity exchanges like Nasdaq, moments of crisis are always times when transaction volumes spike. Volatility attracts trading activity, and a precipitous event like the Lehman collapse was bound to spark a panicked sell-off. Could we handle the trading volume?

Thankfully, Nasdaq systems were up to the task. My CIO, Anna Ewing, and her team did a fantastic job of keeping everything up and running. Admittedly there were a few scary moments— times when our systems seemed to be bending like a sapling in a November nor'easter. Our transaction technology was pushed to the very edge over the days and weeks following the Lehman bankruptcy. We bent but didn't break. We regularly test transaction volumes in our laboratory that exceed normal operations by two or three times. But in that period we were far exceeding even our test volumes. Every day I was relieved when we successfully processed the morning rush of orders. It was a testimony to the investment we had made in our transaction services over the previous years, beginning with the purchase of Instinet, and the subsequent consolidation and improvements we had made around that core technology.

The increase in transaction volume also meant a large increase in associated revenue. This created an incongruous situation: While everything else was crashing around us, Nasdaq revenue was going through the roof. But I knew that it was temporary. Like a drug-induced high, the crisis-driven revenue surge never lasts very long, and the eventual hangover is brutal. Indeed, the backside of any crisis in the economy is usually a significant recession, entailing a painful drop in transaction volumes, which can linger for some time, compounded by other knock-on effects, like the inevitable disappearance of the IPO market. So I had no illusions about the significant but short-lived profits suddenly appearing on our income statement.

The Great Credit Ice Age

Trust is essential in the development of any well-functioning society or economy. The political scientist Francis Fukuyama points out that successful societies are characterized by wide and efficient networks of trust that allow them to develop the social, political, and economic institutions that are critical to long-term thriving. The social capital that flows out of those trust networks is, like economic capital, an important part of what makes an advanced economy truly work. Trusting and being trustworthy tend to beget more of themselves in a win-win virtuous circle, but the opposite is true as well. Distrust can feed on itself, in a lose-lose deal that ultimately leaves everyone worse off. A circle of distrust was exactly what was set in motion when Lehman failed. Suddenly no one on Wall Street seemed trustworthy. And when trust fails in an economic system that runs on social capital as well as financial capital, the results are disastrous.

The first consequence of the Lehman bankruptcy was a freeze in lending activity. As if someone had injected a heavy sludge into a finely tuned machine, the financial industry began to gum up and grind to a halt. The markets absolutely rely on credit. It's the oil that makes the entire engine run smoothly. And credit depends on trust. We all know that a credit card company will lend money to a consumer only if they calculate that that person is likely to pay the money back. The same goes for the billions of dollars in short-term loans extended every day between institutions in our global financial ecosystem. As with a personal credit card, the moment there is a loss of faith that an institution will repay the debt, credit lines get cut and lending stops.

That was what happened after Lehman—en masse. Trust started to break down. After all, who knew what monsters lurked on other people's balance sheets? What if more Lehmans were out there, getting ready to implode? Even a business that was perfectly healthy for the moment might have significant exposure to Lehman's failure. What if it had money owed to it that now would never be paid back? With stock markets going south, assets that were once perceived as rock-solid might suddenly look a lot less valuable. The insurance giant AIG was rumored to be the next institution teetering on insolvency. Maybe Morgan Stanley, whose stock was dropping every day like a stone, wasn't far behind Lehman—or so people whispered. Perhaps even Goldman Sachs, the gold standard of investment banking, would require capital infusions to stay afloat? The rumor mill went into overdrive, and every counterparty, every trade, and every transaction was subject to heightened scrutiny and suspicion.

As these fears started to metastasize on Wall Street and spread throughout global markets, interbank lending rates soared. The market for commercial paper, an indicator of lending activity, shrunk dramatically. The so-called TED spread (the difference between interbank loan rates and rates on short-term Treasury bills), a key risk indicator, reached an all-time high. "Credit Markets Frozen as Banks Hoard Cash," announced one typical headline of the moment. A high-trust network had quickly devolved into a panicked race for survival. Now the only counterparty that anyone truly trusted was the "lender of last resort," the federal government. The government had to act and provide a backstop to the spiraling crisis. Soon, a massive bailout was on the way.

Should federal regulators have tried harder to save Lehman and prevent the fallout of that bankruptcy? Without question, I think the answer is yes, assuming it was possible. In retrospect, letting Lehman fail was like taking the pin out of a financial hand grenade and hoping it wouldn't blow up. Clearly, Lehman was only a symptom of the global financial crisis, not the cause, but it was a precipitous decision nonetheless to allow it to collapse. But hindsight is always twenty-twenty, and such decisions are never so simple in the heat of the moment.

Our nation's economic leaders—individuals like Hank Paulson, Treasury Secretary; Tim Geithner, President of the Federal Reserve Bank of New York; Ben Bernanke, Chairman of the Federal Reserve; Chris Cox, head of the SEC; and Sheila Bair, head of the FDIC—were already operating in ambiguous territory, where the rules were not prescribed precisely and they had to fill in the gaps. They were trying to respond to the unfolding crisis with appropriate speed while acting within their actual legislative authority. There were no finely honed and tested tools to easily unwind an institution like Lehman, only blunt instruments. There was also the issue of moral hazard, the concern that if the government set a precedent of stepping in to rescue a major institution, it could actually set the stage for more risky behavior by institutions that now knew the downsides of that risk could be borne by others.

Among the architects of the crisis response, I interacted on occasion with Geithner, Cox, and Bernanke. Each earned my appreciation and respect, but the individual I knew best was Paulson. My first meeting with him was in his office in Washington, early on in his tenure. I recall him wondering, almost wistfully, what he would be able to accomplish at the Treasury, given the seeming stability of the economy at the time, his truncated term, and the meager bipartisan support for other needed reforms. He mentioned getting rid of the penny as one of his initiatives, which, though a laudable goal (and one that no one has yet achieved), is almost comically insignificant compared to the actual issues that he would be confronted with. I guess the lesson is: Be careful what you wish for!

On a more serious note, I believe that Paulson is a hero for the unprecedented actions he took, along with Bernanke and others, to prop up the national and global economy. I don't hand out such compliments casually. The country was lucky to have a public servant of his temper and stature in such a critical role during one of the most dangerous periods in our history. Despite his Goldman Sachs roots, he never seemed to be merely a creature of Wall Street. He always struck me as a grounded, everyday man—refreshingly unconcerned with his own position. He wasn't a natural politician—neither a gifted orator nor a reliable partisan of Left or Right. But clever verbosity is often overrated in business and life. And overt partisanship would have been a disaster during the financial crisis.

After the worst of the crisis was over, and the country was slowly and painfully recovering, I attended a conference at which Paulson, now retired, was a keynote speaker. At the end of his talk, I was the first in the audience on my feet. It was the only time I have ever led a standing ovation, and it wasn't because of what he had said but because of what he did—for all of us. God help us if there had been someone less suited in the office of Treasury Secretary in late 2008. The moment demanded heroism, and Paulson delivered. He is, in my book, a great American.

I watched the unfolding crisis from the relative safety of the stock exchange, where things were less catastrophic. Indeed, the most important thing from my vantage point was how the equity markets as a whole performed in the midst of the chaos. In fact, they performed admirably—an untold story amid all the doom and gloom.

Indeed, it's worth emphasizing that while Wall Street often gets painted with a broad brush, the equity exchanges were not responsible for the crisis. Rather, it started in the housing market and festered in the over-the-counter, nontransparent, bilateral trading venues where new financial instruments like credit default swaps helped create unseen risk. Nor did stock markets freeze up, like so many other trading venues. Indeed, once Lehman failed and credit markets ground to a halt, the equity exchanges, including Nasdaq, continued to function amid the spreading global panic, day after day after day. Trades were made and cleared, and the system continued to operate. Trust was maintained. People didn't stop believing that their trade on Nasdaq or

NYSE would get properly processed. They didn't lose trust in the counterparty on the other side of the trade. The federal government never had to step in. That speaks to the resiliency of our model.

Of course, like everyone else, we were deeply concerned about how equity markets were dramatically falling during that period, and the impact on our nation's economy and the wealth of hard-working Americans. We were constantly reviewing possible changes to our structure to make sure that trading practices like short selling were not fueling negative sentiment or interfering with appropriate price discovery. But ultimately our job is not to make the market go up or down; it is to make sure it doesn't break down, which would have been its own kind of disaster. That was our responsibility; the one thing we could do in our corner of Wall Street to help. Consider this amazing fact—the primary thing we had to worry about during the crisis was *too much volume*, while the main concern with many of these other venues was *no volume at all*. They had broken down completely.

To Short or Not to Short

In my office at Nasdaq, there were a number of monitors playing financial news channels and displaying market data. Most days, they barely received a glance, but in the fall of 2008, my executive team and I were often glued to the drama unfolding in the market. On one particularly brutal day, Chris Concannon was my viewing partner. The market was dropping precipitously, and even as we stood on the fiftieth floor of a Wall Street tower, you could sense the fear in the streets. It seemed to permeate the very atmosphere of the city during those days, as if a massive low-pressure system had just parked itself over Manhattan.

"I've never seen the market fall like this." Chris's voice wavered slightly, betraying his own concern. Morgan Stanley was just one of the stocks falling, as if there was nothing between it and a fire-sale bankruptcy. Could things really be that bad? As the numbers flashed red on the screen, I turned to him, trying not to look as worried as I felt. "Short sellers are just hammering Morgan. And Goldman. The shorts are going to burn down the market."

Short selling, for those not familiar with the term, means that an investor essentially bets that a stock price will fall, and seeks to profit off that decrease in price.* At the height of the financial crisis, with prices plummeting, short selling was rampant, and some were concerned that it was contributing to the downward spiral.

"Should we try to do something more?" Chris asked, unable to take his eyes away from the bloodbath on the screen.

Ask me on a normal day if short selling is a positive thing for the markets, and I could give you solid reasons why the answer is a resounding yes. Arguably, the ability to bet on the decline in the share price of a company brings needed discipline to markets, facilitating better price discovery. If you can only bet that the price will rise (by going long), that is an unbalanced situation and stocks will be overvalued. In theory, short selling can keep

---

* In short selling, an investor borrows a stock from an owner (paying a nominal fee) and sells it for a profit. If it then goes down in price, the investor buys it back and returns it to the original owner. The difference between the price earned from selling it at a higher price and buying it at a lower one is the profit earned on the short sale.

a certain "irrational exuberance" from taking hold in equities, allowing diverse voices to express their opinion on the direction of a stock price. It can also help root out fraud in markets, making it hard for companies like Enron to hide their duplicitous accounting practices. But during the financial crisis, short selling was like throwing gasoline on a forest fire that was already burning up capital at an alarming rate. So I appreciated Chris's question. It was one I'd been asking myself. I wondered if maybe we should try to influence the SEC to further curtail short selling, at least temporarily. I also appreciated, however, that this was a step with far-reaching consequences that we currently could not see.

"Normally, I would say that's a bad idea, but…" My voice trailed off. At that moment, despite my position at the top of Wall Street's machinery, I felt buffeted by forces far beyond my control. Between the two us, Chris and I probably knew as much about market structure as any two people on the planet. But in the whirlwind of that period, it was hard to know how much to trust your own experience. It was the classic dilemma of the philosophical ideal versus the pragmatic reality. None of us had lived through anything like this before. Who were we to play puppet master to the markets, especially at such a delicate point in their history? Maybe it was all going to burn down, despite our elegant theories, hard work, and idealistic motives. I looked at Chris and completed my thought: "…but what the hell do I know?"

Such doubts often swirled around us as we watched the market swoon, flinching at the body blows it was receiving. Sooner or later, it was going to be a knockout punch. We put our heads down and did our jobs amid the gathering gloom, but our usual optimism was in short supply.

Soon after that conversation, I was at home over a weekend

when I received a call from Chris Cox just before dinner. He had just been discussing the issue of short selling with Geithner. Already in the summer, they had cracked down on the practice, and attempts had been made to tighten restrictions. They had even banned short selling outright for a period in some financial stocks. Now Geithner was looking to implement further protections. I was sympathetic to the idea.

"Bob, sorry to bother you. But Geithner wants to get this done immediately, if possible," Cox explained. He sounded exhausted, urgent, and worried—all at the same time.

He wasn't the only one concerned about the issue. In fact, Cox was also getting pressure from the banks and politicians about it. Both New York Senators, Chuck Schumer and Hillary Clinton, were urging a short-selling ban. At one point, during the crisis, TV personality Jim Cramer went after Cox personally for not reining in short sellers, and then presidential candidate John McCain called for him to be fired. Personally, I found Cox to be hardworking, nonideological, and responsive—all good qualities for running the SEC. But justified or not, he was being held accountable for allowing short sellers, the bogeymen of the moment, to further destabilize markets.

"Chris, I agree," I told him, "but as you know better than anyone, the SEC is not an organization known for its adaptive agility. It isn't designed to move fast on anything." It was a simple fact. The SEC is required to meticulously follow sunshine laws requiring transparency. You can't even have more than two Commissioners talking to each other at the same time; otherwise, these laws require a full public hearing of all five Commissioners. The public has to weigh in on new regulations. There is a comment period. It's an orchestrated process. Indeed, I had come to realize an inconvenient truth—when it comes to government institutions, you can have transparency or you can have speed, but you can't have both.

"Dad, are you ready for dinner?" Katie's voice rang out as she entered my office. My daughter and I had made plans to go out, and she was hungry. Normally, she would have looked irritated and urged me to hurry up and get off the phone, and like most teenagers shown little concern for her father's business dealings. This time was different, however. As soon as she entered the room, she got very quiet and still. She suddenly looked concerned— for me. I was amazed at how the very atmosphere of the room and the gravity of the moment cut through all of her teenage self-absorption.

Cox soon explained to me that he had a new plan. "Bob, since the SEC can't self-propose this, I want Nasdaq and NYSE to join together and do it themselves. That could be approved quickly."

Cox's plan was sound, and that was exactly what we did in the following days. The SEC passed a temporary ban on most short selling, which lasted several weeks, and ended in early October 2008. At the time, it felt good to have done something. But of course banning short selling doesn't stop selling, or prevent the markets from falling. I've come to regard it as a cautionary tale about what can happen when one acts too quickly to fix a perceived problem and in the process interferes with natural market forces. Even at the time, the consensus was largely that the ban did little to help stabilize markets, and a number of careful studies afterward came to the same conclusion. If anything, it might have been counterproductive. Before he departed the SEC later that year, Cox also said that he regretted the decision. "Knowing what we know now," he said, "I believe on balance the commission would not do it again."[1]

The Perils of Leverage

"There are only three ways a smart person can go broke. Liquor, ladies, and leverage," is a saying attributed to legendary investor Charlie Munger.[2] There are a lot of smart people on Wall Street, and it's true that the three *L*s have taken down more than a few, but in 2008, one stood out far above the others—leverage. There was no single cause of the crisis; many events came together and conspired to set the system on fire. But the dangers of leverage were at the center of it all, and that stands out to me as a lesson that must be learned if we are to avoid repeat performances.

Leverage is not all bad, of course. I went deep into debt to acquire some of the assets that were essential to the transformation of Nasdaq, like Instinet. In those days, we were temporarily nine times leveraged. That means, for example, that if our business declined for some reason, it could impair our ability to pay off the debt. We knew that Nasdaq was temporarily in a delicate position, but given the synergies of the deal, we also knew that we could quickly bring it under control. That was a unique circumstance. In general, I was careful to keep our debt well within reasonable limits. I also avoided acquisitions that I felt would have left Nasdaq too highly leveraged, as demonstrated when we walked away from the LSE bid.

Perhaps my most relevant experience with leverage came as the new owner of OMX, which owned a clearinghouse in the

Nordics. This was a business I was familiar with but had never overseen operationally, so I had to get up to speed fast. Any CEO worth his or her paycheck needs to understand any business he or she is overseeing and find the right comfort level in terms of the degree of oversight. It can be surprising how many CEOs, especially in large corporations, don't truly know important details about their own businesses. So I had to learn the essential components of the clearinghouse business—one of which was managing the margin. In the context of clearing, that means knowing how exposed the positions of your member institutions are and how much capital is needed to account for that risk. We employed a number of high-IQ mathematicians to help us do exactly that.

Soon after the acquisition, I met with the team managing risk. This was many months before Bear Stearns and Lehman Brothers made everyone rethink our risk models. This team was using sophisticated mathematical profiles to measure correlations among different assets, and the risks entailed in those relationships. So, for example, if a big institutional client had a $100 million portfolio that was cleared with us, we might demand a $7 million margin at the clearinghouse. However, in this meeting, our team was telling me their models showed that declines in certain assets weren't historically correlated with declines in other assets. Since the model showed the risk profile was reduced in such cases, perhaps we should relax the margin requirements on those types of portfolios containing these noncorrelated assets.

Thankfully, our team decided not to change our margin requirement based on those calculations. We stayed conservative. I had no idea then how grateful I would be for that decision. In retrospect, it looks prophetic. Now we know that too many such models proved disastrously inaccurate. In a real crisis, everything is correlated. But in those days, I didn't know the storm that was coming. I decided not to ratchet up our risk, no matter what the smartest guys in the room suggested. A few months later, as we found ourselves closely monitoring our risk levels on a daily basis through the crisis, there were several cases when we were forced to make margin calls on our member firms.

Here is where one of the most important leadership lessons applies: *Don't fool yourself.* It's a hard lesson to learn. There are always ways to convince yourself of things that don't deserve your conviction. It's always possible to talk yourself into a conclusion that owes more to the climate of the moment and the temporary incentives of the day than to any independent assessment of the situation. And leverage is one of those matters about which it's all too easy to fool yourself, assuming that the future will look like the past.

But the reality is that the future doesn't always look like the past. That may sound obvious, but humans always like to interpret their current experience through the lens of what's come before. Computers (programmed by humans) often do the same. Just because something has not happened doesn't mean it won't. We all learned that critical lesson in the financial crisis. Some models seemed rock-solid until the very day they failed completely. Don't get caught fighting the last battle. Don't fool yourself.

"Beware of geeks bearing formulas" is another pearl of wisdom from Warren Buffett, urging investors to be skeptical of history-based models. It's sound advice, although I might phrase it differently. After all, Nasdaq has built a multibillion-dollar business while relying on many geeks bearing useful formulas and models—likewise with many of our listed firms. But like any sophisticated tool, mathematics can become one more way to fool yourself—like the investment bankers on Wall Street before the financial crisis who somehow convinced themselves that a 30:1 leverage ratio was acceptable. In other words, they were putting up $3.33 in actual capital for every $100 invested, meaning that if their portfolio declined 4 percent or more, they would be insolvent! Yet CEOs armed with formulas talked themselves into thinking such leverage was manageable. I have made plenty of mistakes in my career, but that was one I never would have made. I could not have slept soundly with that kind of risk hanging over my head.

In an era in which the investment banks were still organized as partnerships and not as public corporations, I find it hard to imagine that such high-risk levels would have been employed. The incentives of the partnership—the skin in the game, so to speak—would surely have exerted greater discipline, and that would have mitigated some of the assumed risk. No crisis on the scale of 2008 has one or even two causes; inevitably, it's a confluence of many events. But leverage, the failure of leadership, and the different organizational structure of Wall Street investment banks each played a significant role.

What about the SEC? How much blame should they get? Regulatory failure also contributed to the crisis, and the SEC was obviously ground zero of that issue. But rather than point the finger at one person, or even the five-person committee, or home in on specific events leading up to the crisis, I think it is more instructive to examine the regulatory culture of the SEC.

Culture may be destiny, as many have pointed out, but in this case, "charter" is also destiny. The SEC's charter is explicitly focused on investor protection and maintaining fair and orderly markets. The stability and soundness of the institutions it oversees are not front and center. This mandate is right there in the founding charter, and arguably it worked fairly well for most of the century since it was set up—until it failed completely. Institutional inertia is a powerful force. The SEC was making sure everyone followed the rules, obsessing over every little change that Nasdaq and other institutions made to their business models—in the name of investor protection—while world-destroying amounts of leverage and risk were building up under their noses. Looking back, the lack of oversight would be laughable if it wasn't so consequential. The SEC simply wasn't designed to look in the right direction.

During the crisis, the surviving investment banks converted to commercial banks, which gave some regulatory authority to the Federal Reserve, changing the dynamic completely. Nevertheless, the financial crisis signaled that it was time for a major update of our nation's regulatory structure—which was exactly what happened after the smoke cleared and some stability returned to the markets.

Dodd-Frank and a Big Bank

"You f——k! You f——king ass! Who do you think you are? What do you think you're doing!?"

The stream of F bombs being hurled at me came as a shock. I had just picked up the phone and was unexpectedly greeted by this tirade before I could even say a couple of words. But it wasn't just the torrent of invectives that was a surprise. It was the person behind them. It's not every day you have Jamie Dimon—CEO of JPMorgan Chase and one of the individuals in the business I respect most highly—call up and curse at you like a drunken sailor.

"Jamie, let me speak," I broke in after about fifteen seconds. But this only seemed to reenergize his rant.

"You don't speak! You listen!" And this was followed by another thirty seconds of shouting and cursing.

Admittedly, I knew exactly what he was upset about. I could even sympathize with his frustration. It was 2009, and we were in the middle of the discussion around the new legislation package that would come to be known as Dodd-Frank, which promised a full overhaul of our nation's financial regulatory structure in response to the systemic breakdowns that had occurred. Dimon had just realized that Nasdaq was involved in a campaign to change the way that certain types of trading and clearing would be conducted—a change that would have significant consequences for the big banks.

A few months earlier, Ed Knight, Nasdaq's legal counsel, had proposed a series of steps we could take to influence the new regulatory structure that would be put in place postcrisis. Every major institution on Wall Street had a stake in it—though Nasdaq's stake was less direct than others'.

The financial crisis highlighted, for me, certain aspects of our model that had proven critical to our resiliency. Equity markets like Nasdaq function using what is sometimes called an "all-to-all" model, meaning that all buyers and sellers come together in an exchange with a central, independent clearinghouse that mutualizes risk. That latter part is key. A clearinghouse legally settles the trades that happen on the exchange. It provides a standard set of rules that governs those transactions. If a retail investor, John Q. Public, puts in a sell order using his retirement account on TD Ameritrade, he may get a confirmation right away, but that does not mean the trade is complete. The trade is not cleared until it is settled at the clearinghouse, and the contract is finalized and the money moves. In a sense, *clearinghouses systematize and institutionalize trust.* Every institution that is a participant in that market has to put up some collateral to the clearinghouse. In turn, the clearinghouse monitors the creditworthiness of member firms and provides a fund that can cover losses if those losses exceed any one member's collateral. Today, the function of a clearinghouse in U.S. equity markets is performed by the DTCC (Depository Trust and Clearing Corporation).

For years, I had been an advocate of open, transparent markets, with competing electronic exchanges and independent clearinghouses. Nasdaq operated that way, and we had pushed regulations that encouraged the evolution of markets in that direction. In the midst of the crisis, the markets that adhered to that model had performed the best, without the hidden risks that had built up in the bilateral, private credit markets. If ever there was a moment when that faith was vindicated, this seemed to be it.

Bilateral, private markets have a tendency to fail; not because of nefarious behavior, but simply because trust is more delicate in those relationships. Without the firewall of a clearinghouse, they are only as strong as their weakest link, and contagion is more of a danger. The rumor mill has more power. A breakdown in trust can quickly infect the whole system. Indeed, failures of trust can more easily infect whole interconnected webs of bilateral relationships. That's why many of those over-the-counter (OTC) trading venues ground to a halt in 2008. Clearinghouses provide an institutional firewall and help inoculate against exactly the type of contagion that attacked our system in the crisis.

Ed's proposal was that we initiate a grassroots campaign to lobby for the inclusion of our proposed changes in the Dodd-Frank rules that were currently being negotiated in Congress. We invested some money in that lobbying campaign, distributing it to civic-minded organizations that were aligned with our goals. We felt it was for a good cause, and we hoped to have a real influence on policy.

During that campaign, one of the more memorable meetings we had was a conversation in the West Wing of the White House with Larry Summers, head of the National Economic Council under Obama. It was exciting to set foot in that iconic building, not as a tourist but on official business that would affect the nation. As we launched into our sermon on clearinghouses, Summers, who is one of the smartest individuals I've been privileged to know, leaned back in his chair and closed his eyes. My heart sank. Was he concentrating? Was he sleeping? I wasn't sure, but I knew he had a reputation for working long hours. Perhaps they had caught up to him (a few days later, the press would actually circulate a photo of him sleeping in a meeting with the President). After a few moments, however, his eyes popped open and he exclaimed, "Clearinghouses, I get it! Basically, that's the reason we invented money."

Puzzled by his statement, I thought, *He must have been asleep.* Then I realized he was right. It was a wonderful leap of logic. Money gives people the confidence to exchange goods and services independent of needing to personally trust each other's creditworthiness. In the same way, a clearinghouse gives investors confidence to exchange securities independent of having to personally trust and verify the creditworthiness of the counterparty. Money may just be pieces of paper (or numbers in an account), but because we're all invested in that medium of exchange and it is backed by the full faith of the federal government, it becomes a way to *clear* hundreds of billions of transactions every day. A clearinghouse performs the same critical function in trading securities, as Summers quickly grasped during our conversation. No one else we'd spoken to had made this unique connection. It's always interesting to see a great mind at work.

In due course, on December 11, 2009, a bill passed the House of Representatives that would mandate the use of independent clearinghouses in many over-the-counter derivatives and take those functions out of the hands of the banks.

When it passed the House, the banks woke up. Suddenly, they realized that there was a possibility they might lose the clearing and trading function in certain derivative markets given the proposed regulatory structure. That hit the bottom line directly, as they would potentially lose significant streams of revenue, like the billions of dollars in profit they earned from trading over-the-counter interest rate swaps for large companies and institutions. In 2008, Chase reportedly earned $5 billion in profit on this one business alone! It's no accident that the internal nickname for the leader of this trading business for JPMorgan Chase was "Matt the Mint."

The House bill threatened to lower the boom on this type of trading and clearing and move it out of the private markets controlled by banks like Chase. When it passed, warning bells went off in executive suites all over Manhattan. In a tough banking environment, that revenue stream was critical. They started asking, "Who is pushing this legislation?" All of which led to that irate phone call from Dimon.

For JPMorgan Chase, the issue was particularly relevant. With one of the biggest balance sheets on Wall Street, they could offer customers a security and certainty that few others could match. They could make trades on derivatives—interest rate swaps, for example—that few others could handle. Bilateral trading venues cleared by specialized, custom-made contracts tend to give an advantage to the person with the biggest balance sheet in the room. In contrast, a mutualized clearinghouse is all about the collective strength of the group, not the individual strength of a particular player. Everyone is treated roughly the same: no sweet deals, no special rates. Everyone puts up collateral. The rules are more transparent and standardized.

In thinking about Dimon's tirade, I could see it from his perspective. JPMorgan Chase had made real sacrifices during the financial crisis, taking on Bear Stearns and Washington Mutual and the liabilities associated with those two troubled institutions. Furthermore, Chase had not been involved in the nefarious activities that led to the crisis. Dimon was fending off politicians out for blood on one end and an outraged public on the other. But if I wasn't going to be an advocate for all-to-all electronic markets with mutualized clearinghouses, who exactly was going to? That's what Nasdaq does! JPMorgan lends money; Nasdaq runs fair markets.

In 2010, Dodd-Frank passed with a version of our proposed regulated structure for derivative markets. We did get clearinghouses overseeing the derivatives market trades, an important

step forward, though it would take many years to fully implement. Moreover, all interest rate swaps now must be reported to
a public database at the DTCC clearinghouse—a move toward
greater transparency, which is also positive. While the OTC markets are still a big step short of where the equity markets are today,
I do believe that they are stronger and better today because of our
and others' efforts, and I take some pride in having helped them
to evolve.

The Madoff Mess

The final coda to the lesson we all learned about trust in the financial crisis was an event that, for many, personified the greed and cor-
ruption that led our economy to the brink of disaster—the Bernie
Madoff affair.

I had been involved in a few dealings with the Madoff brothers, Bernie and Peter, over the years. When I was at ASC representing our software platform, BRASS, I ended up negotiating
with both of them on the price structure of that contract (which
in practice meant negotiating with Peter, as Bernie didn't seem to
be a detail person). He argued incessantly for every extra cent that
they could get from me, even though he had no real leverage in
the discussions. Generally, I'm not one to disparage good negotiating tactics. But it was, frankly, overwrought. In the early days
at Nasdaq, I would find myself in another difficult negotiation
with the Madoffs as I sought to unwind a horrible contract my
predecessors had signed with the brothers for a joint initiative that
went nowhere. While Bernie was never Chairman of the Nasdaq

Board, as some news outlets have reported, before my arrival he was Chairman of an advisory board, a much more ceremonial position, but one that still speaks to his connections at the stock market. I reluctantly settled the contract for more than I thought we should have paid, but I was glad to end Nasdaq's dealings with the brothers.

Still, when I heard the news about the Ponzi scheme, I was as shocked as everyone else. For several days, the news dominated my thoughts and every conversation on Wall Street, although no one I knew was affected personally. Madoff's targets were not professionals in the industry, who would be more inclined to a high level of due diligence.

After the initial shock had passed, everyone in the industry was suddenly a confident Madoff expert. "I knew something was wrong with those guys." "They always seemed dishonest." "It's obvious there was something unsavory about their operation." And yet, right under the noses of all of these self-appointed experts with their perfect, retrospective knowledge, somehow the Madoff Ponzi scheme had lasted for well over a decade, defrauding a whole community of billions and billions of dollars.

If good markets, successful economies, and healthy societies are built on high levels of trust, the Madoff scandal was the polar opposite—an event that degraded our trust in each other and in the markets that support our financial dealings. As with the larger financial crisis that was ultimately Madoff's undoing, it was a moment to appreciate that markets are not abstractions but dynamic systems that are fallible, sensitive, and continually in need of improvement. They exist to allocate precious capital and facilitate its free flow, allowing the entire economy to function better. Like the movement of water in an ecosystem, the functional circulation of capital plays an irreplaceable role in the health of the system it supports. When that circulation breaks down, as it did in the greatest financial crisis of my lifetime, our economies dry up, and we all suffer the consequences.

We are all children of the great recession. It's no exaggeration to say that we will never be the same. A generation of Wall Street bankers and executives had been lulled to sleep by decades of relative stability; it had been several generations since we'd seen a crisis on this scale. When one finally came, after so long, it came with a vengeance. Before 2008, we had risk models and disaster-scenario planning—but let's be honest, it was mostly theoretical. All of our existing models about what could go wrong were swamped in that wave of contagion. The existential threat was real, and we all felt it—the knowledge that we might all go down with the ship.

It changed us. I think about risk today very differently than I did prior to 2008. And I see the same every day on Wall Street—the level of awareness, attention, and concern about what could happen is entirely different than it was prior to the crisis. People are less inclined to underreact. I'm not pretending that our financial system has somehow been derisked. Finance inevitably involves risk, as does all business. It is part of the capitalist endeavor. Nor have the incentives of human nature evolved that much in the last decade. Yet, something has shifted. We all stared into the collective abyss in 2008. Anyone who took a good look into that dark and deep chasm, and came back from the brink, has not forgotten the view.

LEADERSHIP LESSONS

- **The Future Doesn't Always Look Like the Past.** Beware the trap of predicting what's likely to happen only through the lens of what's come before.

- **Trust Is Delicate.** Business is fueled by competition, but it also depends on trust and cooperation. It's too easy to take that for granted—until it fails.

Chapter Ten

The One That Got Away

Nasdaq Drops Bid to Buy NYSE Euronext

New York Times, May 16, 2011

There is a reason why the sleepy, midsized city of Augusta, Georgia, has a regional airport frequented by private jets. The nearby Augusta National Golf Club, home of the annual Masters Tournament, is the most celebrated course in the world. As you drive under the famous canopy of Magnolia Lane, a hush descends, and it is easy to imagine that you are traveling back in time to the antebellum South. For lovers of the sport, the greens and fairways of Augusta have a near-religious hold over the imagination. At this tradition-steeped, invite-only club, there are certain rules and customs that you simply don't transgress—whether a guest or a member. For example, wearing shorts is simply not done. Asking for autographs is forbidden. And, perhaps most difficult for many of the industry titans who make up the membership ranks, mobile phones are not allowed on this immaculately groomed course.

I'm not a member, but I did receive an invitation from a longtime member to play at Augusta one day in the spring of 2011. Little could I have imagined that when I finally set foot on golf's hallowed ground, I'd be wishing I was somewhere else. It was a beautiful afternoon, and I was doing my best to acquit myself well on that celebrated course. I was lying one about 150 yards from the green on the left of the fairway, when my heart lurched at the sound I'd hoped not to hear: my phone vibrating in the pocket of my golf bag.

I swiftly glanced around; luckily no other players were close. I'd had no intention of using the forbidden phone, but I was in a dilemma. The biggest deal of my career was hanging in the balance at the Justice Department, and my general counsel had made it clear: If they called, I was expected to be available. Feeling like a guilty sinner, I had stood in my cabin that morning, phone in hand, unsure what to do. Silent mode? Vibrate? I chose the latter, and slipped it in my bag. *I swear I'll leave it alone*, I thought to myself as I shoved it inside and closed the zipper. At least I'll know if they call and I can hurry to finish and call them back. Even having the phone in my bag was a violation, but I saw no other choice. Now the offending handset was threatening to out me.

Surreptitiously, I opened the bag a little and glanced at the name on the screen. Ed Knight. The call went to voice mail, but immediately he called again. And again. On the third call, I switched it to silent and closed the zipper.

I played the next eight holes in a daze. Every golfer dreams about playing the legendary Amen Corner, yet my mind was elsewhere. I tried to acquit myself with some dignity on the final holes, but all I could think about was getting back to the cabin and returning Ed's call.

When he answered the phone, his voice was calm and collected as usual, but I knew the news must be urgent for him to call me here.

"Bob, sorry to bother you," said Nasdaq's general counsel. "We have news on the deal."

"So soon? How is that possible?"

"I don't know, but a staff person at the Department of Justice called me," he said. "Bob, you're not going to believe this…"

An Intriguing "For Sale" Sign

The lead-up to that fateful phone call had started a few months before, with a surprising public announcement. "NYSE, Deutsche Boerse Agree to Merge" was the CNN headline on February 15, 2011, announcing an agreement between NYSE and the largest European exchange, based in Frankfurt. This deal proposed to create a powerhouse global exchange with Deutsche Boerse shareholders paying $9.53 billion for NYSE and owning 60 percent of the newly combined company. NYSE's CEO was tapped to keep his job postmerger, but the headquarters would be in Europe, and the majority of the Board was going to be from the German company.

In the mid-2000s, both Nasdaq and NYSE had begun to look to Europe for partnerships—Nasdaq with the purchase of the OMX in the Nordics, and NYSE with their purchase of the European-based exchange group Euronext. However, both still valued their independence, or so it seemed until we saw the news story announcing that NYSE was running into the arms of a

German exchange, seeking to make a deal that would change the face of the global equities market if it succeeded.

In the offices of Nasdaq the message was clear—*NYSE is on the market.* And the price was advertised right there in the news stories. NYSE had put into the public domain the value they placed on the company, and the price at which they were willing to give up control. My executive team and I had occasionally mused about buying our rival, but those discussions had never gone very far. But if ever that vision was going to become a reality, this was the moment. For all intents and purposes, the Board of NYSE had just nailed a "For Sale" sign on those massive Corinthian columns with a price attached, and we weren't going to pass up this unique opportunity. They had a fiduciary responsibility to seriously consider higher offers.

Our competitor down the street was still an equities trading powerhouse, the largest stock exchange in the world by trading volume and value of listed companies. But their problems were not small and were not going to go away without significant action from management—which, as far as I could tell, was not going to happen anytime soon. John Thain, CEO from 2004 to 2007, had made some attempts to drag the exchange into the electronic future. But execution was poor, and he wasn't there long enough to make a true difference. Duncan Niederauer, his successor, had come over from Goldman Sachs and said some of the right things about becoming a technology-driven exchange. But he had no experience managing an outfit like NYSE, and I wasn't sure he was proving adept at learning on the job. In a post–Reg NMS world, the equity-trading market had fragmented, leaving NYSE with a much lower market share in trading cash equities, around

26 percent. Furthermore, the exchange still had many of the problems that had plagued all old-school exchanges.

NYSE was a unique mix of a storied American brand, an incredible equities franchise, and an inefficient operation. In the global equity exchange space, it was the last of the large exchanges to not go through the reformation, so to speak—an attractive target for an effective CEO to transform into a lean, mean, highly profitable business.

The proposed deal with Deutsche Boerse would make the combined company the largest exchange in the world, led by Niederauer, though I had to wonder how long that would last given the Deutsche Boerse control of the Board of Directors. Regardless, I didn't intend to find out. We immediately put our heads together to discuss how we might muscle our way between the parties in this proposed merger and make a better offer.

This would be an uninvited bid, which was always a daunting proposition. This was also a deal that would draw massive publicity, with media and investors breathing down my neck, and maneuvers scrutinized every day by financial pundits. Chances of success were not high. I'd been once bitten with the LSE deal, which had been a time-consuming, difficult process. Was I twice shy? After considering it with my team, I finally decided to "screw my courage to the sticking-place" (to paraphrase *Macbeth*)[1] and go for it.

But I would need a partner. We didn't have the size to simply buy NYSE Euronext outright. Moreover, there were valuable assets in Euronext that didn't entirely fit with Nasdaq's business model. So I reached out to Craig Donohue, CEO of CME, the huge derivatives exchange, to discuss a joint bid. After some consideration, he decided to sit this round out. I also approached Jeff

Sprecher, CEO of ICE (Intercontinental Exchange). I knew that Sprecher had created a very entrepreneurial, operationally efficient culture at ICE, and I thought he might just be the perfect partner for Nasdaq on such an acquisition. In some respects, their corporate culture seemed very close to Nasdaq's.

Sprecher was immediately interested. He and I discussed the various assets and how we might split them up. We didn't have access to the internal documents of NYSE Euronext, but as it was a public company, we felt good about the reliability of the company information available. Nevertheless, we spent many long days locked in conference rooms—discussing, negotiating, arguing. How do we slice up the apple? How much does each company pay for each asset? It was a complicated negotiation, and this was just to get to the point of making a reasonable bid.

During those weeks, I walked him through my understanding of the assets of NYSE Euronext, the value to ICE, and how much potential savings and synergies could come from a merged Nasdaq-NYSE. I knew I could cut out a huge percentage of the costs of their operation. We eventually agreed that ICE would take on Euronext's derivatives business, headlined by LIFFE, the London International Financial Futures and Options Exchange.

In many respects, LIFFE was the jewel of Euronext, a high-margin business in a growing market. Once upon a time, in the early 2000s, LIFFE had been independent and up for sale itself. Everyone assumed that LSE would buy it, but somehow Clara Furse (CEO of LSE) had let it slip through her fingers, allowing the Paris-based Euronext to come in and steal one of London's prime financial assets. Now, LIFFE was in play again and a perfect asset for ICE, itself a collection of derivatives exchanges, to pick up.

So in the proposed Nasdaq ICE purchase of NYSE Euronext, we were, in a sense, willing to take the inferior businesses, the lower-margin parts of the acquisition—meaning all of the equities exchanges (NYSE and the European ones). ICE was going to take the high-margin European derivatives exchange, a natural fit for them. It might seem strange to call the massive NYSE equities franchise "inferior," but compared to the margins at LIFFE, it really was. But whatever the margin, equities was Nasdaq's business, and we knew how to run it like a finely tuned machine.

On April 1, 2011, Nasdaq (then Nasdaq-OMX) and ICE launched an alternative bid for NYSE Euronext. Our proposal was for $42.50 per share, an $11.3 billion deal—a 19 percent premium over the Deutsche Boerse offer. We felt it was an offer that the NYSE Board had to take seriously. How could they turn down such a significant premium over the other proposal? As we outlined in the press release announcing the offer, "Given that our proposal is clearly superior, we hope that NYSE Euronext's Board will recognize this opportunity as well as the benefits for NYSE Euronext's employees and customers."

Despite the truth of that statement, there was one major stumbling block to getting the deal done: the Department of Justice. Antitrust scrutiny was going to be intense on this deal, as a Nasdaq-NYSE merger would significantly alter the national trading landscape, changing the competitive dynamics dramatically. I had learned a lot about the rhythms of Washington in my eight years as head of Nasdaq. I knew that antitrust battles are won or lost on the definition of the market. In a national market, a Nasdaq-NYSE marriage would be an uncompetitive monopoly. In a globally defined market, we would be the leader but not without competitors. From that perspective, it was time to pull out the stops to see if we could turn two great national listing franchises into one global powerhouse. What could be better for New York? Indeed, what could be better for America?

A Delicate Dance with the DOJ

The Obama White House was not known for its pro-business stance. Our forty-fourth President came into power at a time when the financial industry had just cratered and was seen by many as having wrecked the economy. The Occupy Wall Street protests were still a few months away, but public sentiment was not exactly friendly toward any business with a Wall Street connection. We knew that there would be some skepticism toward the proposed deal. But in our minds, the issues involved were not about Wall Street, good or bad. Indeed, any sober accounting of the various troubles that led to the financial crisis didn't implicate the exchanges.

Here was a chance, we felt, to build the preeminent global listings exchange. That "strong competitor in a global market" was how we framed our pitch to the DOJ. On the political side, the emphasis was slightly different. On that front, we highlighted how this deal would retain national ownership of one of the jewels of American business. After all, despite the rhetoric of the NYSE Deutsche Boerse proposal, make no mistake: This was an acquisition of NYSE by a German business. The PR departments could spin the narrative however they wanted, but that was the unvarnished truth.

In a globalized business world, such issues may seem insignificant. Already, the American and European financial industries were deeply intertwined. Nevertheless, I had been around Washington's political class enough to know that it was an issue that loomed large in their minds. When he heard about the proposed deal, Senator Chuck Schumer was quoted in the *Wall Street Journal* as asking Niederauer, "Why are you doing this? Do you not care about New York?"[2] Ted Kaufman, then Chair of the Congressional Oversight Committee on the Troubled Asset Relief Program, echoed this concern about the loss of NYSE to a German company, declaring it "a signpost on the road to American decline."[3] Overheated rhetoric aside, a Nasdaq-NYSE merger was a powerful answer to those concerns, and we spent time making that argument in Washington and in New York. Interestingly, one person who did seem to appreciate the patriotic appeal of a combined American equities franchise (and a rebuff of the German company's takeover attempt) was Donald Trump, who sent me an article about our bid from the *Wall Street Journal* with the scrawled message, "Go, Bob, Go!"

In mid-April, we submitted the first round of documents, known as the HSR filing, to the DOJ. A few weeks later this was followed by the "second request," a much more extensive affair. This is the discovery procedure by which the Justice Department investigates mergers and acquisitions that may raise anticompetitive concerns. Or, as I called it, the "proctology exam to end all proctology exams." Fulfilling the second request was an incredible amount of work, and we ended up submitting what seemed like an entire roomful of documents about the proposed merger and the combination of companies—responding as best we could to all of the investigative needs of the DOJ.

Antitrust law in Washington is big business, and we must have had close to one hundred contract attorneys working on this case at the height of the process. Many were formerly at the DOJ in what is largely a revolving door of people going between government and private practice. In fact, Christine Varney, the Obama appointee who headed up the Antitrust Division at the time of our proposal, is a perfect example. As of this writing, she is currently head of antitrust at a major law firm, helping large companies negotiate antitrust scrutiny. In 2011, she was the primary person deciding the fate of our intended merger. Indeed, her position held a unique power. The head of the SEC, by contrast, is one voice among five. Likewise, the Chair of the Federal Reserve is one voice among twelve on the Federal Open Market Committee. The head of the Antitrust Division has more power concentrated in that position than either of those other institutions.

While we complied with the demands of the DOJ, we also had to convince NYSE shareholders to allow time for that process to unfold. Indeed, despite the Nasdaq ICE proposal being a much better deal—more than a billion dollars higher—NYSE was still trying to move ahead with Deutsche Boerse. A few weeks after our announcement, NYSE announced that they had suddenly discovered an extra $100 million in cost savings that could be had from a deal with the German exchange. Clearly, NYSE management was scrambling to make its preferred deal not look so paltry in comparison to ours.

The antitrust concerns didn't help our cause, but the truth was that the rival bid had its own regulatory hurdles. It would have to be cleared by the Committee on Foreign Investment in the United States (CFIUS) and by regulators in Brussels. Our proposal also contained a $350 million sweetener, a cash payment if the deal ended up shareholder approved but killed by the DOJ. Meanwhile, some NYSE shareholders were asking their Board and management to discuss terms with Nasdaq, concerned that the Deutsche Boerse deal undervalued the company. In an effort to win more support, on May 11 we wrote an open letter to NYSE shareholders, imploring them to consider our offer and not settle for an inferior deal. It was titled "What's the Rush?"

"Why are NYSE Euronext stockholders being asked to approve a high-risk, low-value transaction without all of the facts?" we asked. "Why is your Board rushing you into a vote? And why are they refusing to even meet with Nasdaq-OMX and ICE to explore a clearly financially superior alternative?" The letter went on to restate the benefits of the merger and show why the Nasdaq ICE deal offered superior value. It ended with a direct appeal to the shareholders: "The NYSE Euronext Board has rushed to its own judgment without a willingness to consider the facts available to them—don't let them railroad you into the clearly inferior Deutsche Boerse transaction without all the information you need in order to make an informed decision as the ultimate owners of NYSE Euronext. Demand of your Board that they meet with us, and at the same time ask them, 'What's the rush?'"

As we prepared our argument for the DOJ, our biggest concern was the listings business. Our first plan was to argue that the listings market was global. With more and more Chinese and Israeli companies listing in the United States, a number of public companies in Asia listing in Hong Kong or Singapore, and quite a few European and African companies listing in London, we hoped this would be a compelling story. The difficult part was that almost all national companies still listed on Nasdaq and NYSE, rendering our proposed merger an effective national monopoly. So as a backup, we prepared a number of what are known as "remedies." For example, I called up Joe Ratterman, the CEO of BATS, another large national exchange, and had some preliminary discussions about how we might maintain a competitive listings market following a Nasdaq-NYSE merger. Would BATS be interested in taking on a thousand or so selected listings from NYSE? Essentially, we might need to establish a "credible competitor" in the listings business, and BATS seemed the only candidate. On the advice of counsel, we kept these remedies in our back pocket, ready to use after we received a response from the DOJ.

When we finally submitted the second request to the Antitrust Division, we expected it would take them a long time just to wade through the volume of material. After all, we had just landed a veritable tsunami of papers on their doorstep. We prepared ourselves to wait for a response, even as we continued to argue for the merits of the deal publicly and to NYSE shareholders.

In the meantime, I decided to take a brief break. After all, second-round requests can take a month or longer to review. By chance, I had received the invitation to play at Augusta. It was a unique opportunity and came at the perfect moment. Or so I thought. On Tuesday, May 10, I took a much-needed day off and headed down to Georgia. I tried to put the deal out of my mind and soak in the atmosphere of the celebrated course that has been host to the talents of so many great golfers over the last century. Until, that is, the second shot on hole number ten, when my phone blew up and my pleasant interlude in Augusta was superseded, courtesy of the DOJ.

The DOJ was going to sue to block the deal, Ed told me. They would be announcing it Monday.

"What?" It was a punch in the gut. "How can they possibly have considered our proposal? There is no way they could have reviewed a tenth of what we sent them. We haven't even discussed possible remedies." I was exasperated but tried to keep my voice down.

"I think it's quite clear that this has been planned for some time," Ed responded. "Their position was already set. They were just waiting on our submission. They're giving us an hour on Friday to come in and argue our case."

"Varney must be using this as an excuse to hold a press conference, where the Antitrust Division gets to have a nice moment in the limelight—at least that's how it looks to me." Perhaps I was being unfair, but it was impossible to draw any other conclusion.

After all our careful strategizing about how to release our remedies, now we had only one course of action: to fire everything we had, all at once. I intensified my conversations with Ratterman at BATS over the following couple of days. That Friday, we met with the DOJ. We argued that our submission contained valuable information and was at least worthy of their time and consideration. In addition, we explained our plans to enlist BATS as a listings competitor.

The response was warmer. But it changed nothing. They still were going to announce that they were suing to block the deal. Afterward, they were open to meetings with us. It seemed that nothing was going to keep them from having that press conference.

It was possible to beat the DOJ in antitrust court. We had done it at SunGard, but that was a special situation and an expedited process. Plus, it had nowhere near the media prominence that this situation did. Fighting the DOJ might take a year or more, and it would be hard to be in a suspended situation regarding a huge deal like this for any length of time. The whole business would be in a state of uncertainty, and that's never a good thing. And it only heightens the downside if you lose. Fundamentally, I didn't want to risk it.

On May 16, 2011, the DOJ had their press conference, and we announced, with great reluctance, that we were abandoning our pursuit of NYSE. We would not sue for the merger to go through. But it wasn't over yet. There was still a glimmer of hope—once we got through the press conference—that further conversations with the DOJ might be fruitful. We had officially dropped our bid, but unofficially we were still planning a new series of backroom talks with Varney and her team. They were willing to listen. Perhaps we could still salvage the deal with the proper remedies.

After a series of intensive discussions, Ratterman and I had finally arrived at the outline of an agreement. We would sell one thousand NYSE listings to BATS after the consummation of the deal. As we described those plans to the DOJ, they seemed receptive. But somewhere in the discussions, we came to a critical sticking point. We couldn't sell only NYSE listings, they told us. Some would have to come from Nasdaq as well. The whole idea was sounding worse by the minute.

Furthermore, the DOJ told us they would need to verify that this BATS listings proposal was a credible possibility by conducting what they called a "field test." That would mean asking companies directly what they thought about it! That was a line we couldn't cross. I imagined some antitrust attorney from the

DOJ calling up Steve Ballmer: "Hi, Steve, this is the Department of Justice. This idiot over at Nasdaq, Robert Greifeld, is wondering if Microsoft would be okay about Nasdaq selling your listing to BATS exchange. We're not saying this will happen. It may not. But you know, just as a theoretical possibility, how does that sound?"

Replaying that conversation with about fifty of our loyal, longtime companies made me sick to my stomach. There was no way I could allow it. It was one thing to lose a thousand NYSE listings that we never even had. It was another thing altogether to start putting Nasdaq stalwarts on the chopping block. It was an unacceptable remedy.

It was over. I was deflated. At least with LSE it had been our own decision to back away from the acquisition. Here, it was decided for us. But the outcome was the same. I had reached, once again, for that vision of a consolidated global listings franchise and had been beaten back. I had ogled the unobtainable once more, and had paid the price in frustration.

A Painful Postscript

With Nasdaq and ICE out of the way, NYSE was free to complete the deal with Deutsche Boerse. But that would prove more difficult than expected. European regulators took a critical view of the size of the resulting firm, especially in Europe. Many market participants, including Nasdaq, argued against the deal to European regulators. They were going to have a 90 percent market share in the derivatives clearing business in Europe, raising antitrust issues and competitive concerns for our own much smaller derivatives clearing business in the Nordics. The review process dragged on over the summer and into the fall, and by early 2012 the merger looked increasing unlikely. By February it was dead. On the mergers-and-acquisitions front, it was a year of much ado, and nothing came of it in the end.

Well, almost nothing. The postscript to our "almost merger" was an actual acquisition—but Nasdaq wasn't involved. On December 20, 2012, our former partner ICE announced its own plan to acquire NYSE Euronext, and the bid was successful. For the first time in its 220-year history, NYSE was no longer an independent organization. That's what a decade of failed leadership will get you in the world of business, even for an institution like NYSE. ICE wasn't in the equity business, so they had none of the antitrust issues that Nasdaq had. It was clear sailing from a regulatory point of view. From my perspective, management and the Board failed to recognize the true value of NYSE. It was a miscarriage of their responsibility to shareholders.

From my office down the street at One Liberty Plaza, the merger was admittedly hard to watch. It was a fantastic deal for ICE. In the press release announcing the deal, Sprecher noted that there were "massive amounts of synergies that we can realize in two years." And I couldn't help but think to myself, who showed him those synergies? After the ICE acquisition was approved, Sprecher (along with eventual CEO Tom Farley) went into their operation with a knife and a scalpel and cleaned up the place. He cut, he streamlined, and in the end, he probably took more than half a billion dollars in costs out of their operations. One of my great regrets in life was not being able to do that myself—to really straighten that place out. I have real respect for what Sprecher's done with NYSE. I just wish I could have been part of it.

The End of an Era

In the midst of all this high drama, Nasdaq (and I) suffered another difficult loss. During that period, I happened to be visiting our Rockville, Maryland, office, where Adena officially worked and lived, although in reality she traveled extensively and spent a great deal of time in New York.

One afternoon, I dropped by Adena's office to say hello. She invited me in, and as I closed the door, she gave me a somber look. "Please, have a seat. We need to talk." For some reason, I knew immediately what she was going to say.

"Bob, I've been thinking," she began. "I've decided it's time for me to leave Nasdaq. I want to spend more time in DC with my family. And I also feel it's the right time to try something new. I have an offer from Carlyle Group, here in DC, to be CFO. They're going to go public and I can lead them through that process."

Adena had spent her whole career at Nasdaq. Sometimes it seemed she was born and bred in the exchange; I think she probably bled Nasdaq blue. Over the years, I had watched her mature into a remarkable executive and had relied on her support, counsel, and extraordinary work ethic. She had been a valued partner in so many aspects of the business and, in particular, during the many acquisitions (and attempted acquisitions) we had made in the previous years. I did not like to imagine Nasdaq without Adena.

As I sat across from my powerhouse protégé that day, I told her, "Look, I hate to see you go. But I understand. It's good for you to be here with your family and spend more time with your children while they're still at home. The Carlyle opportunity sounds great. Taking them public will be an adventure."

Carlyle Group is one of the biggest alternative asset management firms in the world, based in DC. It was filled with master-of-the-universe types, many of whom ran their own funds and portfolios almost like fiefdoms. The challenge of herding all of those cats to get them in shape to go public was a perfect fit for Adena's talents. She could also work directly with cofounders David Rubenstein, Bill Conway, and Dan D'Aniello, a valuable opportunity. But I also knew that once Carlyle went public, the dynamics of the job would quickly change. Indeed, being CFO at a firm like Carlyle—which is a collection of funds, where most of the operations and real business decisions are made in the subsidiaries—wouldn't be the most stimulating venture. Adena was an operations executive who liked to be involved with everything. Could she really be happy in the long run at Carlyle, which was essentially a nonoperating company?

Losing Adena was not easy. But that's part of being a CEO. Inevitably, you're going to lose good people; you have to lick your wounds and soldier on. No one is indispensable. Nasdaq had also parted ways with Chris Concannon a couple of years previously, when he left to be COO of Virtu Financial. Now Adena was leaving, too. I knew how much she did, how many gaps she covered. As one of her direct reports once told me, "I need to get this work done quickly or Adena will just finish it for me!" I wasn't looking forward to Nasdaq minus her substantial footprint.

Still, I knew it would be good for Adena to get outside of Nasdaq and spread her wings in a different context, and I wanted her to know she had my blessing. Privately, however, I thought, *She'll be back. She'll come home.* No one knew the future then, but I did

think that she would make a great CEO candidate—for someone, someday. Perhaps it would be Nasdaq.

LEADERSHIP LESSONS

- **A Public Company Is Always for Sale.** If it's being run inef-
ficiently, sooner or later someone is going to take notice and
realize they could do a better job.

- **Occasional Failure Is the Price of Big Dreams.** In business, as in
life, when you dare to reach high, some disappointments are
inevitable.

- **Let People Go with Grace.** If you cultivate real leaders, it's likely
that a certain percentage of them will move on. It's not a failure; it's a sign that others recognize your success. Be gracious
and supportive—you never know how your paths will cross
again.

Chapter Eleven

The Facebook Fiasco

Facebook IPO: What the %$#! Happened?

CNN Money, May 23, 2012

One picture captured the moment: Robert Greifeld, CEO of Nasdaq, fist raised in the air, standing next to one of the great technology icons of our time, reveling in the celebration. This picture would come back to haunt me, but for a brief period, just after sunrise on May 18, 2012, I enjoyed the glow of unqualified success. It was a crowning accomplishment in a decade of Nasdaq's relentless resurgence. By any measure, it was one of the stock exchange's most important moments—shepherding to market one of the largest IPOs in history: *Facebook*.

On that morning, I stood on a pristine green lawn, deep in the heart of Silicon Valley, at the former campus of the once-dominant computer colossus Sun Microsystems. Time moves fast in technology's spiritual epicenter, and today the Valley's next great company occupied these buildings. It was an organization with youth, exuberance, and the ultimate network effect—a virtual neighborhood that connected almost a billion people. As a business, it had seemingly unlimited prospects, and Bruce Aust had spent endless hours working and developing his relationships inside the company. A few months earlier, he had called me with the good news: We had landed the IPO. "No one could have done it but you," I told him, as we celebrated over a glass of champagne. It was a happy day, and it represented much more than another name on Nasdaq's IPO list. This was a massive affirmation of our organizational brand—and an IPO that NYSE had desperately wanted.

Upon arrival at Facebook's headquarters that morning, Bruce and I had spent a few minutes with Mark Zuckerberg. It was my first conversation with Facebook's youthful visionary. He was gracious, welcoming, and likable. Wearing his trademark hoodie, Zuckerberg was accompanied by Sheryl Sandberg, Facebook's COO, who would soon become the most famous COO in the country with the publication of her best-selling book *Lean In*. After a few minutes of small talk, we strode outside to participate in the festivities.

Facebook stock wouldn't actually begin trading for another couple of hours, but this was the staff's moment of victory—a chance to recognize the extraordinary journey they had already taken to get to this point. Facebook was finally going public, and everyone wanted a piece of the action, not least the employees. Many had stayed up for a symbolic all-night hackathon, and hundreds were gathered around at the appropriately named One Hacker Way for the festivities.

"In the past eight years, all of you out there have built the largest community in the history of the world," Zuckerberg addressed the crowd. "I can't wait to see what you do going forward!" A cheer erupted from the gathered crowd as we began the count-down to the opening, at 6:30 a.m. Pacific time.

Five...four...three...two...one...The bell rang and the crowd cheered as our faces were beamed around the world on the wings of satellites. Zuckerberg, Sandberg, and the rest of their team were hugging and smiling, and I stood next to them with my fist raised in the air, a snapshot of celebration that I would unexpectedly have the opportunity to revisit in minute detail in the days and weeks ahead.

After the opening-bell excitement had died down, I said my good-byes and quickly jumped in a car to get back to the airport for a flight to the East Coast.

As I watched the morning sun beat back the fog on the hills above Palo Alto, I thought about the milestones in my journey with Nasdaq that had led up to this moment.

It had been almost a decade since I started my journey as CEO of a beaten-down company that was losing money and of diminished significance in a rapidly changing financial industry. In 2003, Nasdaq had been weak, distracted, bureaucratic, facing regulatory challenges, and falling technologically further and further behind. In 2012, it was strong, growing, global, highly prof-itable, and technologically leading-edge. Markets were changing and the power of Nasdaq's technology companies was beginning to rival the old industrial giants that had previously dominated the market. NYSE companies like General Electric, Exxon, and Walmart were beginning to be superseded in market-share equity by Apple, Google, Amazon, Microsoft—all Nasdaq stalwarts. We had the best technology. We had the momentum. We had the expertise. We had the global reach. We had a growing software and services franchise, powering exchanges around the world. We were one of the world's great brands. And now we had Facebook, too.

My phone rang in the car and my reverie was shattered. It was Anna Ewing, my CIO.

"Bob, we have a problem."

I could tell from her voice it was serious. *Oh shit*, I thought to myself, *not now*. "What is it?" I asked.

"It's the IPO," she replied. "Something's not working."

And that was when it all started to go terribly wrong.

Anatomy of a Glitch

The most important periods of the trading day are the opening and closing sessions. Each day at 9:30 a.m., every buyer and seller in a stock order book is brought together in a virtual auction. The institutional dealer, the retail investor, the mutual fund manager, the pension fund advisor, the hedge fund mogul, the day trader— all their orders cross and intermix virtually and a magical event occurs: The true price is discovered. We take price discovery for granted in today's equity markets, but it's the most important function that stock markets perform.

In 2003, when I arrived at Nasdaq, the opening and closing auctions were woefully inadequate, a major gap in our transaction services. At 9:30, our opening bell would ring and the first transaction, large or small, would represent the opening price for the day. That price wasn't a reliable representation of the buying and selling activity in the market. There wasn't adequate price discovery. It was the same at closing: We didn't have what the industry calls a "closing cross," meaning that all the orders "cross" or are taken into account (as in an auction) in the algorithmic determination of the final price.

In 2003, some of our major customers expressed their frustration at having to mark their indices to such a poorly derived opening and closing price. Standard & Poor's approached us and said that they were going to start using the auction of the American Stock Exchange, even with Nasdaq-listed shares. Immediately, this became an urgent issue and, frankly, an embarrassing one. I asked Adena to find a solution—her first real test under my leadership. Together with Frank Hatheway, Nasdaq's Chief Economist, and a small team, she worked on the issue and successfully rebuilt our opening and closing auctions. Nasdaq's transactions market was significantly improved, and our customers were relieved.

In 2005, after the INET acquisition, customers started requesting that our initial price discovery auction for IPOs be reinvented in the same manner as the opening and closing auctions. We carefully sought their feedback to develop the specs for this new IPO process. What could we do better? One customer complaint was clear: In the original opening and closing auctions, we had developed a virtual "gate" that prevented new orders and cancellations of existing orders from getting through, starting two minutes before the final auction was initiated. Customers asked us to decrease that time frame to a few seconds, arguing that two minutes was a lifetime in the increasingly fast-moving equities markets.

Somewhere along the line, our engineering team decided they had a better idea. Wouldn't it be great, they thought, if there was no gate at all, if there was an auction that took into account all existing orders and cancellations and recalculated, if necessary, to include any extra orders or cancellations that had been initiated while the auction process was running?

So they built the IPO auction without a gate. If one person sent a cancellation in during the few seconds the auction was running, the process would reinitiate, just for that one order! Given increases in processing speed and computing horsepower, auctions were running faster and faster, and it probably seemed like a natural evolution of that process. This gateless auction was instituted with hardly anyone knowing about it—just a few individuals on the development team.

It was a classic example of overengineering. Conceptually, it was a beautiful idea—as if that mattered. It was like refueling while in flight—technically tricky, but nice if you can make it work. And it had seemed to work fine; we had already run it 450 times without a hitch. In fact, we might have run that gateless auction for another hundred years and never had a single issue. But with the particular confluence of factors that came together in the unique Facebook IPO—massive interest from retail customers, volume unseen in the history of IPOs, people panicking right before the open about the price, and an influx of sudden cancellations—it became a problem.

The first auction ran perfectly well, but several cancellations came in while it was running. The logic of the programming said, *Run it again.* The initial cancellations were processed, but as it was running again, more cancellations arrived. So it ran the auction yet again. And like a proverbial red queen running faster and faster to stay in the same place, it couldn't get to the end of the auction. Cancellations kept coming, and it kept running and rerunning. It couldn't finalize.

At the time, we didn't understand precisely what was occurring in our IPO code. Later, it would become crystal clear. But for twenty critical minutes, the IPO was unable to settle on an opening price. We issued a statement announcing the delay. We then moved the IPO over to a second matching engine, one with simpler code, and successfully opened the IPO using that engine. For that opening, we used the order book as it had been in our systems at 11:11 a.m. At 11:30 a.m. we started trading Facebook shares normally, based on that order book. By noon we had traded more than 200 million.

The problem came in the information gap we created with the rest of the Street—meaning the big institutions on Wall Street. It took Nasdaq until 1:50 p.m. to get the order confirmations for that opening auction released from the initial engine. Some of those were "too late to cancel" notices, informing customers that their cancellation orders had not been processed, given the issues with the auction. This meant that the investment banks and other institutions trading the IPO had been unable to obtain confirmation on their orders and cancellations (during that critical twenty minutes) for almost two hours, which left them blind as to their exposure. Were their orders filled or not? Had their cancellations gone through our system? Did they own Facebook or not? Many didn't know during those intervening hours.

Like many things in technology (and life), the specific technical problem was small, brief, and quickly contained, but the damage done in the cascading aftermath was consequential and far-reaching. It rippled out across the spiderweb of Wall Street's interconnected trading systems, infecting perceptions of the IPO, and impacting trading behavior. As the day went on, frustration with Nasdaq grew. By the end of the trading session, Facebook was still trading normally, but hundreds of angry customers whose cancellations hadn't gone through were claiming to have lost millions of dollars in the chaos caused by that initial window of confusion.

If Facebook's stock had gone up that day, those customers would have been thrilled with still owning the stock. But Facebook fell that first day—and a few days after—and so investors who had been unable to cancel in those initial minutes lost money (in the short term). Of course, those customers who had wanted to buy Facebook stock at the opening but were unable to get their orders filled actually avoided losing money, and they could now simply buy Facebook at a lower price. Given that it was about to go on a historic bull run, I can only hope they did.

Goldman Sachs were the smart ones that day. They saw that something was not right with our system and shut down their connection to Nasdaq, so the effect of our problems on them was minimal. Other customers, like UBS and Knight Capital, got into trouble by confirming cancellation orders to their own customers before Nasdaq had provided confirmation notices. Under normal circumstances, that might seem a formality, but not in this situation. When a buy order or a cancellation goes to an exchange, it is considered a live round, so to speak, that is still in play until a confirmation notice is actually sent. When our system came back up, we sent out "too late to cancel" notices—with the stock order confirmations. Those customers still owned the stock. But in some cases, they had already confirmed the cancellations to their own retail customers.

On the day itself, the fallout was immediate. The Street demanded explanations and compensation, and generally started taking Nasdaq's name in vain to every journalist in town. The press was pushing for a response. Our competitors were taking shots at us. After taking it on the chin for years, NYSE didn't miss the opportunity to press this brief advantage. Facebook was understandably not happy. By the time I landed on the East Coast, Nasdaq was under siege.

Customer Fallout

"Look, mistakes happen. We weren't happy about it, but we understand." Sheryl Sandberg's generous words were welcome when we reconnected a few weeks after the IPO. I'd flown to California to meet her, and was doing everything I could to respond to all who were affected by the faulty IPO. Facebook was first on the list. Sandberg was being direct but remarkably gracious. Obviously, they weren't happy with the IPO, but she put the best spin on it: "It's going to be about how we both perform over time. It's not just about one day."

I've no doubt the incident was incredibly frustrating to all of Facebook's executive team, who were counting on Nasdaq's reputation for technical excellence when they chose to list with our exchange. It was a blow to their faith, but they stuck with us. Over time, I hope we were able to repair the damage to that important relationship.

The other urgent relationship to repair was with our customers on Wall Street—the investment banks, underwriters, and institutions that were directly affected by the IPO delay and the confusion in orders. How much money had actually been lost during the melee? Lots of numbers were getting thrown around, anywhere from tens of millions of dollars to several hundred million. We were determined to take full accountability, but we couldn't just hand over what people claimed they lost. We needed to determine a reasonable and fair process for resolving claims and determining our liability. Eric Noll, a bright guy who was Chris Concannon's successor as EVP of Transaction Services, worked hard to determine a process for estimating compensation. The SEC also had their own inquiry underway, and they were going to have to approve whatever we came up with.

What was our actual legal liability? Arguably, very little. We had a clause in our rulebook explicitly stating that our liability for trading losses was very limited. But what good would legality do us if we damaged our brand and enraged all of our business partners and customers? After consultation with the Board, we decided to change our policy for this particular situation. It was a delicate decision—we didn't want to open the door to a flood of spurious legal claims that had nothing to do with Facebook and set a precedent that we would regret down the line. But specifically for the IPO and resulting fallout, we decided to make good on the claims against us, where reasonable.

The SEC strongly emphasized that we should adjudicate our claims in as objective a manner as possible and deal with all customers on an equal footing. They wanted to ensure against us giving some customers special dispensation in exchange for future favors or business. This meant we weren't allowed to consult with our customers in the process. Eric analyzed the situation, and we came up with a plan—but largely in a vacuum. The Street panned it. Many felt it didn't adequately address the liability. So Ed Knight headed back to the SEC and convinced them that we had to be able to deal directly with the customers who were impacted. They relented, and we modified our approach.

Over the next weeks, I ended up talking extensively with the leaders of Wall Street financial institutions that had been affected—firms like UBS, Citadel, Morgan Stanley, and Goldman Sachs. While many individual investors were impacted by the IPO, their trades don't come to us directly; they come through these financial intermediaries. Those were our direct customers, and we had to work with them to find a solution. It was not an easy negotiation, and I remember long, intensive days spent working to develop a fair formula and "get to yes."

Finally, we came to an agreement. We decided that during a specific window of time, if you had sent in an order to sell existing shares or had initiated a buy order and then followed up with a subsequent cancellation, we would respect those orders as if they had been confirmed and pay whatever money was lost as a result of the subsequent drop in the stock price. In other words, in the brief period of time that our system was malfunctioning, we compensated people as if it had been working perfectly. We even assumed infinite market capacity to absorb all of those sells and cancellations as part of the agreement. Nasdaq calculated an estimated liability and put money aside to cover the possible claims. The SEC approved it. The Financial Industry Regulatory Authority (FINRA) and its CEO, Rick Ketchum, graciously agreed to audit the process.

I particularly remember one of the last conversations during this period, with the founder and CEO of Citadel, Ken Griffin. By this time, everything had been negotiated, and almost all the major players had accepted our terms. It had been an exhausting process, involving millions of dollars in losses, which adds just a little emotion to such negotiations. In most cases I was sitting across the table from colleagues, rivals, or friends.

After I explained the final agreement, Griffin paused for a

moment on the other end of the line. "Ken, does that all makes sense?" I asked. He replied, "Yes, everything looks good. I appreciate your work on this." Then he added, in a very slow and deliberate way, "We're good here, Bob."

Perhaps it was just the timing, or the way he said it. It had that sense of finality—a signal the process had come to an end. Nasdaq had tried to make good on its obligations to customers and investors—without giving away the farm. Now we could all get back to being colleagues and, in some cases, competitors.

Loser of the Week

In the week after the Facebook IPO, the unfortunate image of my opening-bell fist pump next to Zuckerberg was played on an endless loop on business media channels—my Icarus moment, exposed for all the world to see. I had become used to being in the public eye, and I had been through brief periods in the media superstorm (especially during the attempted takeovers of LSE and NYSE), but this was a darker version. It was hard to escape, and took its toll over the days and weeks that followed. "Robert Greifeld: Fist-Pumping while the Exchange Burned" read one caption.

The Saturday after the IPO was the celebration for my daughter Katie's eighteenth birthday. It was a special moment for her, and as our family and friends celebrated on the lawn of our home, I remember that the beautiful late-spring setting was a marked contrast to the dark clouds swirling around in my own mind. The life of a CEO is demanding, but usually I was able to be fully engaged and present for such an important family milestone. On this day, however, it was impossible to let work just be work. Julia stayed close to my side, a comfort amid the gloom that seemed impossible to shake, even as our daughter crossed a threshold into adulthood.

Over the previous years at Nasdaq, I had naturally developed a public profile in the financial universe. I was a regular on financial channels like CNBC and Bloomberg. Occasionally, I would appear on more general-interest shows or in the print media. Still, I was far from a recognized public figure. I tried to do my part as the public face of a global brand, but I didn't seek out the limelight. But now I had become the infamous CEO at the center of the media furor. Colleagues were questioning my leadership. Pundits were calling for my head. I made the *New York Post*'s "loser of the week" column—always a reliable sign of momentary infamy. Inevitably it would pass, but it was important to come out on the other side of the tempest with minimal damage to Nasdaq's brand.

My inclination as CEO was to dive into figuring out what happened and fixing the problem, and block out all other distractions. But I couldn't entirely do that. In fact, we had to do dozens of things at once—not least of which was manage the media and the public relations fallout from the event as best we could. Complicating matters was that the team around me was in a period of transition. For example, we were in the process of seeking a new SVP of Communications—a rather critical role in this situation. Jeremy Skule would soon fill the position, and do a fantastic job, but that was still many months away.

In consultation with my communications team, I decided that I should do a major interview. We chose Maria Bartiromo, then at CNBC. Popular and ubiquitous on the business channel, she had a reputation for balanced interviews. She wasn't a journalist who was just looking for "gotcha!" points. We hoped she would provide a forum in which I could clearly explain our efforts to respond to problems of the IPO and make our customers whole. We held the interview at MarketSite. Bartiromo and I knew each other, and so as we sat down together, there was a sense of familiarity, even friendship. But that quickly changed as the cameras rolled.

"Where were you, Bob? Who was in charge?" she challenged me right off the bat.

It wasn't an easy interview. She implied that our response was too little, too late. Quoting NYSE's PR, she listed their problems with our approach, and suggested they might have done better.

Still, she asked fair questions and gave me the opportunity to respond. That was all we could ask. It was the one interview in my life where I knew everyone in the business, all of my friends, colleagues, and competitors, was watching—to see how Nasdaq would respond, and to see how I would handle the moment. It was important to be frank and responsive, defend the company but not be defensive, apologize for our missteps but limit our circle of liability, be forthright, responsible, and forward-looking, but also apologetic and empathetic. Oh, and not to say anything that would further complicate our media situation or legal liability—you know, just your everyday conversation.

Her final question was one of the toughest: "Is anybody's job on the line? Whose head is going to roll over this?" She paused, then continued. "Is your job on the line, Bob?"

"That's not for me to say," I responded. "But I think my track record speaks for itself. This was not a high point for us; it was a low point. But we're going to be a better company as a result of it."

Honestly, I never really felt like my job was on the line. I had a supportive Board, and while no one was happy with the situation, they weren't out for blood—at least not mine. Ed Knight had some good advice for me during those difficult days. "Keep the pressure on yourself," he suggested. "That keeps pressure off of everyone else, including the Board of Directors. It's when the Board itself is being publicly shamed or called out, when they feel direct pressure, that the CEO gets in trouble."

So I tried to be the public face of this mistake and take the heat. It just seemed the right thing to do—strategically, organizationally, and most important, ethically. Sooner or later, the media would move on, the Facebook IPO would fade from the headlines, and I could go back to spending all of my time responding to the internal issues that were revealed as a result of this failure.

A Good-Luck Charm

A few weeks after the original incident, I was sitting in my office one Monday morning when my assistant announced that Adena Friedman was in the building and asking to see me. As CFO of the Carlyle Group, Adena spent most of her time in Washington, DC, these days, but we would occasionally get together when she was in New York. This visit was unexpected, however.

Adena walked into the office with a friendly and sympathetic expression. "I just wanted to stop in and say hello. I can only imagine what it's been like the last few weeks around here."

She was just there to offer her support. After all, she had worked at Nasdaq for almost twenty years, and nearly a decade under me. Even at Carlyle, she had felt the trauma of Nasdaq's public shaming. After several weeks of disaster management, long days, endless public relations strategizing, and getting battered by prognosticators and pundits in the media, it was nice to see a friendly face with no problem to solve or ax to grind. As we briefly caught up with each other's lives, the drama of the ongoing fallout from Facebook momentarily faded. After a few minutes, Adena got up to leave.

"Before I go, I had something I wanted to give you." She reached into her pocket and pulled out a small four-leaf clover. "I picked this at my son's Little League baseball game over the weekend. I thought you could use it." She laid it on the desk and walked to the door before she turned and said, "Good luck with everything."

I was surprised and touched by the sweet gesture. I could imagine Adena—powerful CFO of one of the biggest private equity companies in the world—sitting for hours and hours on a weekend watching her son play baseball. I knew one of her natural talents was pattern recognition. There she was, one eye on the game, and all of those IQ points looking for an outlet on a summer day at the park. What better opportunity for a momentary distraction than looking for patterns in the clover patch? And how thoughtful that she would save one as a good-luck charm for me.

As with several of my former executives, Adena and I had formed a bond in the midst of our working life at Nasdaq that endured after she was gone. This was actually common with my teams at Nasdaq. Even today, I regularly spend time with old colleagues who spent time in Nasdaq's executive suites. People often talk about the competitive dynamics of business, and that is certainly part of the story, but in my experience it's the collaborative bonds that are memorable and lasting. I believe this was especially true for those of us who shared the intensity of Nasdaq's years of upheaval and change.

Though she had moved away from Nasdaq, Adena was still a favored daughter of the exchange, and I continued to hope that a time would come when I would reach out and invite her to rejoin Nasdaq. But such thinking was for another time and place. Now wasn't the time to contemplate who was already gone, and their future. The question for the moment was: Should I add anyone's name to the departure list?

Taking the Fall

Who was really to blame for the Facebook fiasco? To a significant degree, I saw the culture created in my Nasdaq engineering team as being responsible for the troubles we ran into with the IPO. Indeed, my übertalented development team had decided to make the perfect the enemy of the good. But that didn't mean that there was a natural person to let go. It would have been easy if there had been malfeasance, or even incompetence, but no one came to work at Nasdaq looking to do harm, and the troubles of the IPO couldn't really be blamed on incompetence.

I relearned a critical lesson on the day of the Facebook IPO—*the right approach at one moment is not necessarily the right approach at another moment.* Nasdaq's development team had been forged during the ECN wars of the early decade, running lean and fast, almost like a startup. With my blessing, after the Instinet acquisition, they had largely left behind Nasdaq's previous IT culture, the every-change-to-code-must-be-signed-in-triplicate-by-three-departments approach of the previous era. The times had demanded it. It was also an era built around efficiency, as we beat back the bloat that had once been too common in Nasdaq's halls. But the business environment was now changing. The existential threat was greatly reduced, and the fundamental restructuring of the equities industry based on electronic trading had largely run its course. Once again, stability was taking precedence over speed in Nasdaq's transactions business.

However, institutions, like organisms, tend toward a certain inertia, meaning that without new input, they will mostly continue on an established trajectory, unless something—usually a crisis—jolts the system into a new direction. My initial arrival at Nasdaq in 2003 was a jolt that had changed the trajectory of the entire company. To a lesser extent, Facebook was another.

I had helped to create an engineering-friendly culture and placed enormous trust in developer hands. I don't regret it. Nasdaq was immensely better off because of it, and we were able to stay ahead of a market in transition. But now we were in a different part of the business cycle. We were no longer under immediate threat from falling behind technologically, but another PR disaster would be just as threatening. The pressure of technological evolution was now cutting the other way—toward a more conservative approach. My trust-the-developers culture met its Waterloo in the Facebook IPO. We had to evolve again, and quickly.

At the time, I was acutely aware of the peril we were in as an organization. For months afterward, I felt like I was walking on eggshells. We might have weathered the Facebook storm, but another high-profile issue could have multiplier effects that would be disastrous. We had to avoid that at all costs. Not only did we have our own exchange to worry about; we provided the software that essentially ran ninety different exchanges around the planet! We were updating that code all of the time. Were there further surprises lurking out there, hidden away by our well-meaning engineering teams? Moreover, some of our customers ran their systems fast and loose. But I knew who would be blamed if something went wrong—especially during this period. Whatever reservoir of goodwill we had developed over the years was momentarily depleted by the Facebook IPO crisis. We needed to be perfect, even in a world where computers and software never are.

I offered a companywide "amnesty" to our engineering teams. If anyone was aware of any code lurking in our systems that might now seem problematic in light of recent events, I announced, please tell us immediately. I wanted to make sure we had complete disclosure of any potential issues. Full absolution would be granted for all such confessions.

Still, should anyone take the fall for Facebook? Given the engineering team's role in the debacle, the natural person was the leader of that group. But as I considered the question, I realized that this was not a sin of incompetence; it was ultimately a sin of culture. And as I have often said, culture comes from the top. I'm not saying that person was blameless, but neither was I, and that was the point. After all, I had encouraged the culture that allowed this failure. It seemed disingenuous to ignore that inconvenient truth. I knew we needed meaningful changes to our technology team and our engineering culture, but I thought we could get some new blood in the door without spilling more of our own. So after the media storm had died down, I began a search for a new executive who could lead our post-Facebook revamp.

We needed to get outside of our own box for answers. We asked IBM to perform a system-wide audit of our IT situation. An external perspective was critical. In general, we didn't use a lot of consultants. I took to heart the old joke that you hire a consultant to tell you what time it is, and they look at your watch to give you the answer. But in this case that was exactly what we needed: third-party validation. IBM was thorough, and they gave us a comprehensive report, analyzing how we did everything and making suggestions for improvement. We already knew almost everything they would say, but nevertheless it was useful, and it helped us move forward.

I also spent time with my executive team carefully thinking about system reliability. We lived in a business environment where the expectation was that we be 100 percent reliable. But software systems never are. Every few weeks, we learn of a major corporate system undergoing a dramatic failure. So how do you negotiate those expectations of perfection in the noticeably imperfect world of technology? As part of our process, the Nasdaq team studied other industries where reliability is absolutely paramount. We adopted some of the practices of the telecommunications industry and also the airline industry, where system confidence is a life-or-death matter.

For years, our system had achieved high reliability— approaching 99.99 percent. That sounds impressive, and it is, but while "four nines" is nice, it's the fifth one (99.999) that gets you close to zero breakdowns. But to get to five nines, you're talking about a system that is so locked down it becomes almost impossible to innovate and compete. While I was ready to embrace a more conservative approach to our IT systems, I was also aware that there were still trade-offs involved. If our future IT regime decided to lock things down too much, Nasdaq's own technological innovation would stall. That wasn't the threat that it might have been in the previous decade, and certainly not the immediate concern, but it still could prove problematic down the line. If anything, we were becoming more of a technology company, not less of one. We might not have needed the speed and nimbleness of our prior incarnation, but we still needed to innovate and lead the market if we were going to thrive.

By the end of 2012, my search for new IT talent had settled on two potential hires. One was at a European bank. He was professional, buttoned-down, and had a regimented, formal, conservative persona. He was just what the doctor ordered for the immediate needs of our situation. But as I considered the hire, I was concerned that despite the expertise that he would bring to the job, there was a longer-term horizon that I needed to consider. I didn't want to fall into the trap of fighting the last battle. This was a few months later, and the fog of Facebook was beginning to lift. I worried that if I hired this person, it would solve one problem but create another down the line. How to bring in a more conservative mandate and an innovative spirit at the same time? Somehow I needed to find an individual who could move between these dual mandates with both a dancer's grace and a soldier's gait.

Enter Brad Peterson. He had been CIO of Charles Schwab and before that eBay—giving him a background in both finance and Silicon Valley. I suspected Brad might not be the buttoned-down type when he showed up to an interview in jeans. In his defense, it was a Saturday, so I pressed on:

"Why are you interested in the job?" I began.

"I'm not really interested in the job," he replied bluntly.

"And yet, you're here," I replied after a moment, slightly confused.

As it turns out, he had agreed to the last-minute interview without having time to truly consider it. It was a strange start to the conversation, but as we continued to talk, I began to warm up to this bright, interesting technology executive with a West Coast vibe. At one point he asked me directly, "What do you think went wrong with the Facebook IPO?"

I responded, "You may not like this answer, but our technology development team had too much power, and if you come here, that's got to change."

Brad wasn't fazed. We spoke for a couple of hours about technology, business, finance, and the history of Nasdaq. I sensed he was a creative thinker, someone who might not only be able to fix what ailed us but also shape the next generation of our technology platforms. By the end of that conversation, I knew that Nasdaq had found its future CIO.

The Long-Term Fallout

Two years later, Brad and I sat in a conference room in Hong Kong with Joe Tsai, cofounder and Executive Vice Chairman of Alibaba, discussing their impending IPO. Alibaba was the biggest Chinese IPO ever and the most sought after since Facebook. Glenn Hutchins, my negotiating friend from the INET deal, was on the Board of Nasdaq and had connections to Tsai, and he joined the meeting. Börje Ekholm, former head of Investor AB and current Chairman of the Nasdaq Board, came along as well. Tsai had once worked for Ekholm, and would later put him on the Alibaba Board. In other words, our connections with Alibaba ran deep. Normally, this all-star team would have boosted my confidence that we could win the day. But nothing was normal post-Facebook when it came to winning big IPOs.

That day at Alibaba, as Brad walked all of us through Nasdaq's new, radically simplified IPO process (it was now only about sixty lines of code), I knew that we had put to bed the internal technical issues that led to the Facebook debacle. I was confident that the technological and cultural changes in our engineering teams were upgrading the organization on many levels. But that was only one part of the story. We also had worked hard to regain the industry reputation and momentum that we had pre-Facebook. Thankfully, memories can be short in business, and most new technology companies considering IPOs weren't concerned about what had happened with Facebook. We won lots of new IPOs in 2013 and 2014, and much of the noise of the disaster quickly faded. But one issue remained. Bankers have a longer memory than technologists, and unfortunately, their opinions mattered more with the big IPOs, like Alibaba. Despite our efforts in Hong Kong, we lost the Alibaba IPO, and it wasn't because of Joe Tsai or Jack Ma. It was pressure from the banks and IPO underwriters, many of whom were pushing big clients like Alibaba toward NYSE, "just to be safe."

As our team considered what had happened with the loss of Alibaba, we radically revamped the nontechnical side of our IPO process as well. It was the last step on the journey that began that morning at One Hacker Way. We approached it from a customer-service perspective, speaking to the banks and asking what they would like to see us implement as part of the service. Some of this was an evolution of our thinking—from identifying as an exchange to thinking of ourselves as a tech company. Exchanges have member institutions who trade on their systems and are primarily concerned with lower costs. Technology companies have products and software services, and the customer experience is paramount. We began to think of the IPO process as belonging in the latter category. I even moved responsibility for IPOs out of the transactions business into the Corporate Client Group (listings), an important step.

Today, Nasdaq's IPO process is not just an automated auction, as it was in 2012. A Nasdaq IPO auctioneer oversees everything carefully in a high-touch, curated, customer-centric process. It's a better process, a superior product, and a much-improved experience for our customers. Over time, we won high praise for our new process, and I think it is fair to say that by the end of my tenure, we had largely recovered from any reputational damage we had suffered. In the wake of a crisis, you have to play the media game and go on a PR offensive. But ultimately, the real response is innovation in products and services—talking to the customer and improving your offerings rather than just defending your mistake.

Follow the Turtle

I admire turtles. In fact, I keep dozens as pets. Turtles are steady, consistent creatures with hard shells. They've been around since the time of the dinosaurs, and they know how to survive. Yes, speed is sometimes critical in business. But speed without a clear and consistent direction can lead you nowhere fast. Sometimes, especially in moments of crisis, you need to move slowly and deliberately, and bank on your thick skin. Turtles know how to do that.

The Facebook IPO was one of the most difficult moments of my career. But we didn't panic; we didn't doubt our fundamental business model. I didn't doubt my leadership capabilities. We didn't question the incredible progress Nasdaq had made in the previous years. But neither did we pretend that there weren't genuine issues to be dealt with. As one of my favorite football coaches, Bill Parcells, likes to say, "You are what your record says you are." We had a great record pre-Facebook. That blemish didn't define us, but it was still part of our record, and a spur to the further evolution of the company.

In a competitive environment, no one has a perfect record. Even when you're on top of the world, don't spend too much time patting yourself on the back. It breeds smugness and the wrong kind of satisfaction. While you're celebrating your success, your competitors are eating your lunch. And always be ready to accept a setback and move on. It's never enjoyable, but the capacity to take a loss, and respond well, is a critical leadership skill. And as I suggested to Bartiromo in the interview, we became a better company as a result.

Facebook defined a clear "before" and "after" in my time as CEO. Like a turtle, we put our heads down, worked hard, and slowly, deliberately improved. For all the pain and stress of that spring day in 2012, we didn't allow it to define us; rather, it motivated us.

LEADERSHIP LESSONS

- **Take the Heat.** Sometimes a leader needs to step up and be the public face of a mistake.

- **Don't Gloat over Victories or Obsess over Failures.** While you're celebrating your success or licking your wounds, your competitors are eating your lunch.

- **The Right Approach at One Moment Is Not Necessarily the Right Approach at Another Moment.** What once was a success strategy can later become a liability.

- **The Best Response to Crisis Is Innovation.** Don't spend too much time defending your mistakes. Talk to your customers directly and improve your products or services.

Chapter Twelve

Institutionalizing Innovation

Nasdaq Makes First Share Trade Using Blockchain Technology

Telegraph, December 31, 2015

How do you wake up every day with fresh eyes, ready to pursue change, growth, and innovation? It doesn't matter what company or what industry you work in; this is an ongoing challenge of leadership. A mantra I would often repeat in the halls of Nasdaq was this: *Once you achieve competency, you must battle complacency.*

Ironically, this particular challenge can be easier when times are hard. If competitors are breathing down your neck, it's not difficult to feel the urgency of change. When the business is under existential threat from market forces, the motivation to improve comes naturally. The imperative to evolve is taken care of, we might say, by selection pressures within the market ecosystem. But once you have achieved a significant level of competency in your business, the internal cultural dynamics shift. Success is undoubtedly a wonderful thing, but it comes with new business realities that good leaders must appreciate. Finding the right mixture of consistency and change, institutional stability and constant improvement, efficiency and innovation, is always a critical goal of enterprise leaders.

At Nasdaq, my aim was that we should always be reorganizing a little bit every day. Change, I believe, should be part of a healthy organizational culture. Obviously, there are certain times in the life cycle of a company when larger and more dramatic shifts are needed. My early tenure at Nasdaq was one of those times. But change should not be reserved for moments of crisis and increased market pressure. In fact, when I read about companies undergoing massive reorganizations, I think that more often than not it is the result of a miscarriage of leadership. Dramatic, one-off reorgs are really an admission that management hasn't been doing the hard work of continuously improving the business in little ways, all the time, so now they have to compensate by doing it all at once. Large reorgs are blunt instruments that inevitably cause collateral damage. They are like a massive hammer blow, when a carefully wielded scalpel does the job much more effectively and without the organizational trauma. Indeed, high-functioning organizations are endlessly building on their success; purposefully and actively looking at all the ways that things can be better, smarter, and more efficient; paying attention to their competitors; thinking about the future; and exploring new pathways of innovation.

This was the kind of organization I wanted Nasdaq to be as we moved into the second decade of the new millennium. Up till then, the industry-wide move to electronic markets, internal culture changes, SEC rule changes, a spate of transformative acquisitions, and the great recession had combined to provide a naturally shifting landscape that kept us all on our toes. But now we were entering smoother waters. The financial crisis was a few years in our rearview mirror, and while the economy was still recovering, the markets were generally healthy or moving in that direction. Nasdaq was beginning to reap the benefits of good strategic decisions made in the previous business cycle, and as the economy improved, we started to feel the wind at our backs. That's not to say everything was easy; we were continually pressed by circumstance.

In some respects, in fact, the financial crisis and the ensuing struggles in the economy had just temporarily obscured the success story that Nasdaq had built over the previous decade. The investments we had made and the strategic acquisitions we had pulled off, including the purchase of OMX, positioned us well to ride the emerging economic tailwinds. It can be difficult to know who is strategically well positioned when an economic downturn is depressing everyone's prospects. But as things picked up in the broader economy, our fundamental strength was beginning to show.

There were, of course, plenty of moments of drama in those years—the Flash Crash, Hurricane Sandy, new acquisitions, changing markets. Each of them presented challenges that our team had to rally and respond to. But none compromised the fundamental trajectory of well-functioning markets, expanding business opportunities, growing revenues, and a successful equities franchise. Quarter after quarter passed with larger profits, good margins, and a stock price headed up. Little by little, the IPO market was recovering from the downturn. We continued to win new listings, bringing new tech companies into the fold even as we convinced older technology franchises to switch and join the Nasdaq family.

Our team was also maturing and flourishing. By 2013, Nasdaq had a new Corporate Communications Chief and a new CIO, and our young executives were growing into highly effective leaders. Many of the OMX team had not only adapted to Nasdaq's culture but embraced it enthusiastically and enhanced it. Their abilities boosted Nasdaq's talent pool significantly.

This was a time in which billions of dollars poured into biotech companies and their IPOs, in some cases raising money for promising drugs that were many years away from passing key trials, gaining regulatory approval, and making it to market. Such long-term time horizons are an important function of public markets—to provide that belief and long runway that allow time for a medical breakthrough (and business plan) to come to market. As I watched immunotherapy startups gather investors and capital for their moonshot efforts to improve cancer treatment, I was especially proud of the role Nasdaq played in helping them.

Building a Technology Franchise

In my previous incarnation as an entrepreneur, I had always loved software businesses with recurring revenue. That was what we had built at ASC, and I truly think it's one of the best business models out there. At Nasdaq, in addition to our transactions business, I worked to build our software and services franchise. This was enabled by the purchase of OMX and their exchange technology business. As emerging markets grew stronger, demand was growing all around the world for customized solutions to power market exchanges. Over time, we expanded on the basic order-matching technology of the business and built or acquired significant new functionality.

The 2010 Flash Crash, and subsequent issues, had taught us a number of things about the new world of electronic markets. As markets became more automated, it became more important that the inputs into those massive order-matching engines were carefully reviewed on the front and the back ends of the trade to avoid potential pitfalls. Knight Capital had provided a dramatic example of what can go wrong without that careful analysis, when a software glitch cost them several hundred million dollars of errant trades, forcing their sale to Getco in late 2012.

The existential fear of such disasters helped drive interest in our new suite of tools and spurred us to make them more robust. We developed new surveillance technologies, adding a level of heightened security to our exchange offerings and expanding the reach of our market. We initiated development efforts to integrate machine learning, AI, and big data into Nasdaq's suite of products. Electronic markets were not going away; quite the opposite. But now that they'd been around a few years, and some of their dangers and downsides had been revealed, I wanted Nasdaq to be the best at providing much-needed security and protections. By 2013, our market technology business served over seventy exchanges, clearinghouses, and depositories in fifty countries. It generated nearly $200 million in revenue and was growing quickly.

Consistent, recurring revenue is always a boon for a business, and it protects against the highs and lows of onetime sales or individual deals. As a public company, of course, every quarter you have to disclose your financials. In that sense, running a public company is an endless series of quarters. Many are concerned today that such short reporting periods incentivize companies to focus on short-term returns at the expense of long-term strategic thinking. There is no doubt that as a leader of a public company, one has to quickly adapt to the unique rhythm of quarterly reporting. But in my case, it didn't constrain my focus. In fact, knowing I was going to have to constantly report earnings every quarter helped me concentrate on the longer-term trend line of our earnings. It made me less concerned about the specifics of any single quarter and more concerned about the direction we were headed in.

"*Worry about the trend line, not the slope,*" I would tell my team. Real change takes time. I was always much more concerned about ensuring that change was happening, that we were really moving forward, than I was about the speed at which we were moving. Too often, change is a mirage. The most important thing is to make sure it is real. When you can actually measure organizational change over time, then you know it's happening. The same applies to any kind of change process: losing weight, becoming a faster runner, learning a new skill. Measurable, consistent results, however small, give everyone confidence. Then you can worry less about exactly how fast it's going from day to day or month to month, or quarter to quarter.

I never wanted us to deliver something unnatural in any given quarter. If we were straining too hard to make our numbers, it was a bad sign. It would only compromise the future. Are we improving? Are we headed in a positive direction? Is our competitive standing strong and improving, relative to the market? Are we meeting our customer needs? Those were the more critical issues to pay attention to.

Quarterly numbers should reflect the organic progress of the business. There is a lot of pressure in the markets to have a huge success each quarter, which will boost the near-term stock price, but good CEOs avoid getting caught up in that loser's game. Recurring revenue and the software and services business helped Nasdaq operate on more consistent terms.

In addition to market technology, the other new business line we built around recurring revenue was Corporate Solutions. The ever-complexifying rules and reporting requirements necessary to list on the public markets created a new business opportunity to assist companies in meeting the regulatory demands. This was a natural extension of Nasdaq's expertise. We built Investor Relations websites for companies; offered a press release distribution business; developed a suite of tools for Investor Relations teams; and bought a company called Directors Desk, which helped provide software to administer Board-level meetings with easy-to-use and secure applications. Running exchanges for equities trading in the United States and Europe was still our bread and butter, but little by little, Nasdaq was becoming a larger and broader company.

The Gift Council

Nasdaq expanded through acquisition, but we also grew through internal development and innovation. From day one, I had instituted a high degree of fiscal discipline at Nasdaq, what I called

a weigh-measure-and-count organizational culture, and I made
sure everyone bought into that way of thinking, from my executive team to the troops on the ground. But even as I saw the
success of that approach, I also knew I needed to balance the cost-
conscious culture with an emphasis on longer-term innovation.
Nasdaq ran lean and we ran efficiently. But efficiency and innovation are not generally in the same operational family. They are
distant cousins at best, feuding rivals at worst. How to make both
feel comfortable under the same roof? Indeed, we needed to find
ways to institutionalize an innovative mind-set without compromising our operational mojo.

In order to achieve this, I decided to take a page out of John
Chambers's playbook and create a space for innovation that was
decoupled from people's regular operational budgets. At Cisco,
Chambers set up internal business councils to evaluate new business ideas. I sat through a presentation about Cisco's approach
and loved it. So I did something similar at Nasdaq, adapting it
for our context. We called it the Gift Council, and it basically
functioned like an investment committee at a VC firm. Individuals would present to the council on interesting, innovative opportunities, and if an idea was deemed promising and approved for
funding, the money Nasdaq invested in that project would not
count against the budget in the operational area of the individual
who had proposed it. In exchange, the Gift Council required that
that person give up some sovereignty over the project and submit
to it being closely tracked by the council through its startup-like
phase.

That may sound simple, but for a large company wedded to
fiscal discipline, it was like trying to engage another side of the

brain. The metrics for Gift Council projects had to be entirely different from our normal operational metrics; otherwise, the fiscal discipline of our culture would eat those nascent projects alive before they could show their true potential. We hoped that this approach would provide a way to be respectful of short-term fiscal discipline and cost control while still priming the pump of longer-term innovation.

Some companies create an entirely separate research-and-development structure to nurture new initiatives. On the upside, this can solve the problem of creativity being killed by the thresher of financial discipline, but it has its own built-in problems. Even if you successfully create a highly innovative operation, it's easy for it to become organizationally bureaucratic itself and cut off from the rest of the business. The famous Xerox PARC, the R&D arm of Xerox, was a highly creative organization and the fount of many world-changing ideas (like the laser printer and the graphical user interface), most of which were never taken advantage of by Xerox! With the Gift Council, I was trying to have the best of both worlds, providing a place for business units to protect and nurture innovative ideas while keeping them close to the business and subject to the right kind of discipline and oversight. By the end of 2012, new business ideas that were nurtured under the auspices of the Gift Council had generated $134 million in revenue. And that number was growing quickly.

One of the most interesting projects to emerge from the Gift Council was an initiative called Nasdaq Private Markets (NPM). The development of NPM is a unique story of how Silicon Valley, venture capital, cryptocurrency, and Nasdaq all came together in a happy marriage.

Blockchain and the Rise of the Unicorns

As the economy recovered after the financial crisis, Silicon Valley led the way. By the end of the 2000s, Nasdaq's favorite business corridor was thriving as never before, and money was pouring into the coffers of venture capitalists looking to provide growth capital to the next great startup. It was a boom that resembled in intensity and scale the boom of the late nineties, but the funding model was entirely different. At the beginning of the internet era, it had largely been Nasdaq's marketplace providing public funding to hundreds of early-stage startups, most of whom had few alternative sources of capital. Venture capital provided seed funding in the range of maybe $5 or $10 million, but beyond that, companies needed the public markets. In a sense, we were the primary game in town if you needed significant amounts of money. But by the end of the 2000s, the game had changed dramatically. Billions of dollars were flowing into venture capital, and young companies didn't need to tap the public markets until much later in their evolution. Moreover, regulatory changes and the demands of being a publicly traded company further incentivized growing companies to remain private for longer. Startups postponed their IPOs and raised additional capital, even as they grew into companies worth hundreds of millions, and in some cases well over $1 billion. The number of these so-called unicorns (private startups exceeding billion-dollar valuations) was growing every year.

In some cases, these startups were bought up by bigger technology firms—like Google, Cisco, Microsoft, and others—who were using the growing startup ecosystem almost as a replacement for R&D. Cisco, for example, was a serial acquirer of companies that once upon a time would have gone public and joined the Nasdaq ecosystem. The same is now true of Google, Apple, Microsoft, and many other large technology companies. In addition, many firms launched large venture capital arms of their own, adding bigger and bigger pools of available money to the technology ecosystem.

The advent of these well-capitalized, privately funded teenage companies—like Uber, Lyft, Stripe, Airbnb, and many others—created a conundrum. Employees in those firms naturally had much of their own wealth tied up in relatively illiquid stock options. It's one thing for an employee to hold those options for a few years before they become liquid with an IPO. But now, that time horizon was getting longer and longer. Inevitably, people needed access to their money—to buy houses, pay medical bills, or send kids to college. If they couldn't count on the company going public, they needed ways to cash in those options in some other kind of a liquidity event.

Initially, certain law firms in Silicon Valley would facilitate trading of pre-IPO private-company shares of stock, but as the need increased, so did the opportunity for a new "second market" or "private market"—a venue to facilitate trading in those options. Two new companies, SharesPost and SecondMarket, formed to serve this need. For Nasdaq, this was a call to arms: If a new, semiprivate trading market was forming in startup options, why should we cede the business to upstarts? It was a natural extension of our strengths, and soon we decided to get in on the game as well.

In 2013, using Gift Council funding, we developed Nasdaq Private Markets in collaboration with SharesPost, a new venture designed to bring some order, efficiency, and liquidity to the trading of stock in private growth companies. It also proved to be an important way to develop and deepen our network of relationships with new talent in the Bay Area's significant stable of young companies. A couple of years later, we bought SecondMarket and consolidated this new trading venue around Nasdaq's brand.

It is often said that innovation happens on the boundaries of the establishment, where new ideas can take root without being squashed by the conventional order of things. As an incumbent player in the financial ecosystem, Nasdaq needed to cultivate an awareness of what was going on outside our ecosystem that might be disruptive in the future. And once we had identified those technologies, we needed to figure out how to bring them inside our walls, so to speak, and embrace them, showing a pathway to their adoption without overly compromising existing technological infrastructure.

In this spirit, Brad Peterson, Nasdaq's CIO, started a series of internal conversations among a few leaders about new disruptive technologies that might be coming down the road. During one off-site strategy session in May 2014, we did a session on quantum computing and an interesting new technology called cryptocurrency—including something called Bitcoin, which few people had heard of back then.

As we explored the ins and outs of this exotic new financial instrument, it was hard to ascertain its significance for Nasdaq, if any. It just didn't seem to have any immediate relevance. But at a certain point, we realized that the jewel of Bitcoin wasn't its use as a currency; it was the technology that underlies it—blockchain. Blockchain is the unique database technology upon which many cryptocurrencies depend.

Blockchain is a powerful, decentralized, distributed ledger

system that is highly secure. For a company like Nasdaq, it's a technology that is right in our wheelhouse—after all, we are experts at facilitating trading and transactions, and blockchain is aimed at transforming the way we conduct digital transactions. Brad and I and much of the executive team spent hours discussing this technology—how it worked, how it might be used, how it would change financial markets, and how Nasdaq might pioneer that endeavor. We became early experts on blockchain and its application potential.

Transactions technology in the public market is so well established that it was hard to imagine trying to take this entirely foreign technology and throw it immediately into the mix with the existing networks of banks, clearinghouses, and exchanges. But what if we were to start from scratch in a market that we controlled, one that was not already burdened with so much existing legacy technology? Nasdaq Private Markets began to look like the perfect opportunity to test out this interesting new technology.

In 2015, we launched a service on NPM using blockchain technology that was able to execute, settle, and clear a given trade and then move the money in ten minutes—a fraction of the time it takes in other markets. If you make a trade today in the public equity markets, it takes two days to settle and clear. Rarely has there been a more dramatic example of the future staring us in the face. There is a lot of work to be done to integrate this technology into our financial systems, but I genuinely believe it has tremendous promise. Blockchain is not yet ready for the microsecond, superfast world of equity trading. I believe its real strength, at least for the immediate future, is in settlement and clearing—on the back end of trading, so to speak. That's where its initial impact is likely to be felt. I was thrilled to have Nasdaq be early to market with an application demonstrating its potential. As an established player, Nasdaq needed to embrace the technology, affirm its relevance, and show the evolutionary path to its adoption in the industry. Blockchain has great potential, though the scale of its impact is yet to be seen.

Flash Boys and the Need for Speed

Toward the end of my time at Nasdaq, we received some pointed reminders that stock markets must continue to guard against complacency, and be on the lookout for new forms of inefficiency and new avenues for innovation. In 2014, a particularly public (though overblown) alarm was sounded: According to a new book by best-selling author Michael Lewis, an army of unscrupulous "high frequency traders" (HFTs) were operating in the microsecond gaps between buyers and sellers and profiting from their superior speed at the expense of investors. Furthermore, he claimed, these "flash boys" were enabled by the established Wall Street players.

To understand the HFT phenomenon and separate the facts from the hype, it's important to understand that the search for speed in financial markets is hardly novel. From the fastest horse to the telegraph to the rotary phone to a quick-dialing handset to satellite dishes to fiber optics to point-to-point microwave to the quickest algorithm, traders have always used technology to gain information advantages and outpace competitors. The Rothschilds famously used carrier pigeons in the early nineteenth century to gain an information advantage that would allow them to profit in London's financial markets. And when I was at ASC in the mid-1990s, one of my business lines was selling new wireless communications equipment that would allow individuals standing on the exchange floor to quickly send information up to a trading booth, giving them a brief time advantage over those relying on the less-than-athletic runners.

Later, I was fortunate to be part of a collection of outsiders—motivated by high ideals and armed with ones and zeros—who stormed the castle of old-style, floor-based Wall Street trading, breached the walls, and remade the place in their image. We eradicated inefficiencies and expedited trading, eventually breaking apart what the *Wall Street Journal* in 2003 had bluntly described as a "monopoly" on the part of NYSE, which had "failed to adapt to a world of new technology that allows for faster...electronic trades."

Within a few years of my arrival at Nasdaq, much of the Wall Street infrastructure had radically changed, swept aside by the electronic wave of the future. My own motives in being part of the revolution were more about effective business practices than high ideals. But I certainly shared the *Journal*'s perspective that we were doing the global markets a great service by breaking the hold of floor-based specialists, with their thirty-second time advantage. We changed it to microseconds, and dramatically reduced the friction and inefficiencies of the previous market-making system.

In many respects, we succeeded beyond what I could ever have imagined. In so many ways—ease of access, price of service, capacity for speed, quality of execution, diversity of products, dynamics of competition, transparency of fees—stock exchanges today serve their function far better than they ever have in history.

But conquerors inevitably have a tendency to get complacent. And today's revolutionaries have a tendency to become tomorrow's establishment.

As the markets became more and more electronic, the need for speed moved into the virtual domain with an increasing emphasis on lightning-fast trades made in milliseconds, and even microseconds. Indeed, part of the evolution of markets in my early days at Nasdaq centered on an issue called price-time trading. Simply put, it means that if several orders arrive to an exchange at the exact same price, there naturally has to be some way of deciding which order to execute first. What's the best method for deciding that question? The fair way—and the way the market currently works—is to privilege the order that arrives first. First in, first out. In such a world, speed matters—when price is equal, time is the most democratic differentiator. With that market reality came the need for speed—giving rise to a new kind of high frequency trading operation that bought and sold stocks in the blink of an eye, profiting on microdifferences in the price between two markets or exchanges, measured in pennies, or less. The physical trading floor had been replaced with a virtual "floor"—a series of exchanges competing to offer the best price, and superfast trading operations exploiting the differences between them.

At our data-center headquarters in Secaucus, New Jersey, where the hardware of this virtual world resided, we were developing a new type of business. We decided to sell real estate in our data center. This wasn't just about offering customers greater execution speed; it was also about reliability. If you wanted to ensure continuous, reliable service—avoid nasty interruptions and costly downtime—it's much safer to have a computer in the Nasdaq data center than to rely on some data connection from many miles away. We offered the safe and secure connection of a Local Area Network (LAN) rather than the unpredictability of a Wide Area Network (WAN). The service was available to everyone— big banks, investment banks, HFTs, brokers and dealers, and new trading outfits. In fact, HFTs were a minority of customers. And the critical part was that no one had a speed advantage. Some customers tried. They asked us if their computers could be a few feet closer to the matching engine servers—just as back in the day, traders on the NYSE floor wanted to be a few feet closer to the trading posts. But we built a unique "coil" that slowed down closer connections, making sure there was no time advantage to be gained by the particular positioning of any company's computers. It was a new, cloud-based business, like Amazon Web Services or Microsoft Azure. In fact, many new trading outfits found this was the quickest and most inexpensive way to start initial operations. As with just about everything we did at Nasdaq, we did it all under the close supervision of the SEC.

After the publication of Michael Lewis's *Flash Boys* in the spring of 2014, the furor in the financial media was intense and immediate. Once again, Wall Street was under attack. Lewis has a unique ability to spin an enticing narrative, and he loves to tell lionizing stories of outsider warriors fighting for an enigmatic truth against a blind or corrupt establishment. In this case, the role of "outsider" was played by a small group of individuals looking to understand the role of HFT in markets and build an alternative exchange. The role of "corrupt establishment" was played by all of us who worked at the major banks, exchanges, and trading firms.

Lewis made little mention of how markets had evolved and improved over the previous decades, thanks to the efforts of many of those people he was criticizing. No compliments were forthcoming for the efforts that so many made in the previous era to open up markets, democratize access, reduce costs, and create more efficient markets. Considering that Lewis had talked to almost no significant figures in the industry before publication, you can imagine how my colleagues and I felt about his analysis, or lack thereof.

I understand that *Flash Boys* was not meant to be a fully researched report, weighing the pros and cons of how contemporary financial markets are structured, but many took it as exactly that. In the wake of the financial crisis, it's all too easy to convince the average American of hyperbolic statements like "the stock market is rigged" and "Wall Street is corrupt." I know it's fashionable to look at Wall Street and proclaim, "There be the demons of greed!" In a post–financial crisis world, such claims appeal to our society's natural suspicions.

Of course, if by greed you mean the motivation to be smarter, work harder, compete better, and make money doing it, well, that's not hard to find on Wall Street. But when it comes to protecting and analyzing markets, I don't believe that is the primary issue of concern. The more important question is: Are the players on Wall Street following the rules established by the SEC? And if so, do those rules and regulations need to be updated to protect investors? And finally, do American equity markets compare favorably to alternative markets in the world, and to the financial markets in our own history?

For the most part, Lewis said little directly about Nasdaq in *Flash Boys*, which isn't surprising given that he spoke to no one at the exchange except a former employee who had been terminated a few years before. But he did make a dramatically false claim nonetheless—stating that fully two-thirds of our entire revenue was driven by HFT. I have absolutely no idea where he might have generated such a number, but it is certainly untrue. Again, he never checked that number with us. In fact, after the publication of *Flash Boys* there was such concern about that number that many investors worried Nasdaq transactions revenue might collapse if the HFT industry was regulated differently. We did an internal analysis and concluded that the actual number was well under 10 percent.

Perhaps the most egregious oversight in *Flash Boys* was Lewis's portrayal of the role of the SEC. They come off as minor players in his book, absentee landlords always looking the other way. I found this characterization not only inaccurate but misleading. I could hardly make a change to a line of code in Nasdaq's order-matching computers without approval by the SEC. Our entire business model as an exchange was overseen in great detail. And much of this oversight is not something that happens away from public scrutiny. Significant rule changes at the SEC go through a painstakingly thorough, transparent, and public process. It is carefully orchestrated and open for comment. Smaller rule changes may not have the same level of public scrutiny, but again, every little change that Nasdaq makes in relationship to its exchange is being carefully reviewed and approved by the agency.

Is the SEC perfect? No, of course not. But they are hardly without teeth. They are the cops on the beat, the referees on the field, making sure the rules are enforced and followed, and updating them as needed. In the world portrayed in *Flash Boys*, it often seemed like the SEC was hardly involved—a mistaken impression that may have served the story of rogue foxes rummaging through the henhouse—but it simply is not the case. The SEC is a towering presence throughout the equities industry. But Lewis bypassed this point in favor of making the banks and exchanges the villains.

The book ignored the SEC, but the SEC did not ignore the book. "The markets are not rigged," declared SEC Chairwoman Mary Jo White to a House panel in 2014, soon after the publication of *Flash Boys*. "The U.S. markets are the strongest and most reliable in the world." I agree with her assessment. That does not deny that there is room for improvement. White herself spent considerable effort beefing up the SEC's oversight of HFT firms and their practices.

I would add one thought to White's statement. I also think that today's market is stronger and more robust than any in history. Behind the drama of *Flash Boys* is an unspoken idea that perhaps things were better off before computers came to Wall Street. I think such an impression is wishful thinking.

In the last decades, almost all of the transaction cost has been eliminated from trading in equity markets. One study found that institutional costs for large cap trading fell by more than 20 percent in just the years between 2010 and 2015.[1] Lewis complains that this trend of falling costs has slowed, but that is not surprising. Encroaching upon the small percentage of costs that remain is inevitably going to be more difficult. There is always going to be some friction cost to trading.

With such facts at hand, I don't romanticize Wall Street's past. I try to be frank and fair-minded about its present, and I hope that it will continue to evolve in a better direction in the future. No doubt that evolution will involve some bumps and bruises along the way. But that does not mean apocalypse is imminent. One gets the impression, in the pages of *Flash Boys*, that our current system is on the brink of implosion under the nefarious behavior of the HFT industry, and that massive instability in the market is just around the corner. None of this is true, nor have these warnings played out as he suggested they would. Since the publication of the book, markets are more resilient than ever. What has indeed proved to be true is that progress in the real world is not about moving from black to white, from bad to good, from corrupt to perfect, but rather, from one system with problems to a much better system that solves old problems and usually creates some new ones as well.

To their credit, the protagonists of *Flash Boys* did try to come up with an alternative approach, building an exchange with features designed to curtail HFT behavior. The "speed bump" they developed to foil the industry was innovative, but it is already being replicated and improved upon by others. To paraphrase the words of Oracle CEO Larry Ellison during the dot-com era, I suspect they have created a feature, not a business. Regardless, the market will decide, according to the rules set down by the SEC—as it should be. And a new generation of idealistic young entrepreneurs will seek once again to innovate, improve markets, and overthrow the existing elite to install a better solution. Such is the evolution of business, of markets, and of life.

The Known and the Unknown

In my early days at Nasdaq, I used to have dreams that I was jumping off a cliff, or in some cases falling off a cliff, and tumbling through the air not knowing how or if I was going to land. Sometimes that image would spontaneously come to mind even in daylight. It was a perfect metaphor for how I actually felt during that period. Being CEO of Nasdaq was an experiential leap in all kind of ways. Massive reorganizations, new technologies, global acquisitions, dealing with Washington—all of it was a thrilling adventure, a leap forward into the unknown.

But as a decade passed, that sensation was fading. The job was engaging and consuming. I was deeply gratified by Nasdaq's growth and success. I found satisfaction in working on and solving big problems and watching the ongoing maturation of the business. But that fundamental excitement, that sense of adventure, had diminished. When you can't see the ground beneath you, the thrill of the unknown is real. But now I could see, in some fundamental way, how the future would play out. I was familiar with the terrain. I thought I knew how we were all going to land.

To some extent, I dealt with my own need for new challenges by focusing on the future, digging into the technologies and ideas that would inform the next decade of Nasdaq's growth— blockchain, NPM, Nasdaq Futures Market, and so on. The relative stability of the business also allowed me to make upgrades in otherwise neglected areas of the organization that might not be experiencing noticeable problems but weren't performing to my satisfaction. One of my stock phrases during those years became: *If something is not right, it's wrong.* A good leader should always be looking to upgrade people, processes, and technology.

All of these activities required my full engagement and expertise, but as the novelty and drama of the early days faded, I began to consider my post-Nasdaq life. Watching Nasdaq flourish was its own reward, but the more Nasdaq became a consistent machine, firing on all cylinders, the more I began to recognize that my time at the company was finite. At the very least, it was time to start thinking seriously about who would fill my chair when I was gone.

LEADERSHIP LESSONS

- **Once You Achieve Competency, You Must Battle Complacency.** When the business is under threat from market forces, the motivation to improve comes naturally. When the threats are vanquished, you need to find new ways to encourage change and innovation.

- **Don't Worry About the Slope; Worry About the Trend Line.** Significant change takes time. As long as you're headed in the right direction, it's less important how fast you are going.

- **Carve Out a Safe Space for Innovation.** In a cost-conscious culture, it's hard for innovation to take root. Make sure there's a dedicated space in the culture, the budget, and the institutional structure for new ideas to germinate and grow.

Chapter Thirteen

Don't Look Back

Nasdaq Names Adena Friedman CEO

Reuters, November 14, 2016

"What do you see as the top accomplishments of your career?"

This question was posed to me by Rich Repetto, lead analyst for Sandler O'Neill in the financial sector, onstage at a Securities Trader Association conference in Washington, DC, in 2014. It was the same question that had been asked of Tom Farley, the President of NYSE, who had been onstage right before me. Farley and I were friends and colleagues, having a common background at SunGard. He had spent a few minutes reflecting thoughtfully on his career and I was impressed by what he'd accomplished. But when I was asked the question, I took a different approach.

"The moment I start to think about the past in that way, it's time for the Board to look for a new CEO," I declared to the surprised interviewer as several hundred people looked on. I really meant it. Any moment reflecting on the past is a moment you're not focused on the future. Just because you were successful yesterday does not mean you will be successful tomorrow. No doubt there would come a time to reflect more on the past, but not while I was CEO.

At Nasdaq, I spent more time thinking about how not to become complacent as a leader and how not to lose our edge as a competitive, innovative company than I spent thinking about any of our accomplishments. I pushed our team not to become self-satisfied, and I pushed myself as well. If you're not careful, personally and organizationally, *past success will be a weight on future success, and the greater the success, the heavier the weight.*

That's not to say I didn't take pride in having helped rescue Nasdaq from its doldrums in 2003. But this was more than a decade later. Nasdaq was a different company. I was older. The financial industry had changed. There were no guarantees that Robert Greifeld of 2003 was up to the unique challenges of 2014. Yes, I had gained a great deal of experience, and that was incredibly beneficial, without question. I was more efficient in my day-to-day running of the business. I had seen the ups and downs of the markets. I knew the company inside and out. I knew the players in the industry. My wisdom and skill level had shot up over the years. But in order to truly belong as CEO of a public company, you have to continue to be the right person for the present and the future—again and again, year after year. After all, there are a lot of competent people who are hungry for the opportunity. Every year, I wanted to be at the top of my game, ready for current and future challenges.

I also never wanted to fall into the trap of thinking that Nasdaq's success was inevitable. There was nothing preordained about it. It had to be re-earned every day. Just because we were riding the momentum of past execution didn't mean that our momentum couldn't stall. It was impossible to tell how close we might be as a company to falling behind. I always felt that success and failure were two sides of a thin dime. Indeed, maybe the line between success and failure was thinner than we imagined; maybe we were succeeding by the slimmest of margins. At least, that was how I thought about our performance. I didn't want to start feeling like we had some special privilege—as if the past were always prologue to a successful future. Success doesn't drop out of the sky. We had worked hard to earn it. And each day, we had to do it again. I knew that if I lost that edge, I should seriously consider whether it was time to move on.

Succession

While I didn't spend much time thinking about the past, I did spend a fair amount of time thinking about the future, especially the part that would not include me. Good succession planning is an integral part of being a responsible CEO. It's something every Board should be on top of, even though many shirk that responsibility. I knew I needed a more robust plan for replacing myself at Nasdaq's helm. The most qualified person for the job, in my mind, was Adena Friedman. Since I had first promoted her in 2003, I had watched Adena evolve from a talented young executive to an accomplished, experienced industry leader. Ever since she left for Carlyle, I had kept alive the idea, in the back of my mind, that one day she might make an ideal future CEO for Nasdaq. So in early 2014, I called her up. We met at a restaurant one rainy night in

Manhattan. I had a personal rule that I don't do business dinners unless I'm the one doing the selling. Knowing me, she must have suspected that I had something important to say.

I explained to her that I was planning to be at Nasdaq for a couple more years, but after that, she would be a natural choice to replace me. I asked her to consider returning to the company, and told her that if she did so, and performed, I would help her win the support of the Board. I gave no guarantees, no definitive private or public commitments, but I assured her I would do my best, within my power, to give her every opportunity to prove herself to the Board as the logical choice to be my successor.

She was intrigued, and I was hopeful. However, I wanted her to gain more operational experience in terms of running a large, complicated business. Carlyle was a bunch of operational fiefdoms, and while she oversaw the financial side of things, that wasn't the same as mastering the ins and outs of running revenue-producing businesses. She had been CFO and EVP of Strategy at Nasdaq and had done a great job running the data and indexing business. So I had complete confidence that she could do it, but she would still need a period of proving herself. I assured her that if she did so, I would be her strongest advocate to the Board.

We talked and strategized. By the time our dinner was over, I felt confident that it was an offer she couldn't refuse, and over the next weeks and months, we worked out the details and she completed her work at Carlyle and officially resigned. I personally called David Rubenstein, CEO of Carlyle, to explain to him why Adena was returning to Nasdaq. Carlyle was a Nasdaq-listed company, and I wanted to show them the proper respect. I told him her reasons, as I understood them, for returning to One Liberty Plaza.

He wasn't thrilled but was gracious, and he seemed resigned to the inevitability of losing her. "She did a great job at Carlyle, and I'm sorry to see her go. I guess we just rented her talents for a couple of years," he conceded.

On May 12, 2014, it became official. Adena was returning to Nasdaq and it was obvious to anyone watching closely that she would be the natural person in line to be the next CEO. "Adena Friedman to Rejoin the Nasdaq and Likely Be in Line to Lead"[1] read one headline describing the move. Her official new title was President of Global Corporate and Information Technology Solutions. I hadn't used the "President" title since Magnus Böcker (former CEO of OMX) had left the company, but this seemed an appropriate moment to dust it off. At the same time, I also made Hans-Ole Jochumsen, the current EVP of Transactions, a co-President. He might have had aspirations for the CEO role as well, and he would have certainly been a plausible choice, and a good one. But I explained to him when we made the move that Adena was the clear front-runner.

In early 2015, Adena moved into the COO position, essentially running all of Nasdaq's business lines. I had never had a COO before; I had always considered overseeing the revenue-producing businesses to be part of my job. But giving Adena that responsibility was part of the succession plan. I intended to orchestrate the transition in such a way that the Board never felt the need to do an external search, and letting Adena prove her operational competency was critical. At this point, every single revenue-producing piece of Nasdaq worked for her. If there had been any doubt that she was next in line, it was removed at that point. Three or four highly qualified individuals from other large firms on Wall Street had expressed a desire to run Nasdaq. My intention was for such conversations to seem unnecessary.

One Too Many Mornings

By late 2016, I was finally ready to step down as Nasdaq's CEO. A still-small voice was whispering in my ear, "It's time to move on." Why? In truth, there wasn't one reason. There were many elements that came together to make 2016 the right moment. I had been there for almost fourteen years, a lifetime in terms of global markets. CEOs rarely make it that far. I had the backing of the Board, the support of my team, and a track record like few others. I know that it can be hard for leaders in any field to let go. I've seen too many CEOs struggle to leave behind the job and surrender the trappings of the position—the power, the status, the affirmation, the perks, the limelight, the support structure, the feeling of being at the center of the universe. I didn't want to fall into that trap. When it's time, it's time. No one gains by pretending otherwise. I'd always prided myself on being able to look ahead, see around the next corner. So while I was good at the job, and I was accustomed to the job, it didn't mean I was actually still the best person for the job. In my heart, I knew that it was time to say good-bye.

As Nasdaq got bigger and more successful, it also became a different company. I knew my talents, and while I was skilled at being CEO of Nasdaq, as the company grew and our management team became more experienced and effective, I began to feel that the very qualities that made me so indispensable at one point in the life of Nasdaq were no longer so front and center. There was a moment when my skill set seemed to uniquely fit what Nasdaq desperately needed. I was able to shepherd the exchange through the critical period when new trading technology was dramatically disrupting all exchanges. In a sense, we were the first big one to go through that tunnel of disruption and thrive on the other side. Please don't misunderstand me. I'm not so arrogant as to imagine that no one else could have successfully done the job in 2003. But I think it's also true that I was the right person at the right time.

As Nasdaq grew into a new maturity, however, I felt less essential. My management team had grown up and become a powerful group, highly capable and filled with experience. Every week in our management meetings, I was struck by their independence, foresight, and ability. The reality was that they needed me less and less.

One evaluative method I used to think about my own performance was a conversation in my head between Bob the Nasdaq shareholder and Bob the CEO. How would the former judge the latter? Somewhere along the line, that internal conversation shifted. Bob the shareholder was no longer 100 percent confident that Bob the CEO was still ideal for the job. In my mind, I could imagine the shareholder saying, "You've had a great run. But all good things come to an end. Let Adena have her chance to lead the organization into the future."

There were also family concerns. When I first started at Nasdaq, every night I would come home to Julia and the three kids, and the time with them was always a welcome respite from the intensity of work. Despite the demands of being a CEO, family was central to my life, and Julia and I had shared the many delights, trials, and joys of raising Bobby, Greg, and Katie. That's not to say it wasn't tough. While I had always tried to make time for my family, the reality is that as a CEO of a public company, you're never entirely free of work, and rarely able to be fully present even when you're at home. Mentally, it's a 24/7 occupation. I used to tell my executives that there was no real work-life balance in our particular choice of career. Rather, the better approach was to seek a work-life integration: a healthy and functional relationship between life at home and life at the office. To have a family that was supportive was critical, and I was grateful for the forbearance of mine when those urgent calls came in the middle of dinner or when my mind was otherwise occupied during a family gathering. Inevitably, Julia shouldered an outsized portion of the daily responsibilities in our family's life. That was an unavoidable trade-off of the choice we'd made and my own career commitments. Today, when I look at my children's successes with pride and admiration, I appreciate all over again the large role that she played in guiding their development.

As the three children grew up, headed off to college, and moved on to new horizons in their twenties, the dynamics of my relationship with them naturally changed. Suddenly, they weren't always there when I had a break. In fact, if I wanted to spend time with them, I had to conform to their busy schedules! The tables had turned. And that's not so easy when you're running a $12 billion company and traveling around the world. As I approached my sixtieth birthday, it became ever more clear to me that time was marching on and no one could say for certain how many years were left. I wanted to spend at least some of that time continuing to be part of my children's lives and the lives of our future grandchildren.

I was also aware that with the kids out of the house, Julia was left alone while I traveled and worked long hours. She'd sacrificed a lot for my career over the years, and it was time to be there for her. There had been one too many mornings when I left the house before she was even awake. Moreover, my own parents were getting older. They'd done so much for me; I felt it was my turn to be available for them as they took their final trips around the sun.

I wanted time to give back, too. After four decades of building a very successful career, I had made more money than I would spend in my lifetime, and it was time to use some of it for helping others and supporting the causes that mattered to me. I decided to focus my giving in a particular area that I'm passionate about: education and opportunity. I'm determined that the upwardly mobile spirit of the American dream should not become unavailable to those from humble circumstances. I wanted to use some of my wealth to provide opportunities for others like myself—who grew up in modest households but are talented and hungry for advancement. As an NYU alumnus, I initially chose the NYU Stern School of Business as an effective vehicle for this: 30 percent of the students in their programs were Pell Grant recipients, with families in low-income brackets. I was able to direct my giving specifically to those students, who have the talent and motivation to qualify for a great education but lack the critical resources needed to make that dream come true. Today, our family foundation is further expanding our investment in programs serving talented, underprivileged children, who have so much promise but lack so many advantages. We're trying to make the rungs on the ladder of opportunity just a little bit easier to reach.

Finally, I wanted to enjoy the fruits of success in a way that is impossible when you're working so hard. I've seen the insides of conference rooms in every corner of the world but rarely had the opportunity to immerse myself in the cultures and landscapes that surround them. I looked forward to enjoying more time with my wife and family, riding my road bike and improving my golf game, traveling around the world, and spending quality time with the many friends and colleagues I had gained over the years.

Don't get me wrong; I wasn't going to stop working. I was just finished being a CEO, with all the demands that come with the job. I still wanted to try new things and take on new challenges, some far outside of my current domains of expertise. I was founder and Chairman of the USATF Foundation and was proud of what we'd achieved over more than a decade, supporting our country's most promising young track and field athletes, but I knew we could do more. Plus, I wanted to get back to my entrepreneurial roots, help create new companies or build up young ones. I was itching to play upstart disruptor again and to mentor young innovators. And as I finally began to allow myself to reflect more directly on the past, I was considering writing a book.

We made the announcement on November 14, 2016. Adena was officially named as my replacement effective January 1, 2017. The weekend before the announcement I sat down in my home office to write a few words to Nasdaq staff. I poured myself a nice glass of wine, and as I took the first sip I thought better of my timing, and decided I'd write it in the morning, when my mind was fresh and less likely to drift into nostalgia. As the sun rose, I put pen to paper, and I thought about all of the various intersecting reasons that made this the right moment to step down. But one truth stood out above the others and seemed to encapsulate my thoughts in leaving. It was about the knowledge that time is a precious, limited resource, and as we get older, we feel it more deeply.

"What I have come to realize," I wrote, "is that the opportunity cost of how you choose to spend your time increases not on a linear but rather a logarithmic scale as your assumption about your number of tomorrows decreases...After careful consideration and discussion, in full recognition that the CEO position will always have infinite and all-encompassing responsibility, Julia and I decided that now is the proper time to plan for a more balanced number of tomorrows."

I was fit, healthy, and mentally sharp, but as I neared sixty, and my number of tomorrows decreased, I knew I wanted to spend them doing other things. I had truly loved being CEO of Nasdaq. But time moves on relentlessly, and Adena had met every test, exceeded every bar, and done everything that I had asked of her. The Board had taken my recommendation and chosen her. It was time for her to put her unique stamp on the future of a great organization.

On the fiftieth floor of One Liberty Plaza, we gathered for a champagne toast as the announcement went out to staff. It was a beautiful and bittersweet moment of celebration, of moving on, moving forward, and moving out. I had cut my leadership teeth on the steel girders of One Liberty Plaza and come away a changed man, a wiser man. Nasdaq, likewise, had found its way, gone from desperately surviving to truly thriving, and I was proud to have been central to that remarkable transformation. I had given the best years of my life to the organization and it had responded in kind.

In a little over a month, Adena would be CEO. I would briefly stay on as Executive Chairman of the Nasdaq Board to oversee the transition. In the words of one of my favorite poets, Bob Dylan, it was time to "strike another match [and] start anew."

A Final Toast

After the resignation letter was released, I found myself in my office, at a loose end. Everyone wanted to talk to me, but I didn't quite know what more to say. And then my phone rang with the best idea I'd heard all day.

"Bob, it's Vinnie. How would you like to meet me for a drink later this afternoon?"

I had known Vinnie Viola, founder of Virtu Financial, since my days at SunGard. A West Point graduate and former army Major, he had become wealthy in the years since we first met, the founder of a successful financial firm, as well as a personal friend. When Chris Concannon left Nasdaq in 2009, he had gone to work with Vinnie at Virtu (before moving on to CBOE). In fact, Vinnie had several times tried to convince me to step away from Nasdaq to come work with him. But it had never felt like the right time.

It was nice to hear from an old friend, and the idea of getting out of the office early was a relief. I quietly slipped into the elevator and headed over to the east side of Manhattan to an old-school Italian restaurant where Vinnie was camped out with a couple of friends.

"Two Dewar's, please," Vinnie said to the waiter as I sat down. Over the years it had become a tradition—Dewar's for both of us, the workingman's Scotch. For two leaders of the financial industry, it was a nod to the time when neither of us could afford anything more expensive. We had both grown up working-class—he was from Brooklyn; I was from Queens and Long Island. The best thing about new money is that you remember what it's like to have none.

"A toast to your success." Vinnie raised his glass, and I joined him.

"And I have news," he continued. "Our President-elect has asked me to be Secretary of the Army."

"Congratulations. That's a real honor," I replied, and we toasted again.

As it would turn out, Vinnie would eventually withdraw his name from consideration, due to business ties that were too difficult to untangle. But for the moment, he was moved and excited by the proposition, which was due to be announced the following month. And he was already making plans for his firm—which was where I came in.

"Bob, come work for Virtu. I'd like you to replace me as Chairman of the Board. I promise it won't be too demanding, and we'll compensate you well. No doubt Doug would appreciate your counsel and expertise." Doug Cifu is cofounder and CEO of Virtu, and he's a great business leader and friend.

With Nasdaq about to be in the rearview mirror, it felt like a day for reflecting on my life and career, both past and future. As I considered his proposal, I imagined how I would have responded to such a proposition at a younger age—incredibly well-paid work, and not exactly backbreaking. Somewhere in the back of my mind, my inner twenty-five-year-old was yelling, *Are you crazy? What's to consider? Take it!*

"Thanks, Vinnie," I said, "but I'm not going to do that."

Vinnie and I had always looked forward to the day we could

spend more time together. And I knew that in the next period of my life, I could easily trade on my name for a few plum Board seats, take a great salary, sit back, and enjoy the perks. That wasn't for me; I was never going to be that guy. I didn't need another job; I'd already had the best one in the world. If I took a Board seat, it was going to be because I had real equity in the company and relished the entrepreneurial challenge of helping the company grow. Still, I knew Doug and the team at Virtu, how smart and capable they were. It would be a thrill to work with them, help build a great company. Maybe something was possible.

"I would love to partner with you on something. Let's do a deal together. What could we do? What could we create? What could we build?"

Vinnie and I explored possibilities. At some point, the name Knight Capital came up. Virtu and Nasdaq had tried to buy the company a few years before but lost out to Getco. Now it was KCG, and ripe for a takeover. Vinnie got excited and called Doug, who was similarly enthusiastic.

I called my friend Glenn Hutchins, a current Board member at Nasdaq. Glenn was looking for new ventures, and we'd already discussed the possibility of partnering. He brought to the table a kaleidoscopic knowledge of the private equity industry. What about it? Maybe we could obtain the financing to help Virtu make a bid? As the idea swirled around in my head and we moved on to a finer Scotch, I could already imagine the synergies.

My phone rang. I looked down at it and smiled. Family trumped business now. Bobby was calling to say congratulations. We spoke for a few minutes before our conversation was interrupted by a call from Greg. Later came a text from Katie, who just happened to live nearby. I invited her to join us; the business discussions could wait. She sat and talked with us as a brisk afternoon melted away into the cold November evening.

Friends. Family. Business. New plans. By the time I stepped out into the night and headed home to spend more time with Julia, the love of my life, I was a happy man. While nothing could ever replace the magic of the Nasdaq years, the future was going to be wonderful.

Acknowledgments

My parents, Adelaide and Robert, raised five children, with limited means and unlimited love. They told me thousands of times, "You can do anything." I am their child and their creation. Parents always want to remain the hero in their children's eyes. My children—Bobby, Greg, and Katie—are adults, and while I will never again be their five-year-old hero, they are my closest friends. Truly, the greatest gift.

This career and this book would not have been possible without the guidance and mentorship of many. The few individuals listed here come first to mind; I apologize to all others. Furlong "Baldy" Baldwin, Evan T. Barrington, Frank Baxter, Steve Black, Michael Casey, Cris Conde, Börje Ekholm, Graham Gurney, Pat Healy, Warren Hellman, Glenn Hutchins, Ira Kirsch, Tom Kloet, Frank Ladwig, Carl LaGrassa, James Mann, Edward Redfield, Arthur Rock, Mike Splinter, and all the members of the Board of Nasdaq.

A leader can never be better than his team. I was fortunate to be surrounded by incredibly talented and motivated individuals. I am in the debt of many; I list a small number here. Rosemary Albergo, Jim Ashton, Bruce Aust, Marianne Baldrica, Marcia Barris, Danny Barsella, Harsh Barve, Magnus Böcker, Terry Campbell, Ulf Carlsson, Mandana Chaffa, Joe Christinat, Dayna Cohen, Chris Concannon, Katharine Cox, Kevin Cummings,

Bobby Cuomo, Ed Ditmire, David Ehret, Paul Erickson, Anna Ewing, Esther Forster, Adena Friedman, Sandy Frucher, Nelson Griggs, Ron Hassen, Doug Hurry, John Hyde, Brian Hyndman, Moss Iman, John Jacobs, Hans-Ole Jochumsen, Jameel Johnson, Will Keh, Tom King, Edward Knight, Carl LaGrassa Jr., Dan Liu, Jean-Jacques Louis, John Lucchese, Bob McCooey, Tom McDugall, Karin McKinnell, Satish Mujumdar, Gerry Murphy, Eric Noll, Bill O'Brien, Brian O'Malley, Jennifer Ok, Matt Orsi, Lars Ottersgård, Vince Palmiere, Brad Peterson, Michael Ptasznik, Nipun Ragoowansi, Steve Randich, Rob Rentenberg, Lauri Rosendahl, Mike Salito, Mark Schroeter, Tom Selby, Dave Shafer, Lee Shavel, James Shedrick, Bethany Sherman, Bjørn Sibbern, Jeremy Skule, Bettina Slusar, Bryan Smith, Rick Tarbox, Donna Thompson, Marc Ulysee, David Warren, Tom Wittman, John Yetter, John Zecca, and Julie Zipper.

I am living proof of the African proverb "It takes a village." Many have helped provide the support that enabled my success in life and work. I mention a few here; thank you. John Bannon, John and Debbie Bunce, John Chambers, Doug Cifu, Steve Cohen, Bill Considine, Jimmy Dunne, Pete Featherstone, Cynthia Forte, Liz and Charlie Frumberg, Steve Goulart, Alex Greifeld, Phil and Carolyn Greifeld, William Greifeld, Ed Herlihy, Bob Hugin, Steve Kandarian, Gloria LaGrassa, Steve Lessing, Mike Oxley, Ken Pasternak, Walter Raquet, Fernando Rivas, Jim Robinson, Rick Rock, Don Saladino, Joey Saladino, Joe Seiler, Kaivan Shakib, John Shay, John and Pam Shortal, Liz and Richard Steigman, Larry Summers, and Vinnie Viola.

CEOs succeed or fail based on how they leverage their time. Deborah Rock had the primary responsibility for deciding who got on the schedule and for how long. She was the secret lever of my time and my success. I'm in Deb's debt for many things, but mainly as a friend. We are both grateful we have our lifetimes to balance the scales.

In the publishing of this book, I've been lucky to have the backing of a top-notch team. Thank you to my agents at Aevitas, David Kuhn, Lauren Sharp, and Nate Muscato, who carefully shepherded this book to a great publisher and have continued to support its progress toward publication. My gratitude also goes out to Gretchen Young at Grand Central Publishing for her thorough and thoughtful editing, and to Emily Rosman for her patience with all the details.

The distillation of fifteen years of memories, many quite arcane, into a coherent narrative seemed quite impossible for quite a long period of time. I certainly believe the task would have remained impossible if not for Carter Phipps and Ellen Daly. Carter's remarkable ability to quickly understand and reduce complex topics to their interesting essence was profoundly unique. And when Carter and I would spend too much time discussing the minutiae of market structure, the significance of the third stanza of "Howl," or the meaning of life, Ellen was there to remind us of the miles to go and how the last chapter might not be quite as good as we thought—and here were eight recommendations for improvement. The best result of this process is that Julia and I have two new friends for life. It has been a pleasure.

Notes

Chapter One: Nasdaq Comes Calling

1. Warren Buffett at the Berkshire Hathaway annual meeting, 1993, quoted in Janet Lowe, *Warren Buffett Speaks: Wit and Wisdom from the World's Greatest Investor* (Hoboken, NJ: John Wiley & Sons, 2007), 143.

Chapter Two: People First

1. Henry Blodget, "Exclusive Interview with Tony Hseih: How Being a Little Bit Weird Made Zappos a Fortune," *Business Insider*, October 18, 2010, https://www.businessinsider.com/henry-blodget-tony-hsieh-zappos-2010-10 (accessed December 2018).
2. Lydia Dishman, "Why Companies Make Bad Hires," *Fast Company*, September 1, 2015, https://www.fastcompany.com/3050570/why-companies-make -bad-hires (accessed December 2018).
3. Jim Collins, *Good to Great: Why Some Companies Make the Leap... and Others Don't* (New York: HarperBusiness, 2001), 42.
4. Thomas Gryta, Joann S. Lublin, and David Benoit, "How Jeffrey Immelt's 'Success Theater' Masked the Rot at GE," *Wall Street Journal*, February 21, 2018, https://www.wsj.com/articles/how-jeffrey-immelts-success-theater -masked-the-rot-at-ge-1519231067 (accessed December 2018).

Chapter Three: Triage

1. Paula Dwyer and Amy Borrus, "Nasdaq: The Fight of Its Life," *Businessweek*, August 11, 2003, https://www.bloomberg.com/news/articles/2003-08-10 /nasdaq-the-fight-of-its-life (accessed December 2018).
2. John Chambers with Diane Brady, *Connecting the Dots: Lessons for Leadership in a Startup World* (New York: Hachette, 2018), 41. Emphasis in the original.

Chapter Four: Buy the Winners

1. Dan Brekke, "Daytrading Places," *Wired*, July 1, 1999, https://www.wired .com/1999/07/island-2/ (accessed December 2018).

Chapter Eight: Grappling with Growth

1. Jim Collins, *Good to Great: Why Some Companies Make the Leap...and Others Don't* (New York: HarperBusiness, 2001), 180.

Chapter Nine: Blood on the Tracks

1. Rachelle Younglai, "SEC Chief Has Regrets over Short-Selling Ban," Reuters, December 31, 2008, https://www.reuters.com/article/us-sec-cox/sec-chief-has-regrets-over-short-selling-ban-idUSTRE4BU3GG20081231 (accessed December 2018).

2. Tae Kim, "Buffett, Quoting Partner Munger, Says There Are Three Ways to Go Broke: 'Liquor, Ladies and Leverage,'" *Squawk Box*, CNBC, February 26, 2018, https://www.cnbc.com/2018/02/26/buffett-says-out-of-the-three-ways-to-go-broke-liquor-ladies-and-leverage-leverage-is-the-worst.html (accessed December 2018).

Chapter Ten: The One That Got Away

1. William Shakespeare, *Macbeth*, Act 1, scene 7, line 60.

2. Devlin Barrett, "Schumer Tilts Toward Offer by Germans for Big Board," *Wall Street Journal*, May 6, 2011, https://www.wsj.com/articles/SB10001424052748703992704576305384222703172 (accessed December 2018).

3. Cyrus Sanati, "The Big Deal About the NYSE's Big Deal: Derivatives," *Fortune*, March 2, 2011, http://fortune.com/2011/03/02/the-big-deal-about-the-nyses-big-deal-derivatives/ (accessed December 2018).

Chapter Twelve: Institutionalizing Innovation

1. Commissioner Luis A. Aguilar, "U.S. Equity Market Structure: Making Our Markets Work Better for Investors," U.S. Securities and Exchange Commission Public Statement, May 11, 2015, https://www.sec.gov/news/statement/us-equity-market-structure.html (accessed December 2018).

Chapter Thirteen: Don't Look Back

1. Brittany Umar, "Adena Friedman to Rejoin the Nasdaq and Likely Be in Line to Lead," Real Money, TheStreet, May 12, 2014, https://realmoney.thestreet.com/video/12704768/adena-friedman-to-rejoin-the-nasdaq-and-likely-be-in-line-to-lead.html (accessed December 2018).

Index

About the Author

Credit: Nasdaq, Inc.

Bob Greifeld is former CEO and Chairman of Nasdaq. He is currently Chairman of Virtu Financial, a leading financial technology and trading firm; Managing Partner and Co-Founder at Cornerstone Investment Capital, a financial technology investment firm; and a board member at Capital Rock and Financeware.

Bob is Chairman and Founder of the USATF Foundation, an organization dedicated to supporting both athletes from disadvantaged backgrounds and our next generation of Olympians. Bob also serves on the NYC Board of Overseers.